HAUNTED HOUSING

HAUNTED HOUSING

How Toxic Scare Stories
Are Spooking the Public
Out of House and Home

CASSANDRA CHRONES MOORE

CATO INSTITUTE
Washington, D.C.

Library of Congress Cataloging-in-Publication Data

Moore, Cassandra Chrones.
    Haunted housing : how toxic scare stories are spooking the public
out of house and home / Cassandra Chrones Moore.
        p.   cm.
    Includes bibliographical references and index.
    ISBN 1-882577-41-8. — ISBN 1-882577-42-6 (pbk.)
    1. Housing and health—Government policy—United States.
2. Health risk assessment in the press—United States.   3. Asbestos—
Safety regulations—United States.   4. Radon—Safety regulations—
United States.   5. Lead based paint—Safety regulations—United States.
6. Electromagnetic fields—Safety regulations—United States.   I. Title.
RA770.M66   1997
613'.5—dc21   97-485
                                                                                                        CIP

CATO INSTITUTE
1000 Massachusetts Ave., N.W.
Washington, D.C. 20001

Contents

Foreword

In his essay *Witches, Floods and Wonder Drugs: Historical Perspectives on Risk Management*, Dr. William C. Clark of Harvard University compares the present-day foreboding over exposure to chemical and mineral pollutants to the witch hunts of the 16th and 17th centuries. In those times, the institutionalized efforts of the church to control witches led to witch proliferation—the more you looked for them, the more you found. Careers were built on the success of the witch assessor, who was rewarded through the confiscation of the suspect witch's property. One of the more notorious of those assessors was one Matthew Hopkins, Witch-finder General, who traveled through the English counties of Norfolk, Essex, Huntington, and Sussex during the mid-17th century for the sole purpose of finding witches. That unsavory character claimed 20 shillings a head for each discovery; but he later overplayed his hand and expired when the populace put him to his own test. Times have not changed; at present, billions of dollars are spent each year to eliminate witches now reborn in the form of chemicals and mineral dusts. As Clark observed, many of the procedures used today to assess risk from exposure to those 20th-century witches are logically indistinguishable from those used by the Inquisition 400 years ago. Cassandra Chrones Moore, in her new book *Haunted Housing: How Toxic Scare Stories Are Spooking the Public Out of House and Home,* presents a brilliant exposé of four of the new-age witches—radon, lead, asbestos, and electromagnetic fields, substances and forces that reputedly haunt millions of homes, schools, and offices.

The public's fear of those and other environmental pollutants is promoted by the "zero threshold hypothesis"—one atom of radon, one fiber of asbestos, or one molecule of ethylene dibromide can initiate the growth of a cancerous tumor. What the public has not been adequately told is that simply living on the Earth exposes us without injury to innumerable naturally occurring carcinogens. Drs. Bruce Ames and Lois Gold and their colleagues at the Department of Molecular Biology, University of California at Berkeley, have published a remarkable series of papers showing that naturally occurring chemical carcinogens (as defined by animal experiments) are ubiquitous in the foods we eat. About 50 percent of the chemicals, both natural and synthetic in origin, that are administered in high-dose animal tests are found to be carcinogenic. For example, of the myriad natural pesticides that occur in plants, only 52 have thus far been tested in animals, and 27 were proven to be carcinogenic. Of the approximately 1,000 chemicals found in roasted coffee, only 22 have thus far been tested in animals and 19 of those 22 were found to be carcinogenic at high dose levels. Thus, one cup of coffee contains 10 milligrams of known animal carcinogens, about the equivalent in weight to the synthetic pesticide residues the average person consumes in one year. Dr. Ames reports that 35 water wells located in Silicon Valley, California, were shut down because the water contains as much as 2,800 parts per billion trichloroethylene (a manmade organic solvent that causes cancer in animals when administered in large doses), even though the water is 100 to 1,000 times *less* "carcinogenic" than an equal volume of cola, beer, coffee, or wine. Those beverages contain animal carcinogens, such as hydrogen peroxide, methylglyoxal, formaldehyde, nitrosamines, and ethyl alcohol. Naturally occurring chemical carcinogens at concentrations of 50,000 parts per billion or greater are found in such common foods as apples, cauliflower, carrots, celery, cabbage, bananas, potatoes, lettuce, broccoli, and mushrooms. We ingest at least 10,000 times more of Mother Nature's carcinogens than of man-made carcinogens.

Dr. Ames's group also considers why so many animal tests are positive for cancer induction. They state that the administration of chemicals at the maximum tolerated dose, as is done in standard animal cancer tests, causes increased cell death that in turn promotes increased cell division and thus greatly increases new cell replacement, a process referred to as mitogenesis. Mitogenesis in turn increases the rate of mutagenesis, the process of producing mutations in the DNA molecules—the carriers of the genetic code. Permanent mutations occur particularly during cell division, when the cell's enzyme repair systems are least effective. As mutations build up in the DNA material, the probability of cancer induction increases. The reason why we humans can consume such a large variety of naturally occurring chemical carcinogens without effect is that we are extremely well protected by highly efficient enzyme repair systems; only by consuming such large quantities of a chemical that chronic cell damage occurs do we increase our cancer risk. In light of the work of Dr. Ames and his colleagues, it is useful to recall the Paracelsus' admonition: Everything is a poison, nothing is a poison, the dose alone makes the poison.

Dr. Richard Doll (the dean of the world's epidemiologists) and his colleague Dr. Richard Peto have shown that human consumption of chemicals that occur naturally in foods and beverages are of importance to cancer incidence when they are ingested in large quantities by special populations. For example, ingestion of large quantities of ethyl alcohol–bearing beverages can cause liver cirrhosis thus increasing the risk of liver cancer, daily consumption of bracken fern containing the chemical safrole increases the risk of esophageal cancer in certain Japanese populations, chewing betel nuts with tobacco is correlated with oral cancer, and ingestion of large amounts of broiled meats and fish containing benzopyrene and other polycyclic hydrocarbons appears to increase the risk of intestinal cancer.

A similar dose response pertains to mineral dusts. We are all continuously exposed, without injury, to asbestos and quartz dusts that exist in the ambient environment (quartz, the main component of beach sand, was recently listed as a group 1 carcinogen by the World Health Organization). Asbestos and quartz dusts, however, are known to cause significant injury in the form of chronic disease (asbestosis and silicosis) and lung cancer after long-term and dusty exposures in the workplace. Yet, the inordinate fear of asbestos-induced cancer led to a multi-billion-dollar removal program in schools, public and commercial buildings, and homes even though the asbestos fiber levels were nearly at the limits of detection.

Asbestos hysteria was particularly evident during the Great New York City Asbestos Panic of 1993. "Hundreds of children are evacuated from their schools. The reason? Possible asbestos exposure. City officials hold a press conference to explain the threat. The press corps bites, and the city is in panic. One question: Did anyone bother to ask if the children were in any real danger?" Richard Vigilante reported in Forbes *MediaCritic*. The panic, so ably described by Vigilante, occurred in New York City just before the opening of schools in the fall of 1993. The public, frightened by the intense newspaper coverage, heeded the advice of their consultants—that the asbestos risk in the New York City schools was large. Demands were made that all asbestos products be removed from over 1,000 school buildings and that the city provide school buildings that were "absolutely safe," but without defining what that meant. The school buildings remained closed, even after the fall term was to have begun, so that they could be reinspected for the presence of asbestos-containing material, which, if found, was to be removed. The reported cost of removal was approximately $100 million. As abatement companies began implementation of emergency remediation strategies, there was no mention in the media, or in any of the reports released by city or federal officials, of the concentrations of fibers in the air upon which the health risks depend. New York City's Board of Education was not required by law to measure the asbestos fiber concentrations in air or ascertain the type of asbestos present before any asbestos abatement took place. In fact, the city's Board of Education, like others nationwide, carried out its remediation on the advice given by the Environmental Protection Agency, which discouraged air sampling before abatement. Health hazard evaluation was based on the presence of asbestos-containing material in buildings, a visual inspection of its condition, and a subjective evaluation by an inspector. No quantitative air data were required for embarking on any remediation course. The officials of the EPA remained publicly silent throughout the 1993 New York City asbestos crisis—despite the 1990 "EPA Green Book" advisory, which stated that most asbestos removal is unnecessary, and despite the need to calm the hysteria generated throughout August and September by daily newspaper articles decrying the dangers of schoolroom asbestos.

Unfortunately the asbestos hysteria, so ably described by Moore, has now spread to France. The French government has just appropriated 1.2 billion francs to begin asbestos removal at the Jussieu campus of the University of Paris. Judging by our experience in the United States, 1.2 billion francs is just "starter money"; the big costs will come later.

The unnecessary expenditure of 50 billion to 100 billion dollars on asbestos abatement has not diminished regulatory activism in the United States for, as is so well described in *Haunted Housing*, we are repeating that costly mistake by promoting home abatement of

radon, lead, and electromagnetic fields. Those abatement initiatives
are justified by alleging that radon causes thousands of lung cancer
deaths each year, that lead causes millions of young children to be
mentally retarded (low IQ), and that magnetic fields cause a variety
of cancers including those of the brain, uterus, and breast. Are those
allegations true? As Moore so thoroughly documents in her book,
those death predictions are not supported by the facts: radon in
most homes is probably beneficial rather than harmful; that exposure
to lead-bearing substances lowers children's IQs is not supported
by rigorous statistical analysis; and electromagnetic fields generated
by such items as power lines, electric blankets, and toasters are
hundreds of times smaller than the earth's magnetic field to which
we are all necessarily exposed throughout our lives.

Cassandra Chrones Moore is uniquely qualified to write a book
such as *Haunted Housing* as a result of both her meticulous study of
the published research and her experience as a real estate professional. She has seen the economic and emotional impact of health
scares on buyers and sellers of homes. After reading this book one
may wonder whether, if these health scares and regulatory initiatives
continue for another decade, it will be possible to sell a house. I
highly recommend this book to anyone in the process of buying or
selling a house and to all working in the real estate and insurance
industries.

A final note: after 40 years' experience as a research scientist with
the U. S. Geological Survey, I am appalled by what I refer to as
"regulatory science." Scientific investigation continually asks the
question, Is it true? The role of science is not only to discover new
facts and phenomena, but to uncover errors in previous investigations. Science is continually in the process of correcting previous
work; no study is fixed in time. As the late Nobel laureate Richard
Feynman stated (to paraphrase), the highest calling of a scientist is
to show that his or her previous investigation is incorrect. But that
is not what happens in "regulatory science." Once a regulatory
initiative, sometimes but not always based on scientific investigation,
is introduced, the initiative persists even when new studies indicate
that the premise upon which the regulation was based is incorrect.
It is only with great effort, generally through legal or political challenge or an act of Congress, that a health or environmental regulation
is changed or withdrawn. To avoid costly regulatory mistakes, such

as the asbestos abatement program, procedures need to be established for a periodic review of the science supporting a particular regulatory initiative. If new research does not support previous studies, then the regulation must be amended. The premise that radon, lead, asbestos, and electromagnetic fields found in homes are major health hazards must be reexamined at the highest levels of scientific and governmental inquiry.

MALCOLM ROSS
Scientist Emeritus
United States Geological Survey
Reston, Virginia

Acknowledgments

Haunted Housing began as a series of discussions on the soaring cost of housing at the Competitive Enterprise Institute. The Scaife Family Foundation provided the research funding which made this book possible. Fred L. Smith Jr., CEI's president, and Sam Kazman, general counsel, supplied continuing support. To Professor Bruce Ames of the University of California at Berkeley, I owe a special debt for his list of "sensible experts" who could provide guidance in highly politicized and controversial areas.

The analysis on radon owes a great deal to one of those experts, Anthony Nero Jr., senior scientist at the Lawrence Berkeley Laboratories. For the chapter on lead, Professor Claire Ernhart of Case Western Reserve University supplied a thread through the labyrinth of charge and countercharge; Sanford Weiner, research associate at the Massachusetts Institute of Technology, decoded the methodology of the original study on dentine lead. Dr. Edgar Schoen, clinical professor at the University of California at San Francisco, provided a "sensible" perspective on universal testing.

It is a particular pleasure to acknowledge my debt to Professor Brooke Mossman of the University of Vermont for her balanced appraisal of the asbestos debate. The debt is equally profound to Malcolm Ross, scientist emeritus at the U.S. Geological Survey for his careful reading of several drafts, his corrections, and his detailed suggestions. I am equally pleased to acknowledge my profound indebtedness to Professor John Moulder of the Medical College of Wisconsin, who, in addition to maintaining the Internet's Frequently Asked Questions on EMF and Cancer, found the time to answer innumerable queries and to provide a tutorial on electric and magnetic fields.

As editor, Paula Duggan first gave shape to the lead chapter. Over the following months, the editorial skills of Michael Gough, director of science and risk studies at the Cato Institute, made the analysis more cogent, despite the problems posed by international e-mail and fax. To Darren Donnelly and Jennifer Brooks, I am grateful for analytical perceptions that went far beyond routine research assistance.

To my husband, who suggested resources and who helped me to navigate around the shoals of endless computer glitches, I owe a profound debt for his computer skills, as well as for his patience and understanding.

The insights of those whom I have mentioned and the advice of many others have been of the greatest help; but I, of course, accept full responsibility for any errors or omissions.

Introduction

It is man's indomitable nature to scare himself silly for no
good reason.

Calvin and Hobbes

Buying a home used to be a relatively simple procedure. Purchasers looked at the ads, visited open houses, and worked with a broker or negotiated directly with an owner. The concerns were mainly practical or aesthetic. Would the bank or savings and loan grant the mortgage? Was the back yard big enough for a swing set and a garden? Would the kitchen accommodate a breakfast table and chairs? Fanciful anxieties sometimes intruded. Several years ago, a broker recalled, a customer made a bid on a house, then spent sleepless nights unable to remember whether the bedrooms had closets. They did, of course—the large walk-in variety—but, feeling foolish about the question, she waited a week before calling to find out.

Today those concerns pale in comparison with deep-seated anxieties about health risks. Is there asbestos in the ceiling? Is there radon in the basement? Is that lead paint on the walls? Do the power frequency fields (more often called electromagnetic fields or EMF) from nearby transmission and distribution lines pose a cancer risk? An army of inspectors, contractors, and attorneys derives its livelihood from inspection for, discovery of, and remediation of those problems, if problems they be.

And therein lies the rub, for the perception of a menace and the reality of a hazard may lie far apart on the spectrum of risk, and it has become exceedingly difficult to differentiate between the two. The media assault homebuyers with stories that radon causes somewhere between 5,000 and 30,000 lung cancer deaths a year (it's remarkable that the 30,000 remains in the mind while skeptical scientists' questioning of the lower estimates doesn't make the news), that asbestos in buildings is another cause of lung cancer, that lead paint can reduce children's intelligence, and that EMF causes brain tumors. Cautious, fact-based analyses that challenge those scary

1

connections surface in the scientific literature, but the potential homebuyer rarely reads or even hears of them.

More troubling is the government's role in escalating anxiety. The Environmental Protection Agency, supported by the Centers for Disease Control, has been in the vanguard, publicizing high estimates of lung cancer cases from asbestos and radon and urging universal testing of children to determine concentrations of lead in their bodies, regardless of need or cost. The popular press has been vigilant in alerting the public about EMF, and state legislatures and public utilities have reacted with alarm, proposing and sometimes implementing costly measures to mitigate the supposed threat.

And costs mount. Testing each home in the United States for radon, as the EPA urged in 1986, would cost from $10 billion to $20 billion. "Remediating" homes to reduce radon concentrations in indoor air to the current "safe" level that the EPA says can be achieved in most homes would require from $500 billion to $1 trillion. Redoing the job in homes where the initial effort was unsuccessful would increase the bill, perhaps by several billion dollars. State legislatures debate "radon abatement" bills that would require testing in homes and schools at a cost of additional millions. The total cost to homeowners and taxpayers has yet to be calculated.

If the costs from radon are generally prospective, the past and present costs of asbestos are all too real. Through the 1980s, the EPA's insistence on the unproved theory that "one fiber can kill" led to panic and wrecked budgets as school boards ripped out asbestos-containing materials and owners of apartment and office buildings spent millions on asbestos removal rather than be saddled with unmarketable real estate.

Here as nowhere else, the costs of litigation loom large as suits originating from the World War II use of asbestos in shipyards and in the construction industry during the building boom that followed wend their way through the courts. Claims against the U. S. government alone have amounted to $14 billion. In general, the federal government's immunity to suit in such cases has held, but suits against asbestos mining and manufacturing companies have resulted in the payment of billions of dollars in settlements and damages. There may be 100,000 more suits in the next decade, and the end is not in sight.

Suits brought by people who claim their health was damaged because they lived or worked in buildings that contained asbestos have had little success. In contrast, billions of dollars are at stake in suits brought by school boards against former manufacturers of asbestos-containing materials and by those manufacturers against their insurance companies.

In 1990 the EPA conceded reluctantly that it was better to "manage asbestos in place" than to rip it out. In practice, that meant leaving the asbestos-containing materials alone until the building was renovated or demolished. But the fear lingers and so does the "rip-it-out" management approach. As a result, the discovery of asbestos in a house that is for sale is likely to force reopening of negotiations, trigger costly delays and higher closing costs, and, perhaps, expensive and unnecessary removal. With asbestos, as with other risks, homebuyers must often add the cost of removal to the other expenses of buying a house. Can they still afford the house? If not, how do they decide between skipping the removal and the fear of harming their children?

Lead awakens even more deep-seated anxieties. The fear of irremediably harming the mental abilities of one's children looms as a specter over the purchase of any home built before 1978, when lead paint was banned. "Getting the lead out" of housing is expensive; to remove all lead paint from housing would cost $30 billion, a total that bids fair to rival the national debt. Congress was aware of the impact of those costs on the federal budget when it passed the Residential Lead-Based Paint Hazard Reduction Act in 1992, and that awareness forced retrenchment from the all-out program to remove lead paint from all public housing and most rental properties. But, as of December 1996, the seller in every real estate sale and rental transaction involving housing built before 1978 must disclose all known information about lead in the unit and give the buyer a pamphlet about the dangers of lead, or face imprisonment and a $10,000 fine.

The expenses of litigation for lead are less daunting than those associated with asbestos. The numbers of suits and dollars are smaller—so far, anyway. But the associated problems of appearing in court, endless delays, and legal fees eat up the resources of defendants, and any payout to plaintiffs is a small part of the total that goes into the legal maw.

The fourth major hazard—the power lines that march across the landscape and deliver electricity to homes—is far more visible than the costs it imposes. Fear of cancer from EMF has led to vast present and projected expenditures in the name of "prudent avoidance." It is estimated that it would cost $200 billion to bury certain transmission lines nationwide and far more to reduce exposure to EMF from all transmission and distribution lines. The total cost of prudent avoidance, according to some estimates, approaches half a trillion dollars. Despite the repeated assertions of reputable scientists that such expenditures are virtually pointless, utilities and the government continue to pour additional funds into studies of the possible health effects of EMF.

The following chapters analyze the alleged risks from those hazards, the scientific debates surrounding them, and the federal policies that lead to vast expenditures to correct them. Have those outlays been necessary? The evidence induces skepticism. Credulity and fear have created an atmosphere of hysteria inimical to reasoned argument, diverting resources, burdening the taxpayer, frightening the homebuyer, and putting at risk the long-cherished goal of many Americans to own their own home.

Fluctuating mortgage rates and the specter of the loss of the mortgage deduction are less at issue than the creeping tide of even more stringent standards and even more graphic scare stories about residential environmental hazards. The widely publicized risks from asbestos, lead, radon, and EMF have raised the costs of buying and selling a house and renting an apartment and caught everyone involved in a squeeze. Sellers are raising asking prices to cover expenses while many landlords, unwilling to "delead" apartments and rental homes, are simply opting out of the game. That further distorts the housing market, making a home less affordable and an apartment more difficult to find.

As obstacles mount, disclosure forms grow even longer. Costly inspections, often followed by far costlier removal or mitigation of the hazard, complicate negotiations for purchase or rental, delay settlements, and add to the overall costs. Currently, disclosures are mainly voluntary, urged by brokers, although some states have now made them mandatory. The federal government has intruded with its disclosure rule on lead, and Congress considered a similar disclosure rule for radon in 1994. Additional intrusions will surely be attempted, and each success will increase the presence of the federal government in housing, traditionally a state and local issue.

Conceivably, the homebuyer could face expenditures ranging from $100 for a bedroom carbon monoxide detector to $25,000 for

4

a radon ventilation system to make the home conform to some recommendation, rule, or regulation. As this book shows, the federal government need not write a regulation to bring about such outcomes. It probably could not. By raising fears it coaxes brokers, sellers, and buyers to protect themselves against potential future regulations and liability, and inspections, disclosures, and remediation follow without any federal regulation.

The threat of suit is omnipresent. In today's litigious climate, real estate agents and brokers are finding it increasingly difficult to obtain errors and omissions insurance—that is, malpractice coverage—even if no grievance has ever been filed against them. Few insurance firms are willing to take on the task. Premiums for the handful of policies available mount steadily.

The sole winner in this new version of "Monopoly" may be the plaintiffs' bar. Those injured and those who believe they have been injured file suit for huge sums. They may receive little in return, even from favorable verdicts, but the attorneys generally reap rich rewards.

As the following chapters document, a large part of those costs—many of the rules and regulations, much of the litigation, and most of the anxiety—is unnecessary. For every hazard discussed—radon, asbestos, lead, EMF—the same scenario unfolds. The unveiling of a health menace, however doubtful, brings on a cascade of headlines, then a series of congressional hearings, then the passage of well-intentioned but often poorly designed legislation. The legislation provides for an expensive bureaucracy to administer new programs. The hypothetical man in the Calvin and Hobbes quote may have no good reason to scare himself silly, but many a bureaucrat has plenty of good reasons, including larger budgets, public recognition, and advancement in the agency, to scare lots of people silly.

The legislation, the rules, and the regulations often rest on a foundation of flawed research and politicized science. A vicious circle begins. Finding it safer to mount large-scale campaigns against small and doubtful risks than to question popular (if ill-informed) views, agencies and the bureaucrats who run them raise the level of anxiety. The media, uncertain of the science and unwilling or unable to spend the time necessary to understand the underlying scientific and political issues, fan the flames. Scare stories, after all, sell more papers than good news. To deepen the confusion, scientists qualifying as "sensible experts" are too often preoccupied with their own research, teaching, and pursuit of research funding to play a significant role in the debate. Reluctant to become involved, many scientists abdicate, allowing the politicization of science to proceed almost unchecked.

The general public, however unwittingly, plays into the hands of the journalists, the bureaucrats, and the purveyors of defective studies. Frightened by the horror stories publicized by their government, many people become totally risk averse, unwilling to tolerate even a scintilla of menace. Insistent on absolute safety, however impossible that goal may be, they help to perpetuate the vicious and expensive circle of doubt and anxiety.

This book is intended as a resource for those dealing with such problems—the prospective buyer and seller of a home, the landlord and tenant, the real estate community, attorneys weighing the merits of a case, legislators looking for an assessment of risk. Faced with an inspector's report of asbestos in the ceiling, consumers and those on whom they depend should have at hand a reference to help them evaluate the threat. Asking the critical questions may not only allay anxiety but may also help the puzzled buyer or renter to decide on a reasonable course of action. Students in courses on environmental policy may also find the book of interest because it outlines the policymaking involved in those issues and suggests approaches for improvement.

Risk assessment is central to the debate about what has come to be called "haunted housing." Risks from radon, asbestos, and lead are based on adverse effects seen in people who were exposed to far greater concentrations in the workplace. The government makes extrapolations from those exposures and those effects to predict the effects of far lower residential exposure. In the cases of asbestos and radon, the predicted effects are so small that they cannot be seen against the "background" rates of lung cancer. The decreases in IQ that have been associated with lead exposure in homes are highly suspect on methodological grounds. The issue of EMF is different in that the evidence for its effects comes almost entirely from studies of residential exposure, and none of those studies has established a tie between measured EMF and disease.

Risk dominates the policy debate, but government at all levels is reluctant to deal openly with the uncertainties in the risk estimates. Those uncertainties can be addressed through a series of questions:

What is the level of the risk? How confident are we of the government's estimate? Are there opposing estimates? How credible are those? What alternatives are there to letting government agencies, with vested interests in the outcome, decide on the risk? Is the risk great enough to warrant attention? What methods can reduce it? How significant are the reductions? Will the methods work? How well? What will be the benefits? What will be the costs?

Federal, state, and local policymakers and the popular press make little attempt to discuss those issues in depth. Sophisticated analyses are relegated to academic journals. The resulting drive to mitigate questionable environmental hazards penalizes not only buyers, sellers, and landlords but all taxpayers. Unnecessary initiatives bloat government budgets, imposing outlays with little or no regard to expected benefits.

This book attempts to redress the balance.

1. Radon: The Spectral Presence

For more than 20 years, radon has been a concern for Congress, the Department of Energy, and the Environmental Protection Agency. The EPA has issued bulletin after bulletin warning home dwellers to test and remediate for the gas that, it claims, causes between 7,000 and 30,000 cases of lung cancer annually. The public, however, has remained generally apathetic: perhaps 5 percent of homes have been tested; fewer still have been "mitigated" to reduce radon concentrations.

In yet another effort to galvanize buyers and sellers of homes into action, Congress drafted the Radon Awareness and Disclosure Act of 1994. The legislation would have mandated that sellers provide buyers of commercial or residential structures less than three stories high with a pamphlet detailing the hazards of radon and containing a list of EPA-approved firms that could measure radon and implement mitigation procedures to reduce concentrations of the gas.[1] The pamphlet would also have included a roster of government offices to be contacted for further information and recommended testing procedures for those who wished to do the testing themselves. At the time of selling, purchasers and sellers of homes would have had to acknowledge having received and read a Radon Warning Statement and buyers would have received notification of their right to conduct an independent radon test.

Before that date the government had relied on voluntary actions to reduce exposures. As drafted, the 1994 act would have moved toward mandatory testing and mitigation at a cost, projected in

---

[1]Three stories is a curious limit since even a 100-story building has lower floors and, presumably, a basement where radon exposure would be higher. In some measure, the EPA would have been denying the "protection" of disclosure to those living on the lower floors of tall buildings.

1991, of \$44 billion.[2] It is likely that the final cost would have been much higher.

To justify proposing such an expenditure, radon must surely pose a deadly threat, but many respected scientists have voiced doubts about the nature and extent of the menace. The EPA and Congress have generally disregarded the skeptics; the Department of Energy has been more circumspect in its evaluation of a possible hazard but has found it difficult to make itself heard, and the public remains largely unmoved by EPA exhortations.

Radon and the Specter of Radiation

Radon is a naturally occurring gas, neither mysterious nor necessarily fearsome. Produced by a nuclear decay chain beginning with uranium in rocks and soil, radon is colorless, odorless, and tasteless. Because uranium ores are widespread, uranium-238, a precursor of radium-226, which in turn produces radon-222, is present in soil and rock virtually everywhere in the United States. Granite igneous and metamorphic rocks, black shales, and phosphatic rocks, as well as certain glacial deposits, are all rich in uranium. The richest uranium ores, however, occur in the sedimentary rocks of the Colorado plateau in western Colorado and adjacent parts of Utah, Arizona, Wyoming, and New Mexico. The black shale underlying parts of Tennessee, Kentucky, Ohio, Indiana, and Illinois contains lower grade deposits; the most important phosphate areas in the country lie in north and west-central Florida. Maps released by the EPA in 1986 and 1987 identify those areas as having potentially high radon levels.[3]

Wherever uranium occurs, radon escapes constantly into the atmosphere.[4] Well water that has passed through uranium-bearing rock

---

[2]Tony Snow, "Writing Radon into Every Homeowner Deal," *Washington Times*, August 8, 1994, p. A18. Update: State of Wisconsin, Department of Radiation, telephone conversation, July 23, 1996.

[3]Kenneth Q. Lao, *Controlling Indoor Radon* (New York: Van Nostrand, Reinhold, 1990), pp. 27, 28. For a more detailed analysis of the various deposits, see A. Bertrand Brill et al., "Radon Update: Facts Concerning Environmental Radon: Levels, Mitigation Strategies, Dosimetry, Effects and Guidelines," *Journal of Nuclear Medicine* 35, no. 2 (February 1994): 372–73.

[4]Ibid., p. 1; Ben Bolch and Harold Lyons, "A Multibillion-Dollar Radon Scare," *Public Interest*, no. 99 (Spring 1990): 62.

and water from certain deep aquifers also emit radon into the atmosphere. In other words, radon is part of the air we breathe and constitutes a significant element of the background radiation that is always with us. Like cosmic rays, a major constituent of natural radiation, it is unavoidable.

Why has radon elicited such an intense reaction? It is radioactive, an attribute that evokes fear, perhaps dating from the anxieties raised by the nuclear testing of the 1950s and 1960s and, even further back, from the explosions at Hiroshima and Nagasaki that ended World War II.[5] The outrage that greeted France's decision to resume nuclear tests in the South Pacific in 1995 had its wellspring in those earlier events.

Radon, one of the "noble gases," is chemically nonreactive and relatively free to move through other gases, liquids, and porous solids; once it is released into the air, water, or soil, it tends to travel around. Unlike the other noble gases, however, radon is unstable and decays to other elements, called "daughters" or "progeny." Each of the decays releases packets of radioactive energy.

Despite the attention given to radon, that element, itself, poses no substantial health risk. Instead it is the chain of radioactive particles released from the decay of radon that poses the risk.[6] Radon is not a major risk because it has a half-life of approximately four days, meaning that, on average, four days will pass before a radon atom decays to release radioactivity. As a result, a molecule of radon that is breathed into the lungs will almost certainly be exhaled before it decays. On the other hand, the short-lived radon progeny, or radon daughters, have half-lives measured in minutes to microseconds, and once in the lung, they are very likely to decay and release

[5]Elizabeth Whelan makes this point when discussing the fear of nuclear power in *Toxic Terror*. "The 'environmentalists' of the 1950s had a *genuine* cause for alarm, with some hard data to back up their demands for more discriminate use of nuclear testing devices. Today's environmentalists, however, seem to be constantly groping for a cause and so often those causes turn out to be those of combating purely hypothetical risk." Elizabeth M. Whelan, *Toxic Terror* (Ottawa, Ill.: Jameson Books, 1985), p. 63.

[6]William W. Nazaroff and Kevin Teichman, "Indoor Radon," *Environmental Science Technology* 24, no. 6 (1990): 775.

radioactivity.[7] This distinction, in fact, makes little practical difference because measurements of radon provide information about
expected exposures to its decay products. The progeny (or daughters) continue to decay, finally resulting in nonradioactive lead
atoms.

Radon and its daughters release alpha particles that, when
released in the lungs, can collide with and penetrate into cells, deliv-
ering a large amount of energy and damaging DNA and other cellu-
lar components. Alpha particles, the nuclei of helium atoms, constitute the largest and slowest and therefore the least penetrating form
of radiation. They generally pose no risk when emitted outside the
body; the skin can stop them. They can penetrate lung cells, however,
with unstoppable force. The decay chain also produces beta particles.
Far smaller—the size of an electron—more penetrating, and faster
moving, beta particles deliver smaller packets of energy to cells, and
they are not the major source of risk from radon. They too can be
stopped by a thin barrier, such as aluminum foil.[8]

Lest this scenario set the stage for another round of "toxic terror,"
it is worth noting that humans have a remarkable capacity to repair
DNA damage. Dr. Leonard Sagan, for example, notes that "human
beings are about one-fourth as sensitive to radiation as was previously expected from forecasts using studies on rats, that statistical
studies of survivors of atomic bombing have failed to produce statistically significant results, and that the ability of human DNA to
repair itself is indeed remarkable."[9]

Because radiation is so often perceived as a fearful specter, the
source of deformity and disease, the potential for reversal and recovery is worthy of emphasis. Elevated doses of radiation can indeed

[7]Lao, pp. 6, 13, 264; Mueller Associates, Inc., SYSCON Corporation, Brookhaven
National Laboratory. *Handbook of Radon in Buildings: Detection, Safety, and Control*
(New York: Hemisphere Publishing Corporation, 1988).

[8]The EPA has also proposed a theoretical risk of stomach cancer from the ingestion
of radon-rich water, but the proposal has received relatively little attention. The
presence of food readily stops the alpha particles and "there is no known direct
evidence linking ingested radon to the increase of gastrointestinal cancer incidences."
Lao, pp. 56–58.

Nevertheless, the EPA based its so far unsuccessful attempt at regulating radon in
water on the stomach cancer risk. See U.S. Congress, Office of Technology Assessment,
"Indoor Radon," in *Researching Health Risks*. OTA-BBS-570 (Washington: Government
Printing Office, November 1993), pp. 156–65.

[9]Bolch and Lyons, *Public Interest* 99 (Spring 1990): 67.

cause somatic damage by destroying tissue or causing burns; lower exposures, such as those experienced by miners, have increased cancer rates. Obviously, caution is warranted for radiation exposure. At the same time, a number of the studies outlined below suggest the existence of a threshold below which radiation does not increase cancer rates.

Historical Development

Before outlining the development of radon policy, a historical perspective may be helpful. The radon controversy has its roots in the proliferation of uranium mines after World War II, when the Atomic Energy Commission made the development of domestic sources of uranium a high priority. Without doubt those early mines were extremely unhealthy—dusty, unventilated "dog holes."[10] For the miner, ventilation ran a poor second to extraction of the uranium ore. To make matters worse, most of the miners smoked, so cigarette smoke mingled with mineral dusts containing uranium and its decay products. Not only radiation but the dust itself irritated the lungs.

An officer of the U.S. Public Health Service who monitored the uranium mines of the Colorado plateau from 1951 to 1971 reported the primitive conditions. Attempting to improve radon monitoring, he noted the difficulty of obtaining reliable measurements. The miners themselves made many of those measurements and tended to underestimate exposures.[11]

A link between radioactivity in the mines and lung cancer had been suspected as early as the 1930s, and, in the 1950s and 1960s, epidemiologic studies of miners in Europe and the western United States confirmed that prolonged exposure to radon gas in mines causes cancer. In the late 1960s the U.S. Public Health Service responded by setting an occupational limit on the amount of gas to which any American miner could be exposed.[12]

---

[10]Philip H. Abelson, "Radon Today: The Role of Flimflam in Public Policy," *Regulation* 14, no. 4 (Fall 1991): 95, 96. Abelson cites John Morgan, a purchasing agent for the Atomic Energy Commission, as calling the mines "dog holes."

[11]Ibid., p. 95.

[12]Leonard A. Cole, *Element of Risk: The Politics of Radon* (Washington: AAAS Press, 1993), pp. 9–10; U.S. Congress, Office of Technology Assessment, *Researching Health Risks* (Washington: Government Printing Office, November 1993), p. 153. [Hereafter this document is referred to as "OTA" in this chapter.]

Emerging Concern

Radon remained for many years largely a concern of miners. In the 1960s, however, high levels of radon were discovered in Grand Junction, Colorado, where homes had been built atop waste products ("tailings") from uranium mines. Utilization of the tailings from the mines is traceable to the Atomic Energy Commission's failure to supervise the milling industry on the plateau, and large volumes were used as fill for new houses. Although anxiety over radon has ballooned out of proportion to the risk, its origins have a basis in fact. In response to growing concern, Congress passed the Uranium Mill Tailing Radiation Control Act (1978), directing the EPA to promulgate health standards for areas near uranium processing sites.[13]

A few years later, however, radon in homes jumped from being the concern of a small number of people in a remote area in the West to being characterized as a threat to as many as 80 million of the 240 million people in the United States. In 1984 an engineer named Stanley Watras set off a radiation detection device on his way *into* work at a nuclear power plant that was under construction in Pennsylvania. Investigation revealed that the source of the radiation was a radon level in his home 16 times that permitted by occupational standards for uranium mines.[14] It also disclosed that Mr. Watras's house was built above an old mine. Neighboring homes did not have elevated radon levels, foreshadowing the common finding of very localized "hot spots" and "hot houses" in areas characterized by lower levels of exposure.

The discovery created widespread consternation. It appeared that radon was to be found not only in mines but in homes, not only in Pennsylvania but throughout the United States. Since uranium miners who had inhaled radon had shown a high incidence of lung cancer, it was quickly inferred that radon in the home posed a similar threat, despite the much lower concentrations and the quite different conditions. Exploration of the possible radon menace rapidly involved the federal government, initiating a complex interplay among the EPA, the Department of Energy, the U.S. Public Health Service, and the Congress that has consistently raised the stakes ever

[13]Jeanne Prussman, "The Radon Riddle," *Boston College Environmental Affairs Law Review* 18 (1991): 716 n. 8; 719 n. 23.

[14]OTA, p. 148.

since. The threat to health is uncertain; the potential cost to the consumer and taxpayer in dollars is staggering; the regulatory threat and the menace of liability may be as frightening to homeowners as the specter of radiation.

How Radon Risks Are Estimated and Why Risks from Indoor Radon Can't Be Measured

The EPA, like every other organization that estimates radon risks, bases its estimates on the results of occupational epidemiology studies that examine lung cancer rates in workers exposed to high levels of radon. Few of the many studies of possible relationships between the lower exposures to radon that are experienced in the home have shown any association. Although the EPA touts the few that do as "smoking guns" that prove the risk, careful analysis shows that "residential studies" can neither detect the risk from radon, if there is one, nor prove that there is no risk. Scientists whose research is supported by the federal government have done analyses that show residential studies will not provide definitive information, but the government continues to fund those studies. Finally, "ecological studies" that compare lung cancer risks with average radon levels in states or counties demonstrate an inverse relationship—cancer rates fall with increasing radon levels.

Because we lack, and probably always will lack, direct information about risks from indoor or residential radon, there will always be arguments about the risk estimates. At the bottom of those arguments are disagreements about the extrapolation models (generally called simply "models") used to estimate risks at low exposures.

Risk Models

Over 15 years ago, the EPA adopted the convention of a no-threshold linear model for indoor exposure to radon.[15] The following outline presents that model succinctly:

> Also known as the linear model, the linear, no-threshold model assumes that the risk of cancer is linearly proportional to the absorbed dose. If the absorbed dose is ten times higher, then the number of cancer incidences is also ten times higher. [And] any radiation exposure may carry some risk.[16]

[15]Frank B. Cross and Paula C. Murray, "Liability for Toxic Radon Gas in Residential Home Sales," *North Carolina Law Review 66* (1988): 696, n. 61, 62.

[16]Lao, p. 63. The author cites a 1981 report from the General Accounting Office.

The EPA has clung to this convention like a limpet to a rock despite growing criticism from the scientific community.

Although research to date has failed to invalidate the linear model, some researchers view it skeptically. It has been criticized as "a naive way to predict most phenomena ... used only ... when so little information is available that no other technique seems possible,"[17] and, indeed, examination of all the information about radiation risks has been unable to demonstrate that the linear model is the only one that fits the data.[18] The EPA's continual adherence to the linear model, with no serious consideration of any other, has the important consequence of predicting higher cancer risks and providing more justification for a regulatory program.

The linear model runs counter to most observations of cause and effect that result in "S-shaped" dose-response curves. The linear model also rules out a "threshold," the possibility that there is some low level below which there is no appreciable effect. Use of either an S-shaped model or a threshold model greatly reduces the cancer risks associated with indoor radon.

Differing even more sharply from the linear, no-threshold approach is the concept known as "hormesis,"[19] which is the idea that exposure to radiation [or some chemicals] at low levels may be beneficial because they could stimulate the body's defense mechanisms. Philip Abelson notes:

> Some experimental data indicate no effect or a beneficial effect for small radiation exposures. ... Moreover, it has been shown that low-level radiations make the cells less susceptible to subsequent high doses of radiation. This adaptive response has been attributed to the induction of a chromosomal break-repair mechanism.[20]

Phrased more colloquially, people are more resilient than prophets of doom would have us believe. Abelson continues, "Moderate but

[17]Bolch and Lyons, p. 64.

[18]Committee on the Biological Effects of Ionizing Radiation, National Research Council, *Health Risks of Radon and Other Internally Deposited Alpha-Emitters, BEIR IV* (Washington: National Academy Press, 1988). Referred to hereafter as BEIR IV.

[19]Ibid., p. 67. See also T. D. Luckey, *Radiation Hormesis* (Boca Raton, Fla.: CRC Press, 1991); cited in Competitive Enterprise Institute, p. 15 n. 21.

[20]Abelson, p. 96.

higher than average levels of radon correlate with beneficial lessening of the incidence of lung cancer ... a finding that appears to hold elsewhere in the world."[21] The German scientist Klaus Becker asserted, "The biopositive, therapeutic effects of radon in moderate concentrations appear to be much better established than any possible detrimental effects on man."[22]

Hormesis is probably not "an idea whose time has come"; it is too radically different from the conventional wisdom that anything that causes harm at high exposures will also cause harm at lower exposures. Nevertheless, county-by-county studies of radon levels and lung cancer as well as other comparisons of average lung cancer rates and average radon levels support a hormetic effect.

The Health Physics Society and Risks from Indoor Radon

Probably no professional group has better credentials for having opinions about radiation risk than the Health Physics Society, "a non-profit scientific organization dedicated exclusively to the protection of people and the environment from radiation."[23]

> In accordance with current knowledge of radiation health risks, the Health Physics Society recommends against quantitative estimation of health risk below a dose of 5 rem [a measure of radiation dose] in one year, or a lifetime dose of 10 rem in addition to background radiation. Risk estimation in this dose range should be strictly qualitative accentuating a range of hypothetical health outcomes with an emphasis on the likely possibility of zero adverse health effects ... Below 10 rem (which includes occupational and environmental exposures) risks of health effects are either too small to be observed or non-existent.[24]

Discussion of risks from radon requires the use of measurements of doses of radiation or exposures to radiation. The "rem" is a unit of exposure that is used in the radiation protection community, and

[21]Ibid., pp. 96, 97.

[22]Klaus Becker, "How Dangerous Is Radon in Buildings? Some Reflections from Europe," *Risk Analysis* 14 (1994): 1–2.

[23]Health Physics Society, "Radiation Risk in Perspective," position statement, 1996, McLean, Va.

[24]Ibid.

a worker in a modern nuclear facility will be exposed to less than 5 rem per year.

A different measure, "picoCurie per liter" (pCi/l),[25] is used in discussions of indoor radon exposures. The EPA has decided that indoor concentrations above 4 pCi/l are cause for concern, and 4 pCi/l has been set as an "action level," at which efforts should be made to reduce radon exposures.

The EPA's action level, 4 pCi/l, is equivalent to about 2.4 rem/year,[26] if a person spent the entire year in a part of a house at that level. In fact, people spend time outdoors and in upper floors of multistory buildings where exposures are lower. Leaving aside those complications in estimating exposures and following the recommendations of the Health Physics Society, no efforts should be made to estimate the risk from indoor exposures less than 8.2 pCi/l (equivalent to 5 rem/year). In contrast, the EPA makes its quantitative estimate of lung cancer mortality risk by assuming that any exposure above zero increases the risk. The EPA's predictions of 13,000 or so annual deaths from indoor radon exposure should be dismissed as wild speculation and replaced with a sober statement that all exposures below 8.2 pCi/l can be described as having some "hypothetical health outcomes with an emphasis on the likely possibility of zero adverse health effects."[27] The risk from exposures above 8.2 pCi/l amounts to about 1,000 lung cancer deaths a year.[28] Even that number is speculative, and, as is discussed below, there is no way to be certain that the risk is even that high. Incorporation of the Health Physics Society's recommendation or any other recommendation like it would lead to a much different discussion of indoor

[25]A pico (p) Curie is a measure of radioactivity. "Pico" means one-trillionth, so a picoCurie (pCi) is one–trillionth of a Curie. One Curie is equal to 3.7 × 1010 radioactive disintegrations per second or 2.2 disintegrations per minute. The measure 4 pCi/l means that the radioactivity in one liter (l) of air (or water) produces 4 × 2.2 disintegrations per minute = 8.8 disintegrations per minute. Other countries commonly use "becquerels per cubic meter" (Bq/m3) to express concentrations of radioactivity, and 1 pCi/l is equal to 37 Bq/m3. See OTA, p. 146.

[26]Bruce Busby, University of Michigan, stated that exposures to 4 pCi/l are equivalent to about 2.4 rem/year. Electronic communication to Michael Gough, director of science and risk studies, Cato Institute, September 8, 1996.

[27]Ibid.

[28]OTA, figure 6-1, p. 156.

radon, but the EPA and its allies can be expected to fight the society's recommendation to the bitter end.

The next three subsections discuss the kinds of information available about radon risks. The occupational studies show that high radon exposures increase lung cancer rates, the residential studies show that low exposures do not cause observable increases, and the county-by-county comparisons show that lung cancer rates decrease with increasing levels of radon. The Health Physics Society's recommendations change none of those conclusions, but the society would reject making estimates of risk by making extrapolations from the results of the occupational (miners) studies to estimated risks at indoor exposure levels. Instead, the society would say that while there may be some risks at indoor levels, it would place "an emphasis on the likely possiblity of zero adverse health effects."

The society's recommendations would not affect interpretation of the county-by-county studies. Those interpretations do not involve any extrapolation because they depend on measured cancer rates that are compared with measured radon levels.

The Bases for the Estimates of Risk from Indoor Radon

The EPA relies heavily on two analyses of occupational radon studies as the basis of its risk estimates: One, published in 1984 by the National Council of Radiation Protection and Measurement, is the NCRP study (NCRP),[29] and the other is the BEIR IV (Biological Effects of Ionizing Radiation) Report produced by a committee of the National Research Council, an arm of the National Academy of Sciences, in 1988.[30] The NCRP report cited studies from Europe and Canada, as well as the United States, and BEIR IV drew heavily on a survey of literature about uranium miners on the Colorado Plateau. As complete as those reviews are, Philip Abelson captured their shortcoming when he said of BEIR IV, "It is a careful study, but it can be no more reliable than the fragmentary data available to the committee."[31] In particular, there is very little information about exposures (there were very few measurements in the 1940s and

[29]National Council on Radiation Protection and Measurements. *Report*, no. 78 (Bethesda, Md.: NCRP, 1984).

[30]National Research Council, *Health Risks of Radon and Other Deposited Alpha-Emitters. BEIR IV* (Washington: National Academy Press, 1988). [Called "BEIR IV" hereafter.]

[31]Abelson, p. 96.

1950s, and the few that are available are of questionable value). Therefore, as rigorous as the process may be, "exposure reconstruction," which is at the heart of risk estimation, remains something of a guessing game.

Equally fundamental are the problems with the extrapolation models. There is no way to verify that predictions made with them are accurate—the predicted numbers of lung cancers at low exposure levels are too few to be detected against the usual "background" number of lung cancer cases if, indeed, they occur.

Both the NCRP and BEIR IV calculated the risks from miners' exposures to high levels of radon, and both pointed to other factors, such as smoking, that contributed to the risk. Philip Abelson stated, "The one conclusion of the [BEIR IV] report that is valid beyond doubt is that at high doses of radon, miners who are cigarette smokers experience an enhanced incidence of lung cancer. The data with respect to nonsmokers are less impressive."[32]

The BEIR V report, published in 1990, considered some of the special conditions in mines and modified BEIR IV's quantitative risk estimate. In particular, mines are far dustier than homes and radon progeny that are attached to dust particles are more likely to be inhaled and more likely to remain in the lungs, and miners are working hard, breathing deeply and inhaling more air than most people engaged in indoor activites. Those considerations led the EPA to reduce its risk estimates, but not significantly. The director of the EPA's Office of Radiation Programs announced that the estimated lung cancer risk for smokers exposed to radon dropped from 4 chances in 100 to 3 chances in 100. He continued to caution that "radon is still one of the larger health risks people face."[33]

To their credit, NCRP and BEIR IV also underscored doubts about risks at lower levels, leading Philip Cole, the author of a popular book about radon, to conclude, "Virtually every scientific report on the subject [recognizes] that the effects of radon levels commonly found indoors are speculative."[34] Similarily, Brill and his associates conclude, "The shape of the dose response curves for miners exposed

[32]Ibid.

[33]Quoted in Warren E. Leary, "U.S. Study Finds a Reduced Cancer Danger from Radon in Homes," *New York Times*, February 12, 1991, p. L10.

[34]Cole, p. 29.

... in the workplace ... is linear." But they limit that conclusion when it comes to risks at low exposures: "No detectable increase in lung cancer frequency is seen in the lowest exposed miners." And they go on to say that "no compelling evidence for increased cancer risks has yet been demonstrated from 'acceptable' levels (<4–8 pCi/l)."[35] The "acceptable" levels are three to six times as high as average indoor radon concentrations.

Those quotes illuminate the quandary. At high levels, lung cancer increases with increasing radon concentrations. At lower occupational levels and certainly at levels found in homes, there is no verified increase in cancer. That is consistent with either of two conclusions: (1) that there is no effect at low levels or (2) that the effect is so small as to be undetectable in the number of people who have been studied. Laying those reservations aside, "The EPA continues to base its estimate of annual lung cancer deaths from radon on incomplete data, a statistical method [linear, no-threshold] of questionable validity and a glaring lack of evidence from epidemiological surveys that would substantiate such a large number."[36]

While everyone would like better evidence to support or refute the EPA estimate, no better evidence is likely to be forthcoming. Occupational exposure is far lower now than in the past; there will be no more highly exposed populations (unless there are nuclear accidents or nuclear war), and direct studies of people exposed to indoor radon cannot distinguish between no effect and an effect so small as to be undetectable. That quandary, the same seen in studies of low-level occupational exposure, has not stopped such studies from being done.

Studies of the Effects of Indoor Radon

Case-control methods are used to investigate possible relationships between diseases and exposure. In most studies of indoor radon, the "cases" are women (women are less likely to be smokers) who have been diagnosed with lung cancer, and "controls" are women of similar age, background, and areas of residence who do not have lung cancer. Then the investigators measure (or, less satisfyingly, estimate) radon levels in the women's homes. Because

[35]Brill et al., p. 368.
[36]Cole, p. 27.

radon exposure years ago might contribute to risk, measurements or estimates often have to be made in several dwellings for every case and control. If indoor radon contributes to the causation of cancer, concentrations of radon in the homes of the cancer cases should be higher than in the homes of the controls.

The Office of Technology Assessment has provided a readable review of the residential studies (and ecological studies discussed in the next section) that were published before 1993, and the interested reader is directed to that source.[37] Most of those studies failed to find any association, and since then researchers at the National Cancer Institute have published a careful examination of more than 500 Missouri women with lung cancer that failed to find any association.[38] Canadian investigators concluded: "After adjusting for cigarette smoking, education, ethnicity, and occupational confounders, no increase in the relative risk of any of the histologic types of lung cancer observed among cases was detected in relation to cumulative exposure to radon."[39] More recently, a group of Finnish scientists published very similar results from the study of a slightly larger and more heavily exposed population. They concluded,

> In the analysis stratified by age, sex, smoking status, or histologic type of cancer, no statistically significant indications of increased risk of lung cancer related to indoor radon concentration were observed for any of the subgroups ["stratification" is various techniques to separate out the effects of age, sex, etc. from the effects of radon].[40]

The Finnish scientists summarized their results and the implications of those results as follows:

> Our analyses do not indicate increased risk of lung cancer from indoor radon exposure. *Implication:* Indoor radon exposure does not appear to be an important cause of lung cancer.[41]

[37]OTA, pp. 145–70.

[38]M. C. R. Alavanga et al., "Residential Radon Exposure and Lung Cancer among Nonsmoking Women." *Journal of the National Cancer Institute* 86 (1994): 1829–37.

[39]E. G. Létourneau et al., "A Case-Control Study of Residential Radon and Lung Cancer in Winnipeg, Manitoba," *American Journal of Epidemiology* 140 (1994): 310–22.

[40]A. Auvinen et al., "Indoor Radon Exposure and Risk of Lung Cancer," *Journal of the National Cancer Institute* 88, no. 14 (1996): 966–72.

[41]Ibid.

Regardless of how many such studies are done and of the number of studies that do or do not find an association, that approach will never settle the question of the size of the risk from indoor radon, or even whether a risk exists. This conclusion follows from the fact that the predicted risks from indoor radon are so small that they cannot be detected in any conceivable residential study.

Michael Gough, formerly at the OTA and now at the Cato Institute, wrote Dr. Richard D. Klausner, director of the National Cancer Institute, in early 1996 to question the continued funding of residential studies.[42] Gough cited a 1990 paper[43] that concluded that it is a practical impossibility to design and mount a sufficiently large study of residential exposure to test the predictions from the occupational studies and a later paper[44] arguing that pooling data from all such studies will not resolve the issue.

Gough characterized the studies that have been done as showing "the detected cancer incidence . . . is in a range that is consistent both with no radon-associated lung cancer increase and with an increase as large as that predicted by the miners studies."[45] "Why," he asked, "do the National Institutes of Health continue to spend money on studies that have insufficient power to test the hypotheses about lung cancer risk that are based on the miners data?" The letter was not answered.

Ecological Studies and Hormesis

Curiously enough, data from the EPA itself suggest the fallacy of the linear approach. An agency survey of 34 states showed that exposure in five midwestern states was about twice the national level. Yet "the lung cancer incidence in those five highest radon states was reported as only about 80 percent of the national average."[46] That result was no aberration. In a study of 750 people who had lived in

---

[42]Michael Gough, letter to Richard D. Klausner, director of the National Cancer Institute, April 3, 1996. Copy in the possession of the author.

[43]J. H. Lubin, J. M. Samat, and C. Weinberg, "Design Issues in Epidemiologic Studies of Indoor Exposure to Radon and Lung Cancer," *Health Physics* 59 (1990): 807–17.

[44]J. H. Lubin, J. D. Boice Jr., and J. M. Samat, "Errors in Exposure Assessment, Statistical Power and the Interpretation of Residential Radon Studies," *Radiation Research* 144 (1995): 329–41.

[45]Gough, letter.

[46]Abelson, p. 96.

houses with high radon levels over the past 60 years, the New Jersey Department of Health could draw no statistically valid link between radon and lung cancer: "White males had slightly higher rates of lung cancer deaths compared to the general population, but in homes with the highest radon concentrations the incidence of lung cancer deaths was lower." Ralph Lapp, a radiation physicist, reported that natural radon levels were seven times greater in New Jersey than in Texas, yet lung cancer deaths as a ratio of total cancer deaths were almost the same for the two states.[47]

Nobel laureate Rosalyn Yalow summed up the results of several epidemiological studies:

> In the three states with the highest mean radon levels in home living areas (Colorado, North Dakota, Iowa: 3.9, 3.5, 3.3 pCi/l respectively), the lung cancer death rate averages 41 per 100,000, and in the three states with the lowest radon levels (Delaware, Louisiana, California: 0.75, 0.96, 0.97 pCi/liter respectively), the rate averages 66 per 100,000.[48]

In other words, the average lung cancer death rate was 39 percent *lower* in the states with the highest levels, a result that would give pause to anyone but an EPA administrator.

A descriptive study of lung cancer death rates versus county levels of radon in Washington State showed a significant lung cancer excess in the lowest radon counties. Furthermore, "The trend in rates was statistically significant: the rates decreased toward the highest radon counties."[49]

Studies that compare average radon exposure with lung cancer rates in a county or state are viewed with great suspicion because they suffer from the "ecological fallacy." The fallacy arises because nothing is known about the exposure of the individuals who develop cancer. The EPA, at least, uses that criticism selectively. It dismisses ecological studies that show no connection between radon and lung

---

[47]Leonard A. Cole, "Radon Scare—Where's the Proof?" *New York Times*, October 6, 1988, p. A31.

[48]Cited by Abelson, p. 97.

[49]John S. Neuberger, Floyd J. Frost, and Kenneth B. Gerald, "Residential Radon Exposure and Lung Cancer," *Journal of Environmental Health* 55, no. 3 (November/December 1992): 23.

cancer but bases its claims about the health effects of airborne particulates on ecological studies.

Professor Bernard Cohen of the University of Pittsburgh and his associates have completed a series of papers that contradict the linear model and support the concept of hormesis and have addressed the criticisms that are raised against the studies. As the organizing principle of his study, Cohen ranked counties from highest to lowest on the basis of their lung cancer rates and then determined radon levels in each county. According to theories of increasing cancer with increasing exposure, the average radon level in the counties with the highest lung cancer rates should have been about three times higher than in the counties with the lowest lung cancer rates. Instead, preliminary data showed that the average radon level in the *highest* lung cancer counties was only about one-half that in the counties with the lowest lung cancer.[50]

Subsequent studies confirmed the observation. Professor Cohen's analysis of 965 counties nationwide found "a strong negative slope [lung cancer rates decreased with increasing radon levels], which is highly significantly different from the slope predicted using linear/nonthresholds models and BEIR IV data."[51] To "significantly different," "contradictory" can be added.

The study was then extended to 1,600 U.S. counties.[52] Professor Cohen states, "After correcting for variations in smoking frequency, . . . there is a strong tendency for m[ortality] to *decrease* with *increasing* r[adon], in contrast to the sharp increase expected from the theory" (emphasis added). He concludes,

> The principal conclusion from this work is that the conventional linear, no-threshold theory . . . fails badly, greatly overestimating the health impacts of low dose, low dose rate radiation. One is further tempted to conclude that low level

---

[50]Bernard L. Cohen, "Expected Indoor 222 Rn Levels in Counties with Very High and Very Low Lung Cancer Rates," *Health Physics* 57, no. 6 (December 1989): 897, 906.

[51]Cited by Brill et al., pp. 381, 385. The study appeared in *Indoor Radon and Lung Cancer: Reality or Myth*, ed. F. T. Cross (Columbus, Ohio: Batelle Press, 1992): 959–75.

[52]Brill et al., pp. 381, 385. The study cited by Brill et al. appeared as "Relationship between Exposure to Radon and Various Types of Cancer," *Health Physics* 65 (1993): 234–51.

exposure to radon is protective against lung cancer, as proposed in the theory of hormesis.[53]

Professor Cohen's analysis has been attacked on methodological
grounds by several scientists who suggested that other factors might
have confounded his results. In particular, questions were raised
about smoking rates and the frequency with which people move
(for instance, a person who lived most of his life in a high-radon
area might move late in life to a low-radon area and die there,
leading to a spurious association). Professor Cohen has addressed
the issues of "smoking prevalence" (though not of rates, which
would require a long, expensive, and difficult case-control study)
and "migration" and has concluded that they do not explain his
findings. Moreover, he has explored the possible effects of every
factor suggested by his critics that might affect his results—geography, climate, altitude, smoking rates, and socioeconomic conditions
that vary from county to county—54 socioeconomic factors in all.
None explains the discrepancy between the increase in lung cancer
rates expected from increased exposure according to the linear model
and the tendency of those rates to *decrease* as exposure rises. By
extension, Professor Cohen's results lend weight to the findings in
the studies in the Midwest, New Jersey, and elsewhere that do not
confirm the linear model.[54]

In a summary of his research, Cohen states, "In spite of extensive
efforts, no potential explanation for the discrepancy other than failure of the linear, no-threshold theory for carcinogenesis from inhaled
radon decay products could be found."[55] His work is a serious assault
on the linear hypothesis, and the EPA's general response has been
to ignore it.

Summary of the Models and the Evidence

The EPA and this chapter discuss what may appear to be precise
estimates of the numbers of cancers to be expected from exposure

[53]Bernard L. Cohen, "Test of the Linear No Threshold Theory of Radiation Carcinogenesis in the Low Dose, Low Dose Rate Region." Xeroxed copy in the possession
of the author, n.d., pp. 1, 35.

[54]Ibid.

[55]Bernard L. Cohen, "Test of the Linear No Threshold Theory of Radiation Carcinogenesis for Inhaled Radon Decay Products," *Health Physics* 68, no. 2 (February
1995): 157.

to radon in homes. The numbers are only estimates; there is no way to verify them, and there is room for skepticism about the model that is used to generate them. There is even evidence for an inverse relationship between radon levels and lung cancer.

Although the numbers of cancers that might be averted by reducing radon exposures are very uncertain, there can be no doubt about the costs of reducing radon exposures. The costs, as we will see, would be very large.

Enter the Federal Government

In 1983, to comply with the Uranium Mill Tailings Radiation Control Act passed five years earlier, the EPA set 4 pCi/l of air radon as the level that would mandate an "action response" for homes on tailings. There would be a maximum limit of 6 pCi/l. At that point, the agency was willing to acknowledge uncertainty: "We recognize that the data available [do not preclude] a threshold for some types of damage below which there are no harmful effects. . . ."[56] Such doubts all but disappeared as EPA launched and maintained its crusade against indoor radon.

The EPA found receptive ears and strong support for its crusade in Congress. Congress's nine "radon hearings" between 1985 and 1992 focused on the testimony of administrators, effectively cutting off the findings, insights, and criticisms of scientists and greatly expanding the EPA's reach. In 1985 the House Subcommittee on Natural Resources, Agricultural Research and Environment heard in detail about the new threat to the citizenry posed by radon and indoor air pollution. Then as now, the EPA relied on the studies of uranium miners to validate its declaration that indoor radon was causing between 5,000 and 30,000 lung cancer deaths every year. The popular press trumpeted the news: radon posed a greater threat than asbestos, toxic waste dumps, dioxin—indeed more than all other environmental hazards.[57] That the danger from asbestos and dioxin has recently been shown to have been grossly overestimated suggests the reliability of such pronouncements.

In 1986 the EPA appointed Richard J. Guimond as director of the newly created radon division in its Office of Radiation Programs.

[56]Cole, p. 11.
[57]Cross and Murray, p. 687 n. 3; 688 n. 4.

At that time, the agency began to assume the lead government role in radon policy, and Title IV of the Superfund Amendments and Reauthorization Act (SARA) of 1986 authorized the EPA to conduct research and supply information on radon and other indoor air pollutants.[58]

The emphasis on information was significant. Short of suing nature, the EPA could do little but pursue an "inforegulatory approach," since there was no individual or large industrial company to blame. By 1987 A. James Barnes, the agency's deputy administrator, was able to point with pride to his agency's accomplishments. In addition to instituting surveys in various states, the EPA in 1986 had published and disseminated *A Citizen's Guide to Radon*, a document notable for its disregard of the *combined* effects of smoking and radon on EPA estimates of radon risks.[59] Barnes also defended the 4 pCi/l action level as a practical standard given the technology available, a position he was to emphasize in 1987 hearings.[60]

Whatever misgivings scientists might have voiced about the levels of risk and EPA policies, the EPA was and is diligent in spreading word of the radon menace. It highlighted the menace in 1988, when, together with the U.S. Surgeon General, it issued an unprecedented nationwide health advisory, urging that virtually every dwelling in the country be tested for radon.[61] Testing would be costly. To inspect every home in the country would cost an estimated 10 to 20 billion dollars. Mitigation of "unsafe levels" would cost more, from 50 billion to 1 trillion dollars. Considering the uncertainty of the risk, the approach is best characterized as "Damn the torpedoes; full steam ahead," regardless of the cost or the need.

To provide the EPA with additional ammunition—that is, federal funds—Congress enacted the Indoor Radon Abatement Act in October 1988. The act articulated a national goal, that the air within buildings "should be as free of radon as the ambient air outside

---

[58]Prussman, p. 739; Rita M. Nichols, "Construction Contractors Confront the Indoor Radon Hazard," *Journal of Urban and Contemporary Law* 37 (1990): 135–38, 161–65.

[59]Cole, p. 13.

[60]Cole, pp. 85–86.

[61]Larry B. Stammer, "Levels of Radon Low in Homes in California," *Los Angeles Times,* March 29, 1990, pp. A3, A28.

of buildings."[62] That is, in fact, *sheer nonsense*, since the pressure differentials of man-made constructions will always suck in soil gases, giving rise to radon levels above those in the atmosphere, where radon is diffused.[63]

The pronouncement was virtually equivalent to the famed Delaney clause, an amendment to the Food, Drug, and Cosmetic Act (1958), which mandated that the Food and Drug Administration ban the addition to food of any chemical that had been shown to cause cancer in animals. Like the crusade against radon, that objective was a costly and basically misguided overreaction to a perceived risk. Delaney is gone, erased by Congress, but the goal of reducing indoor radon levels to those of the air outside remains, although it is neither practical, practicable, nor necessary to the public health.

It took 38 years to get rid of Delaney; let's hope it doesn't take another 38 years to induce Congress to change its mind about radon. It surely will require a major effort in the public policy arena, supported by the scientific community.

As a step toward achieving the impossible dream of reduction to atmospheric levels, the 1988 act required the EPA to establish a radon information clearinghouse that would update the public periodically on radon's health effects and methods of measuring and abating indoor radon. As it had done with asbestos (see chapter 3), the agency was to study radon levels in schools and federal buildings. It was to develop model construction standards and techniques of control in new buildings while ensuring their adoption by the groups responsible for developing national model building codes.

Finally, the EPA was to work with the states to develop the State Indoor Radon Grants Program to help fund the testing and mitigation of indoor radon. The program came with a three-year federal matching grant that ensured the expansion of the agency's bureaucracy and solidified its power. The EPA's regional offices were to act as project directors, distributing largesse to the states and reviewing their quarterly progress reports and work plans.[64]

By 1992, when Congress reauthorized the 1988 Indoor Radon Abatement Act, an increasingly aggressive EPA commanded the

[62]Prussman, p. 740.
[63]Cole, p. 172.
[64]Prussman, p. 740; see also Nichols, pp. 161–65.

field of radon policy. After 1985 the more circumspect Department of Energy, which had actually been carrying on research in the area since the 1970s, was rarely invited to testify before Congress.[65] The tension between the two agencies was an open secret.

In September 1993 Richard Stone, a reporter for *Science*, commented on the bitter dispute: "EPA is at odds with scientists at the Department of Energy (DOE) and elsewhere over whether the effects of high doses of radon can be extrapolated to the low levels found in homes."[66] After noting the EPA projections of 7,000 to 30,000 lung cancer deaths annually attributable to radon, Stone added, "But critics believe the agency needs to temper its radon warnings with an acknowledgment of the uncertain state of the science."[67]

Stone quoted David Smith, director of DOE's health effects and life sciences research division, as arguing against extrapolating from miners to homeowners: "For Smith and others, the jury is still out on radon's effects at low levels of exposure." The EPA had ignored those criticisms, justifying its actions by claiming that "it was necessary to rouse the public from its apathy to radon risks,"[68] that is, by scaring them to death on the basis of uncertain science.

Congress showed itself less than pleased with what one staffer characterized as a "pissing match," and then Rep. Ron Wyden (D-Ore.) was at one point considering legislation to create an interagency committee.[69] DOE, under attack from many sides, decided to close its radon program in 1996, leaving the EPA as the dominant, and practically the only, government voice about indoor radon risks and policy.

Through the early 1990s liberal Democrats, in concert with the EPA, were driving radon policy. In 1992 the Senate put forward an amended Indoor Radon Abatement Act that provided another $31 million in federal expenditures. It also called for the EPA administrator to designate "radon priority areas" in which the average indoor radon level would be likely to exceed the national indoor average

---

[65]Cole, p. 89.

[66]R. S. [Richard Stone], "Radon Risks Up in the Air," *Science* 261 (September 17, 1993): 1515.

[67]Ibid.

[68]Ibid.

[69]Ibid.

of about 1.3 pCi/l of air by more than a de minimis amount, which would have meant that about one-third of the country would be considered high risk. According to the DOE, the bill would cost homeowners more than $50 billion. A less expansive House version would have required the EPA to establish mandatory standards for radon testing technicians and testing equipment while seeking to identify areas and buildings at high risk. The inevitable presidential commission would seek to increase public awareness of the radon risk.[70] Congress adjourned without reconciling the 1992 Senate and House versions, and the Republican Congress elected in 1994 slowed the drive to increase the EPA's authority.

On the other hand, Congress's failure to publicize the scientific debate and to insist on cost-benefit analyses leaves unresolved the underlying problems of finding out the risks and establishing reasonable goals. Moreover, Congress seems reluctant to criticize the EPA radon program. Clearly, that stance benefits both parties, who are thus enabled to claim status as guardians of the public health. In consequence, mandatory testing and mitigation, despite the many voices raised against them, may still become a reality.

Given the tiny amount of support for the idea that indoor radon is a risk that deserves attention, all of the federal efforts directed at it can be seen as "make-work." Nowhere is there greater evidence for that contention than in the saga of AmeriCorps and radon. In low-income communities around the country, AmeriCorps members, part of the Clinton National Service Program, are spreading the word about radon. Boston, Newark, New Jersey, and Atlanta have played host to participants providing information about environmental services, including radon programs. In California, AmeriCorps members working under the direction of the East Bay Conservation Corps have set up booths at shopping malls, libraries, and churches to distribute information. Another project developed a coloring book about radon and lead for children in elementary school.

The EPA's Radon Division liaison to the AmeriCorps projects noted, "All in all, these projects accomplish a lot of good on many fronts."[71] If frightening school children and their parents constitutes

---

[70]Cole, pp. 99–100.

[71]Conference of Radiation Control Program Directors, Inc., *RADON Bulletin* 5, no. 1 (Spring 1995): 10–11.

"accomplish[ing] a lot of good," then Americorps is to be commended. Those with a more balanced perspective may take a less sanguine view.

Scandinavia: Sanity and Relative Risk

A view from across the Atlantic provides a perspective different from that of the EPA. Scandinavia, particularly Sweden, has dealt equably with higher radon levels stemming from use of building materials with high radon content, such as alum shale-based concrete, as well as Swedish energy consciousness, which has prompted very tight construction of new buildings. In fact, the national average for indoor radon is twice the average in the United States—2.7 pCi/l, as opposed to 1.3—but in any case well below the EPA's "action level" of 4 pCi/l.

In 1968 Sweden issued an informational booklet on the hazards of radon from building materials. Six years later Sweden halted the use of alum shale-based concrete in construction. In 1980 the government proposed an action level of 20 pCi/l for existing buildings, 10 pCi/l for rebuilt structures, and 4 pCi/l for new construction. In 1983 the recommended action levels became mandatory limits, and in 1990 the limit for existing housing was lowered by half, to 10 pCi/l, while the Swedish standard for new construction remained at the "action level" operative in the United States, 4 pCi/l.[72] Despite the original emphasis on construction materials, radon from the ground has now been identified as the primary source of radon in Swedish housing.[73]

Three Swedish studies (1979–84) indicated a significant association between radon progeny exposure and lung cancer[74] and may have played a part in the halving of the action level for existing housing in 1990. In contrast to the United States, those limits are mandatory. Unlike the United States, Sweden offered government loans to help

---

[72]Mueller Associates, p. 96; Competitive Enterprise Institute, p. 4. See also Lao, pp. 70, 123, and Cole, p. 173. The National Association of Home Builders notes the precise levels as 10.8 for existing buildings and 3.78 for new construction. Personal communication with the author, November 30, 1995.

[73]Anthony V. Nero Jr., "Radon and Its Decay Products in Indoor Air, " in *Radon and Its Decay Products in Indoor Air*, ed. William W. Nazaroff and Anthony V. Nero Jr. (New York: John Wiley & Sons, 1988), pp. 15, 16.

[74]Lao, p. 20.

with the cost of mitigation, estimated at $2,000 to $3,000 for suction of the gas and subsequent venting if the radon is coming from the ground, $10,000 at a minimum for ventilation if the radon is emitted by structural materials. Response has been minimal. Through 1990 only about 1,700 of the 120,000 homes estimated to have radon levels above 10 pCi/l had been mitigated.[75]

Although government loans may help, homeowners are essentially responsible for the cost of mitigation. Local authorities, however, provide and pay for testing, generally of the short-term or three-day variety, which is often misleading. Again this contrasts with the United States, where homeowners are generally expected to pay. Nevertheless, by 1991, despite years of official urging, only 150,000 homes of Sweden's 3.8 million homes had been tested.[76] Here the parallel with the United States is striking: neither the Swedes nor American citizens are doing much about radon.

Radon is mainly a matter of geography in Finland. The gas comes from gravel deposits created by glacial streams thousands of years ago.[77] Although the deposits have created little public alarm, Finland may have the best technical program for measurement in the world. Since 1980, the Finnish Center for Radiation and Nuclear Safety (STUK) has conducted virtually all testing using alpha-track etch detectors placed in homes for two continuous months, a technique widely considered reliable.[78] Of the 2 million Finnish dwellings, however, only about 35,000 have been tested since 1980 and fewer still, around 150, have been mitigated in the past 10 years. As many as 30,000 dwellings are estimated to have radon concentrations higher than 20 pCi/l; 50,000 have concentrations between 10 and 20 pCi/l.[79] Yet the Finns seem skeptical of the dangers of radon, and despite political pressure to follow Sweden's lead, Finland's action level of 20 pCi/l, set in 1986, seems likely to remain in place.

[75]Cole, p. 174.

[76]Ibid.

[77]Cole, p. 184.

[78]Brill et al., p. 371. The alpha-track etch detectors are sensitive only to radon gas activity; since the tracks etched by the alpha particles do not decay, the detectors can average exposure over a longer period of time than do charcoal canisters, devices usually used for short-term measurements.

[79]Cole, pp. 181–82.

The cost of testing under the auspices of STUK is moderate, about $200. The cost of mitigation is comparable to that in Sweden, $2,000 to $3,000, perhaps $10,000 in difficult cases. Government loans are available, though Finland's program is less generous than Sweden's.[80] In any case, few Finns mitigate radon.

STUK has drawn a "radon map" of Finland, locating areas of high concentration, but its researchers have been unable to find a significant correlation between radon and lung cancer.[81] An epidemiologist, Eeva Ruosteenoja, unable to find a correlation between indoor radon and lung cancer, suggested, "Mainly people should stop smoking."[82] Such a suggestion will likely never be heard from an EPA official.

The EPA Holds the Line

In light of the uncertainty about risk and disagreements about the importance of indoor radon to health, how does the EPA justify its course? Essentially it says, "We know high exposure to radon causes cancer. The evidence about lower exposure is less certain, but it can't be proved that it's not risky. We are charged to act prudently to protect the public health; therefore, we must work to reduce exposure." There is no serious consideration of data and information.

Dedicated to the proposition that residential exposures to radon are dangerous, the EPA denigrates reports that do not support it. Witness the response of David Rowson, acting director of the EPA Radon Division, to press reports about the National Cancer Institute's "Missouri study," which found no association between residential radon levels and lung cancer rates. Rowson first claimed that the press had misrepresented the findings, adding, "There is a wealth of scientific information and strong agreement in the national and international scientific community that radon is a human carcinogen and presents a public health risk in residences."[83] Which studies

[80]Ibid., pp. 186–87.

[81]Ibid., p. 184.

[82]Ibid., pp. 183–85.

[83]David Rowson, "Radon Division Responds to Press Coverage of NCI's Missouri Study," in RADON Bulletin 5, no. 1, p. 4. See also Associated Press, "Study Finds No Household Radon–Lung Cancer Link," San Francisco Chronicle, December 23, 1994, p. A7; M. C. R. Alavanga et al., pp. 1829–37.

has Mr. Rowson been reading? The "wealth of scientific information" does exist, but it scarcely supports "strong agreement in the national and international scientific community" about a threat to public health. If there is agreement, it exists among employees of the EPA and other agencies who believe that any level of risk justifies campaigns to measure and mitigate.

The subtlety of Mr. Rowson's argument would have earned the admiration of the Sophists. He first states a truth everyone accepts—radon is a carcinogen. He then slips into the same sentence a controversial assertion, "presents a public health threat in residences,"[84] to suggest that there is equal evidence and agreement.

In praising the "Missouri study," John D. Boice Jr., former National Cancer Institute chief of radiation epidemiology, noted that it raised questions about the validity of claims about risk from the low doses in homes. He added, "There is no question that radon causes lung cancer. The uncertainty is what is the level of risk from low dose exposures."[85]

Similarly, the EPA shrugged off the finding of the 1996 "Finnish study," which also found no association between indoor radon and lung cancer. Ramona Trovato, head of the EPA division monitoring radon, said the agency had no plans to change its policies. "We are comfortable with the 4 pCi/l, given that radon is a known carcinogen," she said, adding, "If we get new scientific conclusions, we'll certainly take a look at it."[86] It is difficult to understand her definition of a "new scientific conclusion." To an unbiased observer, the Finnish report certainly qualifies. But the EPA prefers to avoid coming to grips with results that would cast grave doubt on its scaremongering policy and, incidentally, save millions for homebuyers and taxpayers.

Let's consider the interpretations of the "negative studies" that find no association between indoor radon and lung cancer. Either those studies mean that there is no risk or that the risk is so small as to be undetectable. Does either conclusion justify expenditures of billions of dollars and government-funded scare campaigns? The

[84]Rowson, p. 4.
[85]Paul Recer, "Home Radon Risk Questioned," *Washington Post*, July 17, 1996, p. A2.
[86]Ibid.

question is left to the reader. The EPA has never asked it of the the public.

Given the level of uncertainty, the EPA's insistence on the risks from residential radon recalls a Pete Seeger lyric of the Vietnam era: "We're knee deep in the Big Muddy; the big fool says to push on."

The Likely Culprit and Solution

The EPA constantly underplays the importance of smoking, rather than radon, as a factor in the incidence of lung cancer. To be fair, the agency often uses exposure to cigarettes as a standard against which to measure exposure to radon. For example, the agency has said that "Exposure to radon at a level of 4 picocuries for one year represents a lung cancer risk comparable to taking between 200 and 300 chest X-rays *or to smoking a half a pack of cigarettes daily for a year*" (emphasis added).[87] It notes consistently that the radon risk to smokers is higher than the risk to nonsmokers. Never, however, does it suggest that changing one's lifestyle by eliminating cigarettes might do much more to mitigate the effects of radon than the expensive strategies it proposes.

William Nazaroff and Herbert Teichman, highly regarded authorities in the field of indoor risks to health, accept the linear, no-threshold model, stating that "no exposure can be considered risk-free."[88] At the same time, they consistently underline the smoking factor, asserting that "more than 90% of the lung cancer risk associated with radon could be controlled by eliminating smoking without any changes in radon concentrations."[89] A recent study from Sweden bolsters the assertion that radon and cigarette smoking act synergistically. "Smokers in the highest exposure group were 25 to 30 times more likely to develop lung cancer than nonsmokers in the lowest exposure group, a risk much greater than simply adding the risks of radon and cigarette smoke." The results indicate that smoking

---

[87]Stammer, p. A3.

[88]Nazaroff and Teichman, p. 777.

[89]Ibid., p. 776. Peter W. Huber makes much the same point in *Galileo's Revenge* (New York: Basic Books, 1991). Smoking, alcohol, and diet—factors all within individual control—are more important than government regulation in controlling the development of cancer.

multiplies the risk, rather than simply adding to it.[90] A change in lifestyle might, therefore, prove more effective than expensive mitigation.

With the drumbeat against smoking throughout the federal government, the EPA has not climbed onto the bandwagon. Why isn't clear, but certainly clamoring for a reduction in smoking, *which is certain to reduce lung cancer rates*, would detract from the EPA's efforts to bring about costly radon testing and mitigation that, if successful, might or might not affect lung cancer rates.

Quantifying the Risk; Estimating the Benefit

The history of the EPA's involvement with radon and even a cursory survey of its critics raise serious questions about the validity of the 4 pCi/l "action level." Canada, our geological neighbor, and Finland set their standards at roughly 20 pCi/l,[91] and Sweden sets its at 10 pCi/l. In addition, many experts in the United States have concluded that levels from 8 to 20 pCi/l are perfectly acceptable. Anthony Nero of the Lawrence Livermore Laboratory in Berkeley, California, estimates that only 2 percent of U.S. homes exceed 8 pCi/l and puts the hazard from radon at that level "on a par with the danger of falls or of fires in the home." The retired director of the Department of Energy's Environmental Measurement Laboratory, John Harley, "agree[s] that the EPA action level should be raised by a factor of two to five."[92]

The EPA, however, has not only resolutely defended its standard but has moved to cut it in half. The revised *Consumer's Guide to Radon Reduction* of 1992 suggests reducing it from 4 to 2 pCi/l[93] because, according to Stephen Page, then acting director of the EPA radon office, "Our research and the experience of private mitigation

[90]Quoted in Richard Stone, "New Radon Study: No Smoking Gun," *Science* 263 (January 28, 1994): 465.

[91]On a microlevel one analyst noted that a glass of milk contains about 18 pCi, a strained analogy because milk is not inhaled, but it draws attention to the ubiquity of radon. Bolch and Lyons, p. 65.

[92]Ibid., pp. 66, 67.

[93]Environmental Protection Agency, Office of Air and Radiation, 6604J, *Consumer's Guide to Radon Reduction* (Washington: Government Printing Office, August 1992), 402-K92-003, p. 3. Referred to hereafter as EPA, 1992.

firms shows levels can be reduced below two pCi/l 80 percent of the time."[94]

The dollars involved in a strategy to reduce radon to 4 or 2 pCi/l fail to concern him, but Nazaroff and Teichman, using the linear, no-threshold model, have calculated the possible benefits as well as the expected costs of reducing indoor exposure. Recall that the costs are real; the benefits are extrapolations—they may be zero and are almost certainly below EPA estimates.

The benefits, whatever they are, would depend, first of all, on the average effectiveness of mitigation. Complete implementation of the 1988 EPA/Centers for Disease Control policy to reduce exposure in all homes to less than 4 pCi/l would lead "to an annual avoidance of 2,500 lung cancer mortalities per year (2,300 among smokers and 200 among nonsmokers)." Nevertheless, "An annual lung cancer mortality rate of more than 12,000 cases would still be attributed to radon exposure."[95] In other words, if the EPA were completely successful and everyone measured and remediated as suggested, the estimated radon-associated lung cancer mortality rate would drop less than 20 percent (from about 15,000 to about 12,500 of the radon-related lung cancer deaths).

That works out to an average cost (net present value) per premature death averted of $270,000, below the range of $400,000 to $7,000,000 per premature death averted that the EPA considers reasonable for controlling an environmental pollutant. The authors are quick to supply a cautionary note, one rarely encountered in the literature: "However, the case of indoor radon is not analogous to the situations in which an activity by some external organization is responsible for the hazardous exposure, and public funds are to be spent for mitigation. *By alternative analogies, radon mitigation is not as attractive*" (emphasis added).[96] That seems to mean that the EPA's forcing private parties to spend money to counter man-made exposure to possible carcinogens is an easier task than asking homeowners to spend their own money to mitigate a naturally occurring substance.

[94]Michael Bennett, *The Asbestos Racket* (Bellevue, Wash.: Free Enterprise Press, 1991), p. 22.

[95]Nazaroff and Teichman, pp. 777, 778. The analysts generally use the standard international unit of measurement for radon, the becquerel. 37 Bq/m3 equals 1 pCi/l. The author has made the conversion to pCi/l when dealing with their calculations.

[96]Ibid., p. 778.

In any case, "the apparent synergistic interaction between smoking and radon" and the mobility of the U.S. population mean that individuals may find the costs of mitigation more or less attractive. Assuming a 10-year occupancy of a given house by a family of four, the willingness of the homeowner to shell out $3,000 to reduce indoor radon concentration from, say, 7 pCi/l to 2.7 pCi/l may depend mainly on his or her lifestyle—that is, whether he or she smokes. Radon remediation would reduce the already low risk of lung cancer for nonsmokers very little. A household of smokers, however, might find mitigation more attractive, even at a cost of $3,000, since it could reduce the lifetime risk of at least one lung cancer death in the family from 0.35 to 0.33, a reduction in absolute risk more than an order of magnitude greater than for the nonsmoking family.

Interestingly, if the EPA were regulating radon, it would find the costs of mitigation even for the nonsmoking family justified. One (estimated) lung cancer death would be avoided for every 900 homes of nonsmokers remediated at a cost of $2.7 million, well within the EPA's acceptable range of $400,000 to $7,000,000 per premature death averted. Clearly there is a difference in perspective. It all depends on whether one is spending one's own money—$3,000 per house to avert a hypothetical risk—or spending anonymous taxpayers' money toward the same end.

Mitigation in the homes of smokers is a bargain, if the estimates of lives saved are correct. Mitigation would, on average, avert one lung cancer death per 60 households of smokers for an average cost per premature death averted of only $180,000. Again the authors sound a cautionary note: "In the absence of incentives such as low-interest loans for mitigation, it seems unlikely that most smokers would make the necessary investment to reduce the radon-related risk of lung cancer *when the dominant cause of their risk is smoking*" (emphasis added). They assert,

> From a public health perspective, the goal of reducing lung cancer incidence also may be more easily met by changing the population's smoking habits than by aggressive measures to reduce indoor radon concentrations. . . . A permanent reduction by about 3% in the number of cigarette smokers would reduce the annual mortality due to lung cancer by the same amount as a radon-mitigation program that succeeded in achieving the EPA/CDC recommendations.[97]

[97]Ibid.

Nazaroff and Teichman estimate that reducing indoor radon levels to outdoor levels (if that is possible) would produce a reduction in annual mortality from radon-related lung cancers of about 11,000 cases per year (10,000 among smokers, 900 among nonsmokers). Even if indoor radon levels were reduced to those in the ambient air, about 4,000 lung cancer deaths would still be attributed to radon exposure. "The implications of measures needed to achieve this goal are staggering." The technical feasibility of achieving the objective in the existing housing stock is unclear, and the costs, assuming feasibility, "would be prohibitively large," on the order of $1 trillion, roughly $10,000 to $16,000 per household times 70 million households.[98]

Since it is a great deal less costly to apply mitigation measures in new construction than in existing housing stock, that approach "would be less impractical, but still difficult and costly." Even implementing mitigation gradually in new housing could require "an annual investment of at least several billion dollars."[99] To quote the late Senator Dirksen, "A billion here and a billion there and pretty soon you're talking about real money."

Health physicists Mossman and Sollitto[100] considered slightly higher estimates of the numbers of "hot" homes and somewhat lower estimates of radon levels, but their analysis also projects a staggering expense. They calculate that the cost of remediating the roughly 4 million homes with radon levels at or above the EPA action guideline would be about $800 million *annually*, whereas the savings in medical expenses and lost productivity would total annually about $200 million. Thus the costs would exceed the benefits by four to one. Even if all 20,000 radon-induced lung cancers were eliminated—an "unrealistic best-case scenario,"—benefits would be "only roughly equal to costs of mitigation."[101] Mossman and Sollitto conclude, "It would appear that regulation of Rn levels in the indoor environment is a case of regulatory unreasonableness." Compliance

[98]Ibid.

[99]Ibid.

[100]Kenneth L. Mossman and Marissa A. Sollitto, "Regulatory Control of Indoor Rn," *Health Physics* 60, no. 2 (February 1991): 169–76.

[101]Ibid, p. 172.

costs would exceed the social benefits without yielding the intended result.

The EPA and Congress have in effect laid the groundwork for a vast and horrendously costly project whose rationale is unclear and whose prospects for success are clouded. The $1 trillion or so required to reduce indoor concentrations in the current housing stock to those encountered outdoors merits comparison with the federal deficit, currently $2 trillion. The outlay of $10,000 to $16,000 per household would take a big chunk out of savings for college tuition, medical expenses, repairing the kitchen, or even a vacation trip. It would make people poorer and, by definition, *less* healthy.

Nor can the embattled homeowner be confident that the expenditure will produce the desired result. According to Nazaroff and Teichman, screening measurements for radon in homes are subject to misclassification and misinterpretation, and quality assurance is insufficient to ensure accuracy.

Water, Water Everywhere

The EPA has found no way to regulate radon that enters homes from the ground. But, in combination with Congress, the agency has identified a regulatory program to deal with radon in drinking water. Under that program, the EPA can impose regulations on water utilities to force removal of radon. Congress paved the way for the program in its 1986 reauthorization of the Safe Drinking Water Act that required the EPA to promulgate a national primary drinking water regulation for radon by 1989. (Eighty-two other contaminants, such as arsenic and sulfate, were also to be regulated.) In 1991 the EPA proposed a standard of 300 pCi/l in water, but Congress suspended action on the regulation pending a review of the costs and benefits of the drinking water standard relative to other risks from radon in the environment and because of complaints that 300 pCi/l of radon in water contributed only about 0.03 pCi/l of radon in air, a tiny fraction of the usual indoor levels of 1.3 pCi/l.

In 1992 Congress directed the EPA to produce a report on the risks posed by radon in drinking water relative to the risks from radon in other media and mandated a review of that report by the Science Advisory Board. Even before a draft was completed, examination of the documents being used by the EPA's Office of Water to construct the proposal led William Raub, the agency's science adviser, to express skepticism about the agency's work. In February 1993, noting the "'enormous uncertainty'" underlying risk estimates from radon, Raub underscored the "inconclusive epidemiological findings as to whether radon (whether ingested or inhaled) actually presents an appreciable risk within the typical American household if none of the occupants smokes tobacco products."[102] Raub recommended a maximum exposure to radon in water equal to that in outdoor air, a "relative-risk" approach that would result in a maximum contaminant level (MCL) of 1,500 to 2,000 pCi/l.

In a letter of July 30, 1993, the chairman of the Science Advisory Board and the chairman of the Science Advisory Board that reviewed EPA's proposed policy about radon in water wrote to Carol Browner, the EPA Administrator, about the costs of the proposed policy:

> It is clear that the cost per lung cancer avoided from mitigation of indoor air radon is substantially less than the cost per cancer death avoided due to mitigation of exposure from radon in drinking water. This difference appears to be at least a factor of 4 ($3.2 million per cancer death avoided related to drinking water and $0.7 million per cancer death related to airborne radon) and may be substantially larger.

They suggested "setting a water standard at 3000 pCi/l, [which] would result in water contributing no more radon to indoor air than is present in outdoor air."[103]

The EPA's report to the United States Congress on Radon in Drinking Water: Multimedia Risk and Cost Assessment of Radon, delivered to Congress in March 1994, ignored those comments and persisted in its recommendation of a limit of 300 pCi/l. Legislators, however, seemed increasingly uncertain of the course to pursue, and the Senate passed an amendment to the agency's 1994 budget delaying the implementation of the proposed maximum contaminant level for radon until October 1994. The delay was extended when Congress refused to appropriate funds that would allow the EPA to set the standard.

[102]Quoted in Richard Stone, "EPA Analysis of Radon in Water Hard to Swallow," *Science* 261 (September 17, 1993): 1,514.

[103]R. C. Loehr and Roger O. McClellan, letter to Carol M. Browner, Administrator, U.S. Environmental Protection Agency. Re: SAB Review of Multimedia Risk and Cost Assessment of Radon in Drinking Water. July 30, 1993.

The EPA estimated that radon in water contributed to 192 excess cancer deaths per year from radon and that reducing radon in water to 300 pCi/l would reduce that number to 107 cancer deaths per year. The annual cost? According to the EPA, $272 million, or $3.2 million per each of the 85 cancer fatalities avoided. Protesting water utilities claimed that the figure could be 5 to 10 times higher.[104]

The 1996 amendment to the Safe Drinking Water Act has canceled any immediate regulation. It directs the EPA to contract with the National Academy of Sciences for a study of the risks of radon in water. After that study is completed and if the study justifies it, early in the next century the EPA can propose a regulation. Even then, states can escape the regulatory burden if they show radon in water makes an insignificant contribution to radon exposure.

Radon in water illuminates the regulatory dance. Congress directs the EPA to set a regulation. When the regulation draws fire, Congress directs all the attention to the EPA, which, after all, has done just what Congress directed. In the case of radon in water, Congress has selected a time-honored solution: Ask for a study and delay any decision.

Points of Radon Entry

Ground Emissions

Uranium-containing rock and soil are the major source of radon in most homes, and the levels of exposure depend on the concentrations of uranium ore in the soil. Concentrations are noticeably high in parts of New England, the Reading Prong (a geological formation running through parts of eastern Pennsylvania, New Jersey, and New York), the Appalachians, the phosphate-mining regions of Florida, the Georgia and Carolina coasts, and scattered areas throughout Wisconsin, Minnesota, and the western states.[105] In general, indoor radon concentrations are higher in those areas. Radon gas moves through soil of all kinds, especially easily through sand, gravel, and fractured bedrock, and enters the home through cracks in foundations, basement walls, sewer and water lines, and dirt crawl spaces.[106]

[104]"Radon Regs Shot Down for Now, "*Science* 262 (October 15, 1993): 337.

[105]Lao, pp. 16–18; Prussman, pp. 718, 719.

[106]Prussman, p. 720; Treffer, p. 21.

Moisture in the soil, up to a certain level, can increase the rate of radon exhalation from the soil. Of greater significance are air pressure differentials between the home and the ground below. When the pressure within the house is lower than the pressure outside, a pressure-driven flow will draw radon gas from the soil into the home. Temperature differences between indoor and outdoor air influence the flow; warmer indoor air tends to rise, allowing displacement by cooler, radon-bearing outdoor air—a tendency termed the "stack effect" because it resembles the air motion in a smokestack.[107]

Wind can also create pressure differences between indoor and outdoor air, inducing air to flow from the soil into the building. Mechanical devices such as exhaust fans in clothes dryers can lower pressure in the house, drawing in radon from the soil. Given that radon is itself a rather heavy gas and that its major route of entry is from the underlying soil into the basement, the highest concentrations of radon and radon progeny are usually found in the basement and on the first floor.[108] Although the gas can diffuse to higher levels in a building, it is diluted by "fresh air," so apartments on the upper floors of a multistory building are unlikely to contain significant amounts.

A recent study indicates that radon can pass through intact concrete, a finding likely to disturb those who have used concrete to seal cracks in basements or slab floors. Although it may look solid, concrete is far from impermeable. Given the large surface area covered by floors and below-grade walls, concrete may constitute the home's dominant entry point for radon. The wetter the original mix, the faster radon diffuses through hardened concrete, but as concrete continues to set over time, the entry of radon decreases, particularly after the first two years.[109]

Well Water

Although the problem is limited in scope, well water constitutes the second major source of indoor radon. Radon is moderately soluble in water, its solubility increasing as the temperature drops. Thus

---

[107]Lao, p. 17.

[108]Ibid., pp. 2, 17, 22.

[109]"Radon: Some Concrete Issues," *Science News* 146, no. 12 (September 17, 1994): 191.

cold groundwater flowing through radon-containing soil and rock can absorb a good deal of the radon. When well water brings dissolved radon into the home, heating and aeration induce release of radon into the atmosphere. Normal indoor activities like showering, flushing a toilet, and running a washing machine or a dishwasher raise the indoor levels.[110]

Overall, radon from drinking water is responsible for only 1 percent to 7 percent of indoor radon concentrations. Generally—particularly in Maine and the Northeast—it is water from private wells that contains high levels of the gas.[111] Moreover, in homes that use public utility systems for water, waterborne radon rarely contributes significantly to indoor levels. Before reaching the tap, such water has spent considerable time in reservoirs, treatment plants, and water towers, long enough for most of the dissolved radon to decay.[112]

Building Materials

Compared with soil gas and groundwater, building materials are the least important source of radon in the triad. In general, unless materials are contaminated with uranium or radium mill tailings— now an unlikely event—radon emissions from such materials will be low.[113]

Construction: Ventilation and Energy Efficiency

In addition to structural factors, ventilation affects the rate at which radon is trapped and concentrated within a building. Ironically, the OPEC oil embargo of 1973 did much to fuel the current controversy by encouraging energy conservation measures that affected indoor air quality. The drive to weatherize new homes and to retrofit existing stock, promoted by the government, reduced air exchange,[114] leading to increased concentrations of radon.[115] Simply

[110]Lao, pp. 18, 20.

[111]Ibid., p. 20.

[112]Ibid.

[113]Ibid., pp. 21, 22.

[114]The rate of air exchange, expressed as air changes per hour, equals the number of times in an hour that a volume of outside air equal to the internal volume enters the house. Mueller Associates, p. 57.

[115]Cross and Murray, p. 694.

put, there was less "fresh air" to dilute the radon (and any other indoor pollutants).

Surveys conducted in the northeastern United States showed that energy-efficient homes had radon concentrations about five times higher than non-energy-efficient homes. Tight construction and insulation for energy conservation reduce air leakage inward through cracks and diminish natural ventilation—that is, the movement of air in and out through intentionally provided openings (windows, doors, or nonpowered ventilators). Solar homes that have heat-storage rock bed with a high radium content tend to have elevated levels of radon.[116]

The Proliferation of State Surveys

Despite the emphasis placed on radon by the EPA and Congress, to say nothing of the media, the states at first pursued far less aggressive policies. By the end of 1989 the EPA had conducted surveys in 25 states, but only 13 states had undertaken statewide radon studies of their own.[117]

The state surveys of the late 1980s and other U.S. measurements indicated that radon concentrations in residences averaged about 1.2 pCi/l, well below the EPA's recommended "action level" of 4 pCi/l. An estimated 1 million homes had concentrations exceeding 8 pCi/l, the action level recommended for remedial action not by the EPA but by the National Council on Radiation Protection and Measurements.[118] Except in "hot spots" like the Reading Prong in eastern Pennsylvania and parts of New Jersey and New York, which correlate with geological factors, concentrations rarely exceeded that figure.

The EPA's 1992 survey of 125 counties in all 50 states basically confirmed earlier findings. Radon levels averaged 1.25 pCi/l, and 6 percent of homes (roughly 4 million) exceeded the EPA action limit of 4 pCi/l.[119] Clearly there was no widespread menace, yet the

---

[116]Lao, p. 23; Mueller Associates, p. 57.

[117]Lao, p. 43; Cole, p. 105.

[118]Mueller Associates, p. 2.

[119]Cited in Brill et al., pp. 374, 384. The "References" list the survey as having been published by the EPA in 1992 as a "Technical Support Document for the 1992 Citizen's Guide to Radon" (EPA 400-R-02011).

EPA knowingly fomented generalized fear in its 1992 *Citizen's Guide to Radon*.

Before passage of the 1988 act, with its impossible goal of reducing indoor radon concentrations to those outdoors, four states—Florida, New Jersey, New York, and Pennsylvania—had established vigorous radon programs. In 1988 Florida became the first state to issue a regulation on human exposure to radiation from natural sources: in new homes, schools, and commercial buildings, *average* annual radon decay product concentration was not to exceed 4 pCi/l in air. Two years later the state legislature established the same standard.[120]

In Florida, according to the 1988 regulation, all parties to a sale must be provided with information about radon; testing, however, is optional. The state also established a radon trust fund to pay for radon programs by levying a tax of 1 cent per square foot on construction or alteration of any building in the state. By 1991 the trust fund, unique to Florida, had amassed $3.6 million to cushion future expenditures.[121]

Of the three states atop the Reading Prong—New York, Pennsylvania, and New Jersey—New York has shown the least enthusiasm for radon programs. It did conduct two statewide surveys, but its radon expenditures fell from $2.5 million in the late 1980s to $1 million in 1992.[122]

New Jersey: The Nightmare Years

Although it, too, sits atop the Reading Prong, New Jersey decreased its expenditures on radon from $4 million in 1986 to $900,000 in 1992.[123] In part, that seems traceable to the state's disastrous experiences with mitigation and cleanup in the town of Montclair. In 1983 the New Jersey Department of Environmental Protection (DEP) announced that several homes in the towns of Montclair, Glen Ridge, and West Orange showed high levels of radon, presumably from radioactive fill transported there from the grounds of the defunct U.S. Radium Corporation, which had been headquartered in a nearby town.[124] Believing that other homes in the state might

[120]Cole, p. 107.
[121]Ibid., pp. 107–108.
[122]Ibid., pp. 109–110.
[123]Ibid., p. 110.
[124]Ibid., p. 112.

contain high levels of radon from natural sources, the DEP intended to treat Montclair as a demonstration project, a model for mitigation elsewhere.[125] The model became a nightmare out of science fiction.

Early in 1985, with the concurrence of the EPA, the DEP announced plans to remove the soil under and around 12 houses at a cost of $8 million. For two to four weeks, the occupants would live in a hotel at the state's expense; if all went well, they would then move back into their homes. Following the successful completion of the demonstration with 12 homes, another 80 homes would be remediated in cooperation with the EPA at an unspecified cost.[126] The residents never moved back into their homes, the demonstration was not successful, and the 80 homes escaped mitigation (and probably a good thing, too).

The well-laid plan went awry almost from the start. In 1985 excavation was completed around eight of the houses at a cost of $600,000 each. Montclair is a pleasantly upscale residential area, but in 1985 the houses were unlikely to have a market value of more than $150,000, so the excavation cost roughly four times the value of the homes. Neither the EPA nor the DEP publicized market appraisals.

After the excavation of the eight houses, the project was suspended, apparently because of the cost. But almost 15,000 barrels had already been filled with radioactive soil. Two-thirds of the barrels were shipped to the nearby town of Kearny; the remaining 5,000 took up residence on the lawns of four of the Montclair houses.[127] No state or local community wanted the soil. A supposed understanding with Nevada collapsed; the Department of Defense rejected storage in a New Jersey arsenal; a nearby township rejected the idea of storage in its quarry.[128]

Negotiations continued for three years in a black comedy unappreciated by the residents of the towns and the displaced homeowners. Some owners moved into temporary lodgings or went to live with friends; some evidently stayed on at the hotel, adding to the costs.

[125]Ibid., p. 113.
[126]Ibid.
[127]Ibid., p. 114.
[128]Ibid., pp. 113–15.

In 1987 the DEP in desperation approached several communities with an offer of $6 million to store the 5,000 drums still sitting in Montclair. There were no takers. In fact, the town of Kearny instituted a suit to force removal of the 10,000 barrels stored on its land. Finally, in September 1987, the DEP contracted for $4 million with a private company to ship the 5,000 drums from Montclair to Oak Ridge, Tennessee, where they were to be mixed with highly radioactive materials and sent to a federally approved depository in Washington State. By the middle of 1988, three years after excavation had begun, all the barrels had disappeared from Montclair and Kearny.[129]

The episode infuriated local residents while undermining the credibility of the DEP and the EPA. The DEP, in particular, consistently mishandled the situation by failing to provide information to people in the areas affected in advance of its pronouncements.

Undaunted by the Montclair fiasco, the EPA in 1990 announced a 10-year program to remove soil from 400 New Jersey houses at a cost of $250 million. The thoroughly discredited DEP would not participate in the far-flung project, which in the end never materialized.[130]

By 1991 the EPA had managed to remove the contaminated dirt from the 4 remaining houses of the original 12 that had stood empty since 1985. (The dirt went to a waste depository in Utah.) One of those four was rebuilt and the owners returned. The EPA purchased the other three, made uninhabitable by years of neglect, and the owners found other housing.[131]

The drive to mitigate regardless of cost or disruption of lives and without regard to alternative courses of action produced dire consequences. Perhaps most disturbing was the recommendation of a report published in 1989 and sponsored by DEP. The authors suggested that "the DEP should refrain from informing the public about uncertainties concerning radon. To avoid giving people excuses not to act. . . ."[132] The bureaucrats are to be omniscient; the public is to be kept in the dark. Consideration of "uncertainties" might have prevented the Montclair fiasco; it surely would have

---

[129]Ibid., pp. 117–120.
[120]Ibid., p. 120.
[131]Ibid., pp. 120–21.
[132]Ibid., p. 123.

caused any organization other than one spending tax money to think carefully before beginning such a project.

Pennsylvania: Renewed Enthusiasm

Galvanized by the Watras incident, Pennsylvania joined with the EPA to screen more than 18,000 homes for radon by the end of 1986. On the basis of short-term measurements, which are likely to give inaccurate or misleading results, 50 percent of the homes showed concentrations above 4 pCi/l. The state did fund a million dollar demonstration project that remediated 105 homes at an average cost of $3,700, almost double the upper limit of the EPA estimate of $1,000 to $2,000 for the mitigation of a home. The project ended in June 1988. Clearly, concern had diminished: Pennsylvania's budget for radon programs, which had more than doubled from 1985 to 1986 (from $1.5 million to $3.5 million), fell to $700,000 in 1992.[133]

Times have changed, however, with the EPA's promotion of radon as a health hazard, and expenditures of public funds have risen. Pennsylvania is again advocating informational and regulatory initiatives. Following is a partial list of outreach programs funded by Pennsylvania with its share of the EPA's Radon Action Program ($5 million annually) and State Indoor Radon Grants ($8 million).

- In October–November, 1994, under a contract with the EPA, the National Children's Theatre for the Environment presented 12 live performances of a musical, "Jeff Meets the Intruders," in elementary schools throughout Pennsylvania. Jeff, the hero, meets and conquers in his home Passive Smoke, Dust Mites, and Radon. After the performance students received coupons for purchase of discounted test kits from the National Safety Council to give to their parents. Under a contract with the EPA, the musical has toured New England and may again tour Pennsylvania.
- During Radon Action Week in October 1994, the EPA awarded mini-grants to 15 nonprofit organizations. The EPA bulletin failed to specify their purpose.
- Welcome Centers along the Pennsylvania Turnpike have issued thousands of copies of the Pennsylvania *Consumer's Guide to*

---

[133]Ibid., pp. 108–109.

Radon, the Citizen's Guide, and the *Home Buyer's and Seller's Guide.* Scintillating reading for the drowsy motorist!

- Through the maternity wards of participating hospitals, the Newborn Project distributes an information guide consisting of a one-page letter of information, a *Citizen's Guide to Radon,* and a certificate redeemable for a free test kit. Those who send in the certificates receive a charcoal test canister from a certified laboratory. After logging the results of the completed tests, the laboratory sends a report to the parents with a copy to the EPA. How can harried parents show their appreciation for such a thoughtful gift? Why mothers of new babies got free tests and the parents of the children who saw "Jeff" got only discount coupons to use toward the purchase of a test kit is not known.

- "The Denial Clinic," a title suggestive of group therapy, constitutes instead a radon public service announcement created in Pennsylvania. Aired on all major state TV/cable and radio stations in February 1995, it brought an upsurge in phone calls to the office of the Radon Control Program.

- On the education front, a contract with the Eastern Region Radon Training Center (ERRTC) would lead to a "Risk Communication Course: Focus on Radon" to be offered to vocational teachers and students and to local government officials dealing with health and the environment in the fall.

The ERRTC was also to market a seven-hour course on radon and radon mitigation to Pennsylvania realtors that could be used for continuing education credits. A member of the Pennsylvania Radon Division staff would teach the section on radon mitigation.

Of the five courses listed in the Bulletin for the fall and winter of 1994, four were noticed as being "free" to teachers of vocational technology, to building code officials, to school officials, and to builders and architects. "Free" in this context meant that the taxpayers were supplying the funding.

- The Radon Division Certification Section was busy with enforcing compliance, imposing the first civil penalty against a company that continued to test for radon in Pennsylvania without proper certification. From July 1, 1994, through April 30, 1995, it conducted 32 laboratory and 42 testing certifications.

- The Penn Radon Division generated two newsletters, a quarterly update sent to the "radon industry (certified community)" and a radon services directory updated on a monthly basis.[134]

As slick promotion, the EPA approach would win awards in the advertising industry. The agency has created a new group of companies, certified by the EPA, that can charge whatever the market will bear for a product that no one wants but that the EPA forces down the throats of the consumers, in this case the citizens of Pennsylvania. With the passage of time and the expansion of its influence, the EPA won't have to play any role: the testing companies will convince real estate brokers that it's in their best interest to test, and the costs will be passed along. The EPA emerges with clean hands.

Hard science, in the form of peer-reviewed journal articles and risk analyses, has no place in this supposedly "informational" campaign. With the help of the federal government, Pennsylvania is simply funding a panoply of goods and services designed to protect its citizens from a menace never conclusively demonstrated. Worse, the state is colluding with the EPA in an effort to frighten its residents without probing the rationale for the flurry of expensive activity. The risk, if risk there be, may stem far less from radon than from the misallocation of resources signaled by those programs.

"Protection Money"

Nothing in Nazaroff and Teichman's careful analysis of the estimated benefits and costs of radon mitigation is more alarming than their conclusion that "most of the mitigation experience in the United States is too recent to yield reliable experience on the long-term efficacy of remedial measures."[135] In other words, the homeowner is buying a pig in a poke. For all the money involved, it should at least be a prize-winning pig!

Depending on the technique and the need for a contractor, overall EPA estimates of implementing radon mitigation measures in the

[134]Conference of Radiation Control Program Directors, Inc. (CRCPD) in cooperation with U.S. Environmental Protection Agency (EPA), "Pennsylvania" in *RADON Bulletin* 5, no. 1 (Spring 1995): 8–10. For figures on national and state expenditures, see Competitive Enterprise Institute, "Eliminate the Radon Action Program" (December 1994), n.p.

[135]Nazaroff and Teichman, pp. 778, 779.

average home to bring concentrations below 4 pCi/l and, if possible, down to 2 pCi/l run between $300 and $2,500, with a mean cost of $1,500.[136] Clearly, costs can go much higher, varying with the location and the type of construction; and, as was seen in the New Jersey fiasco, those averages can have nothing to do with real-world costs.

The EPA, of course, operates on the assumption that no price is too high to pay for projected benefits to health, however uncertain they may be. To keep the radon issue afloat, the agency is shelling out $9 million to $10 million of taxpayers' dollars to support research and the publication of booklets for architects, contractors, physicians, school and government officials, and buyers and sellers of homes. Added to those expenses are the administrative costs of a 90-member radon team in Washington, D.C., to say nothing of the manpower needed for EPA offices focused on radon reduction in the states.

Testing and Its Discontents

Testing for radon is, of course, a necessary precondition to a decision on whether and how to abate it; but the inconvenience, unreliability, and expense of the existing measurement technology demand caution. The EPA has published protocols for seven different types of measuring devices for airborne radon. Homeowners can easily obtain and use only two, the alpha-track detector and the charcoal canister.[137]

The alpha-track detector consists of a small piece of plastic photographic film on which alpha particles leave permanent submicroscopic tracks. The film's container must be carefully placed in the home and beginning and ending times of exposure must be measured precisely. The exposed film then goes to a laboratory that correlates the number of tracks with radon concentrations in the air. To be effective, the test should last three months or longer. On the other hand, it is relatively cheap, about $20 to $50 including the analysis,[138] and its results are considered far more reliable than those obtained from the charcoal canister that is used for measurements over shorter time periods.

[136]Stephen E. Williams, "BUYER BEWARE; Your Time Has Come," *Legal Times*, December 7, 1992.

[137]Lao, pp. 77, 78.

[138]Ibid., pp. 78, 79.

The charcoal canister is also inexpensive, about $15 to $30 including analysis; but it, too, requires placement where it will not be disturbed and stop and start times must be recorded carefully. After a few days of sampling, the canister is shipped to a laboratory that estimates radon.[139] Time is a critical factor. When exposed for a week or longer, canisters produce incorrect measurements. Unfortunately, the usual few days of sampling can produce uninformative results if, for instance, atmospheric conditions favor, or do not favor, the entry of radon into the home.

Those devices are somewhat temperamental. To obtain the most reliable screening results, all short-term devices, such as the charcoal canister, require closure of windows and doors, not only during the test but for 12 hours before measurement. The furnace may operate but air conditioners should not, unless they merely recycle indoor air. Given the resultant level of discomfort, even the EPA at last suggested testing during the colder months in the north and substituting a closed room for a closed house in Florida.[140] Indeed, the closed room, rather than the closed house, has become the norm.

The other devices require trained operators and generally produce results in hours or minutes rather than days. They have at least one factor in common: they are expensive. A continuous radon monitor and a continuous working level monitor can each cost between $2,500 and $10,000.[141] The cost of a radon progeny integrating sampling unit can go even higher: $500 to $3,000 for the sampling device, $5,000 to $10,000 for the analytical equipment.[142] Continuous active sampling is recommended only "when other measures indicate a problem and the source of radon entry needs to be precisely pinpointed."[143]

Generally, the instruments or devices used in the home produce only "screening measurements"—that is, they "indicate the potential of a radon problem." Those measurements then become the basis for determining the necessity of additional follow-up measurements.

[139]Ibid., pp. 79–81.

[140]Ibid., pp. 87, 88.

[141]Ibid., pp. 81–85.

[142]Ibid., pp. 83, 84.

[143]National Council on Radiation Protection and Measurements, *Control of Radon in Houses*, report no. 103 (Bethesda, Md.: NCRP, September 1, 1989), p. 371. Grab sampling, yet another technique, is generally used for industrial monitoring.

The follow-up results will provide the homeowner with the basis for deciding on mitigation actions.[144]

Soil-gas testing and tests for radon in water have more limited applications. Contractors concerned about potential liability may conduct soil-gas testing on construction sites. Otherwise, such testing is generally the domain of scientists. Measurements of waterborne radon are relatively straightforward: the homeowner simply sends one or two samples of household water to a laboratory for analysis.[145]

Undeterred by the difficulties of testing and interpretation, 13 states now have real estate disclosure laws.[146] It has even been suggested that testing be required before the granting of a mortgage. Given the uncertainty and the difficulties in terms of time and expense, more effective methods of hamstringing the mortgage industry and discouraging homeownership can scarcely be imagined. At most, voluntary testing could be helpful in areas known to be high in radon, like the Reading Prong. All-encompassing mandates are likely to produce mainly anxiety.

Testing for radon is spreading insidiously, however. In Montgomery County, Maryland, the tests have become a near-standard part of home sales. Although no ordinance requires them, brokers almost insist on them, arguably as protection against liability. Costs are passed on to buyers and sellers, who are already so enmeshed in writing large checks that they are unlikely to notice them.

The insistence on testing has been one of the EPA's greatest successes. Without laws and without regulations, the agency has devised a method that may eventually force testing on every home sale.

The Protocols of Mitigation

Just as with testing, there's more than one way to go when it comes to mitigation, and there is the same uncertainty about how well it will work.

---

[144]Lao, p. 91.

[145]Ibid., pp. 85, 86.

[146]"Case Study no. 2: Radon," in *Science, Economics, and Environmental Policy*, draft of a research report by the Alexis de Tocqueville Institute, Arlington, Va., July 27, 1994, p. 10.

Passive Techniques

Passive techniques are generally billed as the most desirable because, once implemented, they require "no further action or maintenance."[147] "Source removal" hardly captures the magnitude of the task of digging all the dirt from around a house down to a depth of several feet and backfilling with replacement soil. Alternatively, concrete (painted an attractive green or white depending on the season, perhaps) or some other substance can be applied to the soil and between the soil and the house foundation.[148] That may be the most cost-effective in the long run, lasting the life of the structure, but it adds to construction costs and drives up the price of the home. The average homebuyer, particularly the first-time homebuyer, scraping together a down payment and a mortgage, is unlikely to come up with the cash to dig or seal.

Less costly "passive techniques which inhibit radon entry by employing minor changes to housing design and construction" include "sealing of cracks and utility openings, sump or subfloor ventilation, and placement of impermeable membranes under houses. . . ."[149] Finding and sealing cracks that can run from large to hairline is an elaborate and expensive procedure. Moreover, the sealants themselves may eventually need attention. According to the EPA, this procedure can reduce radon by as much as 50 percent for $100 to $2,000 without additional operating costs, but sealing is "normally used with other techniques," which would drive up the cost.[150]

Active Techniques

Active techniques dilute or intercept the gas or its decay products. Subslab or subfloor ventilation may either be active (requiring a fan) or passive (relying on natural phenomena to provide the suction). In either case, ventilation creates a low-pressure zone in the subslab area, an area into which gas flows and from which it is vented into the atmosphere.[151] The EPA lists costs ranging from $800 to $2,500

---

[147]National Council, p. 371.
[148]Mueller Associates, p. 154.
[149]Ibid., p. 7.
[150]EPA, 1992, p. 16.
[151]Lao, pp. 144–50; Mueller Associates, pp. 7, 163–68.

for an active system, with a radon reduction of 80 percent to 99 percent and annual operating costs for a fan of $75 to $175. For the passive system, less effective in reducing radon (30 percent to 70 percent), the costs can be nearly the same, ranging between $550 and $2,250.

Other active control techniques include "systems that use filtration, electrostatic precipitation, or absorption to remove airborne particles and radon decay products."[152] Those systems require maintenance—filters, for example, must be changed—and they can be expensive. Electrostatic precipitators cost $400 per unit.[153] The techniques also come without guarantees. They are so unlikely to do any good whatsoever that the EPA recommends against the use of air cleaning to reduce radon.[154]

Ventilation

The air-exchange rate strongly influences indoor radon concentration.[155] In fact, doubling the air-exchange rate can cut the radon level by half.[156] Following that logic leads to the conclusion that open doors and windows are the best condition. Why doesn't everyone do it? Oh, yes—people live in houses to get out of the cold or the heat.

With or without open windows, "forced-air ventilation techniques involve the use of fans or blowers to move a large air mass into or out of the house." It increases utility costs, and there are initial costs for the materials, essentially the fan.[157] The EPA estimates the installation costs for such natural ventilation at $200 to $500 if additional vents are installed; *annual* operating costs for a fan, electricity, and heated- or cooled-air loss range between $100 and $700.[158] The estimate makes no mention of the irritation caused by a continuously running fan.

Unless homeowners are Spartan in temperament, comfort will eventually dictate the installation of "mechanical ventilation systems incorporating air-to-air heat exchangers" in which one blower moves

[152]Mueller Associates, p. 7.
[153]Ibid., p. 179.
[154]Lao, p. 129.
[155]Mueller Associates, p. 172.
[156]Lao, p. 129.
[157]Ibid., pp. 130, 131.
[158]EPA, 1992, p. 16.

the outdoor air into the house via ducting while another blower exhausts roughly an equal amount of air to the outdoors. The two streams pass each other in an air-to-air exchanger, which enables the heat transfer to take place.[159] The system "is cost-effective only when the indoor-outdoor temperature differentials are large"—that is, when opening the windows will admit either a chilling blast or a sirocco.

How well does it work? The EPA claims a radon reduction of 25 to 50 percent if the method is used for a full house, 25 to 75 percent if it is used for a basement.[160] How much does it cost? That is equally uncertain. In a 1987 pamphlet, the EPA estimated that installation costs, including material and labor, would range between $800 and $25,000 for duct units and run about $400 for wall-mounted units.[161] Five years later the EPA's 1992 Consumer's Guide to Radon listed "typical" installation costs as ranging from $1,200 to $2,500 with operating costs of $75 to $500 for continuous operation.[162] The entire scenario raises doubts about the effectiveness and the cost-benefit of the procedures in terms of health and economics.

Mitigating Radon in Water

Mitigating radon in water is relatively simple although still expensive. Simply storing the water for 30 days will reduce the radon by more than 90 percent, but the long period of time and the need for a large storage tank make that impractical,[163] at least for private individuals.

Aeration and carbon adsorption are the most common methods of radon removal. Aeration, exposing the water to air through sprays or bubbling, can remove 90 to 99 percent of radon from water for an initial cost of about $2,000.[164] The EPA estimate for 95 to 99 percent removal is higher, $3,000 to $4,500, with $40 to $90 in operating costs.[165]

---

[159]Lao, pp. 131, 132.
[160]EPA, 1992, p. 16.
[161]Cited by Lao, pp. 132–33, 155.
[162]EPA, 1992, p. 16.
[163]Lao, p. 189.
[164]National Council, p. 39.
[165]EPA, 1992, p. 16.

Activated granular carbon (charcoal) adsorbs and retains radon, and the homeowner can expect to pay around $450 for units that remove 80 to 90 percent of radon from water. For a 10 percent increase in efficiency, that is, removal of 90 to 99 percent, a homeowner will pay double, around $900.[166] But that is not the end of it. The adsorbed radon builds up in the unit and its decay can produce radiation fields that require shielding. The total cost then mounts to $2,000, comparable to that of the aeration system, which has no radiation buildup problem.[167] The EPA, when dealing with carbon, does list $1,000 to $2,000 for installation costs but then claims "none" for operating costs. The shield and the problems of disposal would seem to qualify as operating costs.

The expense and the inconvenience would affect very few, "since radon in drinking water is a very small contributor to radon risk."[168] Nevertheless, the EPA has shown itself eager to impose regulations costing millions on water suppliers.

"I'm from the EPA and I'm Here to Help You"

Despite everything, the EPA has been frustrated in its efforts to induce the American public to take action. When public apathy greeted the agency's 1986 *Citizen's Guide to Radon*, the agency became increasingly shrill, resorting to "motivational efforts that depend less on truth and education and more on creating public anxiety."[169]

In the autumn of 1988 Lee Thomas, then the EPA administrator, declared on national television that as many as one-third of U.S. homes exceeded the EPA action level of 4 pCi/l of air. The one-third figure conflicted with scientific studies showing that only about one-fifteenth of homes had levels exceeding that figure, but the EPA forged ahead.

The EPA pronouncements, combined with media coverage, brought Congress into the act, and it passed the 1988 legislation that set the impossible goal of reducing residential levels of radon to those of the outside air. The legislators accepted unquestioningly the EPA's repeated assertions that no level of radon was safe and

---

[166]National Council, p. 39.

[167]Ibid.

[168]Quoted in Richard Stone, "Risk Assessment," p. 1515.

[169]Abelson, p. 98.

enunciated a goal whose attainment could cost $1 trillion. The enormous expense would make each taxpayer poorer; most would reap no benefit.[170]

The public, less impressionable than Congress, maintained a "ho hum" attitude, so a frustrated EPA resorted to creating anxiety about exposure. It first observed that children were three times as susceptible to radon as adults, but it backed away from that statement when researchers at the National Cancer Institute found no support for it.

In 1989 the agency enlisted the help of the Advertising Council in devising a campaign that would play on parents' concern for their children in order to frighten them into following the EPA's recommendations.[171] A 30-second TV spot pictured a child in its mother's lap while a voice intoned that high radon levels in the home was equal to having hundreds of chest X-rays a year. Seven or eight flashes caused the entire skeleton of the child to appear on the screen. Anthony Nero, a scientist well known for his expertise in radon and other indoor pollutants, commented, "The frequent flashes showing us a dead child are not intended to inform, but to cause undue fear, moving people to action with the threat of death. This is terrorism."[172] On a more mundane level, it is false and misleading advertising. Only a government agency could escape legal consequences for having produced it. At the very least, it is ethically reprehensible.

The TV spot no longer runs, and the EPA has turned down the shrillness of its campaign. Even so, the agency still relies, not on facts, but on "strong and unsettling messages," a tactic summarized by one critic as "Do not inform them; scare them."[173] In 1990 the agency circulated the draft of a revised *Citizen's Guide to Radon.* "Designed to raise anxiety rather than to present facts," the guide was denounced by many reviewers and disappeared from view.[174]

The 1992 edition of the guide is designed for those who have tested their homes and found radon levels above 4 pCi/l. There is

[170]Ibid.
[171]Ibid., p. 99.
[172]Ibid.
[173]Ibid.
[174]Ibid.

no question about what the homeowner should do; according to the guide, he or she should mitigate, and the booklet is offered as a guide to help the homeowner select a qualified contractor, determine an "appropriate radon reduction method," and maintain the reduction system. Reassuringly, "With today's technology, radon levels in most homes *can* be reduced to 2 pCi/l or below."[175]

Advice on hiring a contractor illustrates the extent to which the bureaucratic apparatus surrounding radon has grown. The agency recommends hiring a contractor—but, specifically, a contractor listed in the EPA National Radon Contractor Proficiency Report, meaning that the contractor has taken training courses and passed an exam. Homeowners who decide to do the work on their own should obtain "information on appropriate training courses and copies of EPA's technical guidance documents" from the state radon office, and the guide lists the telephone numbers.[176]

In effect, the RCP program is a licensing bureau, raising barriers to entry into the business of radon mitigation and increasing costs. The EPA has thus created a third-party organization dependent on the government for maintaining its business. In order to enhance its operations, that third-party organization will inevitably campaign for more and more regulations.

On the mitigation front, the section titled "What to Look for in a Radon Reduction System" again sounds a reassuring note by soft-pedaling costs: "For most homes, radon reduction measures are no more expensive than having a new hot water heater installed or having the house painted. The cost . . . generally ranges from $500 to $2,500."[177] The costs referenced in the table at the end of the booklet do lie generally within that range, but, as anyone who has dealt with construction knows, the work is likely to exceed the EPA estimates.

The closing section, "Buying or Selling a Home?" sounds a final unsettling note. After noting that buyers and sellers should be informed about radon levels and reduction systems, if they exist, it adds, *"All homes should be tested for radon and high radon levels should*

[175]EPA, 1992, p. 3.
[176]Ibid., pp. 4, 17.
[177]Ibid., p. 7.

be reduced."[178] That is the EPA's version of "Father Knows Best," an assertion meant to evoke unquestioning belief.

The 1993 "Home Buyer's and Seller's Guide to Radon," the next in the series, is remarkable for its unusual emphasis on smoking as a risk factor.[179] At the very beginning, it warns, "If you smoke and your home has high radon levels, your risk of lung cancer is especially high." A table later highlights the differences in risk for smokers and nonsmokers exposed to levels of radon ranging from 20 pCi/l to 0.04 pCi/l. Despite the admonition to quit, smoking is clearly a secondary issue. The guide is much more concerned with "the health of a house" than with the health of an individual.

The second edition of that pamphlet, "The Guide to Protecting Yourself and Your Family from Radon," published in September 1994, while warning once more against smoking continues the EPA's scare tactics.[180] It also soft pedals the expense and inconvenience of testing and mitigation. Having asserted, in boldface type, that "radon is a cancer-causing radioactive gas" that "can be found all over the U.S.," the guide makes a preemptive strike, advising homeowners to "test your home now and save your results" to facilitate a possible sale or rental. If the level is high, no need to worry. "Most homes can be fixed for about the same cost as other common home repairs." Since when is installing a complete ventilation system a "common home repair"?

The guide claims that the risk from radon is well known "because estimates of radon risks are based on studies of cancer in humans (underground miners)." Critic after critic has heaped scorn on this analogy, but the EPA sails blithely ahead.

The final section, "Radon Myths," ignores studies that show no ascertainable relationship or an inverse correlation between indoor radon and lung cancer and claims that "radon testing is inexpensive and easy" with readily available test kits. In the private sector, such claims would constitute false and misleading advertising.

---

[178]Ibid., p. 15.

[179]EPA, 1993, pp. 1, 20, 33.

[180]Environmental Protection Agency, U.S. Department of Health and Human Services, and U.S. Public Health Service, *A Citizen's Guide to Radon* (2nd ed.), 402-K92-001 (Washington: Government Printing Office, September 1994): 3, 7, 10, 11, 13.

The EPA issued in March 1994 a guide entitled *Model Standards and Techniques for Control of Radon in New Residential Buildings*. The Council of American Building Officials has adopted these standards as an appendix to its building code for one- and two-family residences. Jurisdictions—states, counties, or townships—have the power to decide that builders must build according to those standards. In that case, the appendix must be adopted separately—that is, in addition to the CABO code. As government units adopt the appendix, consumers will buy and pay for preventive measures whether or not they want or need them. Remarkably, that cost will be imposed on the public without the EPA's ever having to enact a regulation.

Enter the Litigators

It's impossible to sue Mother Nature, but it may be possible to sue someone who can be found responsible for allowing one of nature's products, radon, to enter a dwelling, increasing risk and, perhaps—and this is a stretch—causing health effects. At the same time, the presence of radon can decrease property values, and perhaps someone can be sued for that.

In "Liability for Toxic Radon Gas in Residential Home Sales," Frank B. Cross and Paula C. Murray provide a veritable "do-it-yourself" guide to suing a contractor.[181] After repeating uncritically the EPA's 1985 estimate of 20,000 lung cancer deaths annually caused by radon, they go on to rehash "The Causes, Nature, and Extent of the Radon Hazard in Residential Buildings." The review notes that the "no threshold hypothesis is an unprovable assumption" but adds that "it is relied on in virtually all government regulation of carcinogens, and the Supreme Court has approved its use in regulation," although not for recovery of damages. That the Supreme Court has set its imprimatur on that regulatory approach apparently obviates all need for qualification or discussion.

After summarizing control measures, the article reaches the nub of the problem, "Establishing Liability for Radon Contamination," asserting that "radon is without question a major public health problem, for which injured individuals may seek remedies at common law." The hurdle that "no clear-cut liability yet exists under any

[181]Cross and Murray, pp. 687–738.

established theory" is brushed aside because "homeowner plaintiffs may be able to recover under common law theories of tort: strict liability, implied warranty of habitability, negligence, or even fraud."

Cross and Murray are quick to evoke the possibility of "expert testimony" to pinpoint the precise source of radon and its effects. They also make it clear that the builder is suspect as a wily entrepreneur with deep pockets.

With apparent regret, the authors acknowledge a possible statute of limitations: "For homes built fifteen or more years ago, before the danger of indoor radon was widely known . . . builders may be able to take advantage of the state-of-the-art defense to absolve themselves of strict liability to injured homebuyers." No such defense will do for "today's builders in high radon concentration areas," who "have a duty to construct homes with radon disperse-ment devices and to warn potential buyers of the dangers of radon contamination." The authors assert such a "duty" but fail to give it a legal foundation. They also assume that the dangers are real and that the potential buyer will be happy to pay for "radon disperse-ment devices," which he may neither want nor need.

The builder, no matter how conscientious, may be unable to escape the dragnet of liability. Noting the possible success of a suit against the builder "for breach of the implied warranty of habitability," the authors are quick to note "a disturbing trend in this area, . . . the ability of the builder to escape liability through a disclaimer." Only the litigious climate of the present day, with its complete dismissal of caveat emptor, to say nothing of common sense, makes the following commentary believable:

> In the typical situation, the builder and the buyer do not share equal bargaining power. Even if the disclaimer is clear and conspicuous, it is unlikely that the buyer realizes that he is waiving his right to receive damages from the builder if the home is not fit for human habitation because of radon contamination. Presumably builders in states that allow dis-claimers will incorporate a clear and concise disclaimer in all contracts of sale. *As a result, a buyer may then have to rely on strict liability, negligence, or fraud as a basis for a cause of action against the builder.*[182]

[182]Ibid., p. 719 (emphasis added).

The buyer, clearly assumed to be an idiot incapable of understanding the disclaimer, must still have grounds on which to proceed against the contractor. This approach, which the attorney-authors endorse, amounts to a game of "Gotcha!"

Costs become increasingly irrelevant as the authors suggest that, "as a matter of course, builders in new home sales and real estate brokers in resale homes will want to suggest to the buyer that a routine inspection for radon contamination be conducted at the time of sale, just as termite inspections are now routine.... A radon test at the time construction is completed, and at periodic intervals thereafter, could prevent or greatly mitigate health problems ... and avoid costly litigation."

The authors turn next to "health-related damages for cancer, whether already sustained or merely anticipated," and the possibility of "demonstrable property damages and the costs of correcting the conditions causing the high indoor concentrations." In discussing health-related damages, the authors note first that lung cancer may lie dormant for 20 years and that the long latency period "presents significant problems for plaintiffs." Nevertheless, they go on to discuss the possibility of recovery for "pure increased risk of cancer," noting that "there is growing support for granting damages for future risk of cancer."

It is reassuring to learn that "the actual probability of future cancer that plaintiffs must prove is somewhat unclear," although "a 50 percent probability of future cancer" seems a fairly reliable standard. On the other hand, even if risk from high indoor radon levels is "in the vicinity of only one percent," plaintiffs who "present evidence of a present injury from chromosomal damage ... may be able to recover for even his slight risk of future cancer."

Whatever the testimony of the alleged "experts," "injury from chromosal damage" is junk science. As Peter Huber notes, "Junk science verdicts may promote and sustain illness even when the electric fields, the microwaves, the trace pollutants, *or the all but unmeasurable radioactivity* have caused nothing but the verdict itself."[183] The remainder of the section on "Health-Related Damages" tends to substantiate Huber's position. Cancerphobia, or fear of

---

[183]Peter W. Huber, *Galileo's Revenge: Junk Science in the Courtroom* (New York: Basic Books, 1991), p. 46 (emphasis added).

future cancer, may present grounds for damages, it is argued, provided that the fear is found to be "reasonable," a term almost infinitely elastic. Recovery for future medical surveillance is another possibility.

In comparison with the putative health risks, the case for property-related damages is relatively clear-cut. As Cross and Murray note, "While somewhat less lucrative than personal injury damages, a homeowner plaintiff exposed to high radon levels has a somewhat greater surety of recovering some level of property damages." Reduction in property value provides the standard measure for damages to real estate; repair costs may be recoverable, especially "when they are less than the reduction in property value."

Whatever the legal footwork, the article evinces over and over again the credulity of its authors in relation to the EPA, indeed their dependence on EPA science, and an almost total disregard of economics. Successful suits alleging damage from radon will increase the price of new construction to cover the expense of additional devices to prevent or mitigate radon and expanded insurance coverage. The price of "used" housing will increase as well, penalizing in particular the first-time homebuyer who generally purchases in this market. Appraisers, brokers, and real estate agents are also concerned with liability. As the premiums for expanded errors and omissions insurance increase and the time required for additional paperwork expands, commissions will almost certainly rise and with them the prices of houses as sellers seek to recover their costs. The litigators will profit while the seller and the consumer become poorer as each pays the potential litigation and clean-up costs.

"The Radon Riddle: Landlord Liability for a Natural Hazard," by Jeanne Prussman, complements the work of Cross and Murray by telling *tenants* how to sue their landlords.[184] Citing the EPA's 1986 *Citizen's Guide to Radon* as her source, she repeats the shibboleth: "Experts believe it [radon] to be responsible for as many as 20,000 lung cancer deaths annually in the United States."

Prussman's concern is with the tenant "injured by radon exposure" who must look to his landlord for compensation. She notes that "the traditional fault-based landlord-tenant theories are unlikely to compensate a tenant injured by radon exposure" and goes on to

[184]Prussman, pp. 715–50.

examine "the possible legal theories under which a tenant could proceed against a landlord for damages caused by radon." Like Cross and Murray, she encourages a tenant to seek compensation "for having been placed 'at risk' for developing a disease and for the anxiety that this increased susceptibility has caused him or her."

Prussman focuses on strict liability because it "eliminates the need to prove misconduct by the landlord and focuses a court's attention on the status of a dwelling," which may be seen as a product that is "unreasonably dangerous." She notes that "the deep pocket and cost-spreading policies behind products liability theory hold true for the landlord-tenant situation," then adds cavalierly, "The landlord may purchase liability insurance and pass the cost on to tenants through rent charges." Evidently, she has never heard of rent control or of a market-clearing price. Undoubtedly, she views those as irrelevant, the landlord being no more than a profit-hungry capitalist, adept at gouging tenants.

"The traditional landlord-tenant theories probably will not provide relief," however, for none of the theories fits radon well, and Prussman concludes that "radon-exposed tenants have a slim chance of recovering from landlords." To compensate, in a concluding section full of questionable assertions, she turns to legislative action to accomplish "the broader social goal of radon reduction." Why that should be a "social goal," she never explains. Evidently she assumes that reducing radon will improve the general health and welfare and that overriding "social goal" would justify legislative action.

Mandatory testing would be the first step in resolving the "radon crisis." Funding from the State Indoor Radon Grant Program and tax credits could be used to ease the burden on landlords. Prussman suggests, however, that those incentives would be insufficient, so "states should enact laws similar to the law existing in Florida and require that a general warning provision about the hazards of radon be included in every real estate transaction." Having created a statutory duty to test, "state legislatures should create a duty upon landlords to abate radon contamination."

Terming "the health hazards of radon severe enough to require abatement," Prussman declares that "the availability and inexpensiveness of many radon reduction methods makes abatement a relatively simple process" since "merely increasing ventilation and installing basement fans" would do the trick. Even the EPA is less simplistic!

Once they have established a duty to test for and abate radon, legislatures must work to enforce their statutes "by providing liability provisions making landlords liable for their failure to test for and abate radon." Statutory liability would ease the tenant's lot, for the mere presence of elevated levels would be sufficient to establish liability, thus negating "the tenant's causation problem."

Who is to set the radon levels? A "legislative forum would allow interested parties to lobby and effect a compromise regarding which radon levels would subject a landlord to what penalty." The legislative forum need include no scientists with knowledge of the issue. Like the uninformed citizens' councils of the French Revolution, the forum will intuit the answer using "democratic principles to solve a widespread national problem."

According to Prussman, the risk of cancer is so grave that state and federal governments should supply incentives, such as tax credits and low-interest loans, for radon abatement. Building codes could be modified to require construction techniques to limit radon entry and increase ventilation.

The author justifies her reliance on the state and the expansion of its already vast regulatory and enforcement powers by asserting that "reliance on common law litigation will not compensate injured tenants and achieve the broader social goal of radon reduction," for "litigation is too uncertain, expensive, and inefficient for society to await accomplishment of these goals through judicial activism." Hence the legislatures should shoulder the burden of ensuring compensation to "the injured victims" by imposing statutory duties to test and abate on the landlord.

The article is remarkable, not only for its assumption of the radon risk and its creation out of whole cloth of a "social goal," but also for the breathtaking nonchalance with which Prussman dismisses the cost in dollars and cents. Indeed, she never discusses the matter, assuming that the landlord will pay, perhaps increasing the rents to cover his expenses. She blithely ignores the wishes of the tenant, who might prefer a whiff of odorless radon to a higher monthly bill, as well as the role of landlord-tenant negotiation. No, the tenant is "the injured victim" to be protected by "Big Brother," the long arm of the state. However baseless the fears, however shaky the scientific foundation of the statutes, the landlord must pay to appease the worries of the tenants and the demands of the statutes. If he fails to do so, he may be hounded into bankruptcy.

He may also abandon his property, thereby decreasing the number of desirable rental units and contributing to an increase in rents across the board. That possibility seems never to have occurred to the author.

Responses, Public and Private

States have entered the radon arena, and some have imposed requirements on real estate transactions. Not to be outdone, and perhaps to ward off government intervention, some associations of real estate brokers have also instituted disclosure requirements.

Florida requires notification of the potential dangers of radon in real estate documents. With admirable restraint, the Florida notice merely says, "Radon is a naturally occurring radioactive gas that . . . may present health risks to persons who are exposed to it over time."[185] A more ambitious Florida regulation that would have required new home construction to maintain radon levels below 4 pCi/l within certain geographic areas was suspended because of debate over geographic applicability.[186] Rhode Island requires sellers to include an advisory in the sales agreement: "Radon has been determined to exist in the state of Rhode Island. Testing for the presence of radon in residential real estate prior to purchase is advisable." Sellers who fail to include the advisory can be fined $100.[187]

New Jersey has followed a similar route, establishing criminal penalties for certain violations. The New Jersey statute provides:

> In the case of a prospective sale of a building which has been tested for radon gas and radon progeny, the seller shall provide the buyer at the time of contract of sale . . . with a copy of the results . . . and evidence of any subsequent mitigation or treatment, and any prospective buyer who contracts for the testing shall have the right to receive the results.[188]

To cover a broader spectrum, the New Jersey Association of Realtors has adopted a contingency clause for buyers that "warns of a

[185]Quoted in Lao, p. 200.

[186]Ibid., p. 175.

[187]Paul Davis, "Radon Law Puts R.I. in New Waters," *Providence Journal-Bulletin* 16, no. 268 (December 31, 1988): p. D1.

[188]Nichols, p. 161 n. 160.

potential radon problem, disclaims the Realtor's ability to give scientific device, recommends professional testing and suggests parties who might pay for mitigation."[189] Clauses of that type are becoming more common, especially in the "hot spots" along the Reading Prong. Though apparently motivated by the desire to sidestep liability, they sound like government regulations; certainly they have all the same effects. The Pennsylvania Association of Realtors has developed a more extensive "Radon Disclosure Addendum" to accompany contracts between sellers and agents as well as between sellers and buyers.[190] Neither the New Jersey nor the Pennsylvania document is alarmist in tone, but each serves as constructive notice to buyers and sellers of the possible existence of a problem. Such an approach reduces the liability risks for the seller, the broker, and the agent, in effect shifting the burden of risk assumption to the buyer.[191]

New Jersey and Pennsylvania have also adopted economic incentives to promote mitigation. New Jersey set up a low-interest loan program to aid homeowners with mitigation; the Pennsylvania legislature voted to establish a fund with a similar goal.[192] Disclosure requirements, rather than incentive programs, however, are still the norm. In response to the perceived threat, 13 states have in fact enacted legislation mandating disclosure.[193] The disclosure forms provide insurance against liability, and their implementation is inexpensive.

Not to be outdone in the race to mandate disclosure, the Department of Housing and Urban Development requires that similar disclosure forms be supplied to applicants for HUD-insured mortgages in those parts of Florida, Montana, and South Dakota "known to have elevated levels of radon." Other federal agencies, such as the Farmers Home Administration and the Veterans Administration, could follow HUD's lead. In the end, Congress will probably decide how far the federal agencies go.

[189]Ibid., p. 156 n. 135.
[190]Lao, pp. 202–5.
[191]Ibid., p. 201.
[192]Mossman and Sollitto, p. 175.
[193]Ibid., p. 171.

Cost Effects on the Market

Radon has been a boon to business as firms have emerged to market radon testing kits and to provide mitigation should the tests reveal a problem. As early as 1987 Radon Detection Services, a New Jersey company, was already operating six franchises, mainly in the Middle Atlantic states. In addition to working with homeowners and the real estate community, the company had established relationships with architects interested in "radon proofing" new construction and with municipalities concerned with including radon reduction measures in local building codes. A New Jersey franchisee quoted a range of $1,500 to $5,000 for its services.[194] By 1989 a state-certified tester in Iowa cost between $225 and $275. Treating problems cost from $900 to $1,500,[195] well within the EPA estimate but enough to spell hardship for a first-time buyer.

Radon testing and mitigation have become a growth industry: the capital cost of setting up a company that simply tests is minimal, and the scare tactics of the EPA may supply a steady stream of clients. The firms have mushroomed, and their profits have zoomed. In 1989 an embryonic company called TEQ, Inc., in Wilkes-Barre, Pennsylvania, expected that it would double or perhaps triple its sales.[196] In Boulder, Colorado, the president of Current Indoor Air Systems, Inc., projected nationwide operations and a $25 million business by 1994.[197] The projections may have been too rosy, but it is unlikely that either enterprise has "gone under."

The strong growth and reports of fraudulent practices spurred fears that companies would take advantage of supposedly gullible consumers by inflating their charges or conducting faulty tests, or both. The response was predictable: a drive for licensing or, at least, certification. The EPA already exercises a form of quality control. Firms can submit their results to the agency for verification; if the EPA finds that they are testing correctly, they become part of the

---

[194]Pamela Fry, "Widespread Radon Information Leads to Area Business Growth," *Lancaster-Reading Business Digest* 6, no. 8 (October 1987): sec. 1, p. 7.

[195]Mark P. Couch, "Radon Complicates Housing Sales," *Business Record* 85, no. 29 (July 17, 1989): sec. 1, p. 1.

[196]Geoff Martin, "W-B Company Fills Radon Market Niche," *Northeast Pennsylvania Business Journal* 4, no. 5 (April 1989): sec. 1, p. 1.

[197]Dinah Zeiger, "Indoor Air Aims at Radon Reduction Market," *Boulder County Business Report* 8, no. 2 (March 1989): sec. 1, p. 16.

National Radon Measurement Proficiency Program, and their names are placed on a list available to the general public.

Some states have embroidered on the federal program. Pennsylvania, for example, passed a certification bill for radon firms early in the summer of 1987.[198] Certification, of course, generally raises the costs, since firms trade on the reliability or "goodwill" generated by the official stamp of approval.

The growing apparatus of regulations and controls has had a ripple effect, raising costs as it expands. Sellers of undeveloped land discover that they must pay for testing and try to pass the costs on to the builder. Builders find that they must build more expensive houses to combat the real or potential radon menace; at the same time, their insurance costs are increasing. Both charges will raise the cost of the finished product.

Depending on the extent of the problem in the community, owners of existing homes may find their equities reduced by the obligation to abate radon and may post a higher sales price or try to split the difference with a potential customer, thereby increasing the cost to the buyer. A seller whose home is the sole "hot spot" in a particular development—a real possibility since the incidence of radon is highly variable depending on construction and environment—may have to bear the entire cost or find that the property is unmarketable. The real estate community adds another disclosure form and may find that the additional risk has caused the premiums for errors and omissions insurance—the real estate version of malpractice insurance—to escalate. Commissions may go up or service may decline.

In the financing area, some mortgage companies now require tests in radon-prone areas while relocation companies are becoming edgy about guaranteeing sales of homes owned by relocating executives before determining the radon risk. Each of these players will try to pass along the increase in costs: some may be absorbed by the purchaser; in others, failing a split, the owner alone will foot the bill. First-time buyers, however, are particularly vulnerable even to small increases in the final price. Faced with an escalation in costs, they may well drop out of the game.

---

[198]Gail S. Bower, "Radon Menace Spurs Testing Standards," *Focus*, no. 963 (September 23, 1987): sec. 1, p. 118.

A Modest Proposal: Go After Big Risks

Having noted the costs and the impossible goal of sampling every U.S. home, Nazaroff and Teichman offer a rational alternative. They estimate that "there are approximately 70,000 homes in the United States in which the average radon concentration exceeds 800 Bq m^{-3} [21.6 pCi/l]."[199] According to their estimates, the lifetime risk of lung cancer for someone living under these conditions is "extraordinarily high, ranging from 2% for female nonsmokers to 33% for male smokers, compared with 0.6% and 12%, respectively, for members of these two classes not exposed to radon." Finding that level of risk unacceptable, they state that "It should be a high priority to rapidly identify these homes and take corrective measures. . . ."[200] While based on "plausible assumptions," all of these estimates are subject to grave doubt. Recall that the Health Physics Society would say that the risks are unknown, with "the likely possibility of zero" for all exposures less than 8 pCi/l.

Nazaroff and Teichman believe that geological information, in combination with measurements in a sample of homes in a region, can identify areas likely to have high radon concentrations. "Greater effort should also be devoted to developing mechanisms for providing information to residents . . . *so they can make informed decisions on whether to measure radon in their homes.*"[201] Given the EPA's efforts and the results thus far, it is difficult to believe that better information will be forthcoming. Nevertheless, the authors' crediting average citizens with the intelligence to make or contribute to decisions about their own lives stands in marked contrast to EPA tactics.

Mossman and Sollitto[202] also conclude that "the approach to standard setting should focus on reducing extremely high domestic levels of Rn rather than meeting a goal to reduce average Rn levels." Only mitigation of high-risk homes would be cost-effective.

They urge that the government focus on identifying those single-family homes with radon levels exceeding 27 pCi/l, roughly 50,000

[199]Nazaroff and Teichman, p. 780.

[200]Ibid.

[201]Ibid. (emphasis added).

[202]Mossman and Sollitto assert that "regulatory programs would be economically inefficient and unreasonable if standards were established at 150 Bq m-3 or less," p. 169. Since 37 Bq m-3 is roughly the equivalent of 4 pCi/l, the authors are stating that EPA insistence on a standard of 4 or even 2 pCi/l is unreasonable.

out of a total housing stock of 60 million.[203] Remediating homes with levels above 20 pCi/l would be more far more cost-effective than trying to remediate every home with a level above 4 pCi/l.[204] Mossman and Sollitto suggest government programs to encourage mitigation of the most affected homes through economic incentives, such as low-cost loans and tax write-offs.

Selective mitigation is also the position put forth forcefully by Anthony Nero. Citing the estimates endorsed by the National Academy of Sciences for the risk of lung cancer posed by "typical" levels of indoor radon—1 in 1,000 for nonsmokers and 1 in 100 for smokers—he notes that the risk is greater than that posed by most environmental hazards and is also based on "a firmer foundation." He is careful to point out, however, that "there is still room for doubt about the reliability of the risk estimates, particularly those for ordinary radon levels." To his statement that "epidemiology may never succeed in demonstrating radon risks for ordinary levels"[205] can only be added the statement that it's almost a sure bet that such risks will never be demonstrated.

Nevertheless, Nero believes that the risk for those living in homes with relatively high radon levels merits mitigation and that this could be achieved in a cost-effective manner. The houses to be most concerned about—"perhaps one in a thousand"—are those with radon levels "far above average: 20 pCi/l, causing exposures at the occupational limit for underground uranium miners." "Finding and fixing the 100,000 'hottest' U.S. homes would probably cost under $500 million. In contrast, reducing radon levels in all homes to below 4 pCi/l, as the EPA has proposed, would cost $20–$100 billion. And lowering indoor levels to outdoor, the present congressional goal, could cost $500 billion." (Nero earlier estimated that the total for this "'Star Wars' approach to radon protection" might reach $1 trillion.[206] Still, one-half or a whole trillion, what difference does it make?) He advocates ventilation systems installed under houses,

[203]Ibid., p. 173.

[204]Ibid., p. 174.

[205]Anthony Nero, "Regulating the Great Indoors," *Technology Review*, August/September 1991, p. 78.

[206]Anthony V. Nero Jr., "A National Strategy for Indoor Radon," *Issues in Science and Technology* 10, no. 1 (Fall 1992), p. 37.

which "can lower a 20-picocurie-per-liter level by a factor of 5 or 10 at a cost of $1,000 or $2,000—a sum within the reach of most homeowners."[207]

Nero finds little to admire in the EPA's handling of the radon issue. From the "misleading and manipulative tactics" to which the EPA resorted after 1986, "in its haste to stir up public concern," to the "short-term screening tests that are inappropriate because indoor levels can vary by a factor of 10" to the Ad Council television spots showing people turning into skeletons, "the agency has shown itself all too willing to delude the public." Unusual among scientists, Nero even draws attention to EPA's mistreatment of those scientists who find fault with the agency. The EPA, he says, has "caused great distress among the community of scientists actually doing research on the behavior and the health effects of indoor radon . . .—seemingly trying to marginalize scientists standing at the center of the radon research community."[208]

His agenda for reform highlights first of all a fundamental flaw: "The EPA's assumption that standard criteria for judging outdoor pollutants apply to radon is premature . . . radon—along with asbestos, some organic chemicals, and tobacco smoke—poses a new problem simply because we don't have a well-developed risk-evaluation and policy framework for indoor pollutants." To come to grips with the problem, "it would be handy to construct a picture of how we think about and value the indoor environment before deciding what level of risk is acceptable and what isn't." Moreover, "An indoor standard would have to acknowledge that people tend to be more tolerant of risks they impose on themselves . . . than they are of risks imposed by outside parties such as polluting industries." The point is worth stressing, since it distinguishes radon sharply from most environmental pollutants.

The control strategy should be "sensible." First of all, the agency should conduct "a more reliable public information program." Such a program would require a major effort, since "Virtually all of EPA's educational vehicles need revision, including the *Citizen's Guide* and other brochures and reports. . . ." This would require re-education at the agency level, that is, "EPA's leaders must make conscious

[207]Nero, "Regulating the Great Indoors," p. 79.
[208]Ibid.

75

efforts to inform and strengthen the staff and to increase interaction with the scientific community." In tandem with its other efforts, the agency "should finally adopt proper detection methods, instead of the short-term monitoring that has led to inflated figures in the past."[209]

He addresses the problems faced by buyers and sellers and suggests that "Hurried testing" in connection with home sales "could be avoided by an insurance scheme that pools the costs of monitoring and mitigation for homes being sold in a given area." The seller would pay approximately $200 for the test; the buyer would receive a long-term detector after moving in. If radon levels exceeded the guidelines, "the pool would cover the cost of remedial action."[210]

That solution, however, is unworkable. Current disclosure requirements specify that a seller must reveal everything about the property that might influence the actions of a buyer. In other words, what is at issue is the level of radon at the time of sale, not the level that may be found after purchase. Nor is a prospective buyer likely to accept a contract offering mitigation of an unknown quantity through an insurance pool that will cover as yet unstipulated amounts. There are too many unknowns to give confidence to buyers, sellers, and real estate brokers.

Nero's comparison of radon testing with a termite report, a comparison made frequently by others, is also misleading. Testing for termites requires two or three hours, and the results are generally reliable. Reliable testing for radon takes days or weeks, a formidable obstacle to a reasonably expeditious negotiation and closing of a sale. At the same time, both the results and the cost and techniques of mitigation are open to question. The key to the problem may be the development of a short-term, inexpensive, and reliable test—for the moment, however, the uncertainties of testing and the costs and techniques of mitigation are still too fallible for comfort.

The suggestion that there be building codes for high-radon areas falls victim to similar uncertainty. A detailed map of high-radon areas, a favorite research topic for Nero, is offered as a prerequisite for successful and cost-effective mitigation. Even accepting his interest in seeing such a map, it is difficult to disagree with him when

[209]Ibid. See also Nero, "A National Strategy," p. 38.
[210]Nero, "A National Strategy," p. 39.

he says, "The decision on where to implement specific codes should be based on the aforementioned radon topology, not the spotty, crude, and misleading screening tests that have been made so far."[211] Whether codes are necessary or desirable remains questionable no matter how good techniques for classification may become.

Of greater importance are two recommendations that might affect EPA strategy. Nero suggests the establishment of a radon advisory committee because the agency must, as part of a long-term strategy, "overcome its reluctance to involve the scientific community substantially." At the same time, the agency should increase the number of its radon staff members "having strong scientific capabilities."[212] Most important would be the development of the conceptual framework for indoor pollutants mentioned above. The advisory committee would play a key role in structuring such a framework, which would "provide a suitable context for adopting long-term exposure reduction goals for homes with near-average radon concentrations." It would also be helpful in figuring out "what to do about nonresidential buildings, such as schools and offices, where exposure patterns differ from homes and where simple, long-term monitoring is not appropriate."[213]

The approach is sensible. Whether the EPA will see fit to abjure scare tactics for a common-sensical and scientifically valid approach remains to be seen. Past experience suggests that it's unlikely.

Conclusion

Indoor radon may be harmful. On the other hand, some low doses of radiation may be without risk and some might conceivably reduce cancer risks, a possibility that the EPA refuses even to contemplate. Open to question, at the very least, are the intensity and duration of the dose needed to cause adverse effects. Open to question as well is the modus operandi of the EPA.

Aided and abetted by rising worry about cancer and health in general, the agency has in essence constructed a house of cards. On the shaky foundation of questionable scientific evidence, it has made

[211]Ibid., p. 40.

[212]Ibid., p. 39. The misleading report of the scientific "consensus" on radon delivered by the EPA's David Rowson makes clear the necessity for such measures. See *supra*, n. 84, p. 23.

[213]Ibid.

a conscious effort to frighten the consumer, responding to the red flag of danger. Congress has passed legislation that has cost as its only certain consequence. With little or no concern for that cost, the EPA and Congress, aided and abetted by fear of liability, have succeeded in complicating further the already complicated transaction of a home sale.

All of which raises the ever-present question of relative risk. It is simple to estimate a risk; to prove that a risk is nonexistent is impossible. As the late Aaron Wildavsky once noted in a lecture, milk is beneficial, but flooding the room with milk would be fatal to trapped listeners. Would anyone be willing to aver, he continued, that it would be impossible to drown in six feet of milk? in one foot? in three inches? in one inch? Not a single person raised a hand.

Given this impossibility, coupled with the uncertainty surrounding radon's effects on health, the debate must center on acceptable levels of risk, which is a political or personal decision. Should the public allow regulatory gurus to implement policy that may depress the equity in 70 million homes? Buying a home is expensive as it is; adding the costs of testing and mitigation may not only restrict the choices available to a first-time buyer but price that buyer out of the market.

Given that breathing outdoor air is associated with a one in 100,000 risk of lung cancer,[214] an individual may opt to spend the dollars required to reduce his indoor radon exposure to outdoor levels, believing he will then maximize his odds against developing lung cancer. That is his choice. On the other hand, should the government spend taxpayers' money to scare people into testing for a risk of uncertain dimensions and to mitigate if the arbitrary EPA "level of concern" is exceeded? There is no technical reason for the 4 pCi/l level. The choice was not made by informed, likely-to-be affected, parties. The EPA made it.

If government exists in part to supply reliable information, the EPA has abdicated all claim to that role. The home-buying public has every right to view its pronouncements with suspicion and mistrust.

---

[214]Mueller Associates, p. 143. The risk is given as one in 100,000 from breathing 0.0048 pCi/l of radon, roughly 1/100th the radon level in outdoor air.

2. Lead: The Ever-Present Specter

In the 1920s the lead industry was proclaiming the adaptability of lead and its many domestic applications. The National Lead Company ran magazine ads headlined "How lead serves in your home," which enumerated its uses: the white enamel on bathtubs and sinks, the glaze on tiles in the bathroom and kitchen, the glossy glaze on china plates and cups in the dining room—all contained lead. Indeed, the ads announced proudly, "Lead is in every room."[1] Because lead paint was considered premium paint, preferred in quality homes, many families were literally surrounded by lead.

By the 1950s no one was advertising lead's omnipresence. Consumers were becoming all too painfully aware of it. Public health officials in some older cities were beginning to trace cases of lead poisoning to deteriorating lead-based paint, and the country was waking up to a problem that still defies resolution.[2] Lead is a naturally occurring element, and nature is immune to lawsuits, so finding a scapegoat—an organization or an industry to blame and fine—has proved difficult.

To make matters worse, the lead controversy is subject to politics. Although the public health risk appears from all credible evidence to have been dramatically reduced, even among the young and poor of the old and crumbling inner cities, the lead hysteria continues. We are all paying for the lack of a sensible and coherent federal policy on this issue, whether in the form of added fees as property owners, buyers, or sellers; more taxes to pay for mandated lead abatement; or higher rents resulting from diminished housing stock.

---

[1]National Lead Company, "How Lead Serves in Your Home," advertisement, *National Geographic* 44, no. 4 (October 1923).

[2]U.S. Department of Housing and Urban Development, Office of Policy Development and Research, *Comprehensive and Workable Plan for the Abatement of Lead-Based Paint in Privately Owned Housing, Report to Congress* (Washington: Government Printing Office, December 7, 1990), 1–2.

As a society, we are also paying in the anxiety generated by seemingly uncontrollable dangers. We need to place the risk in perspective, to counteract vague fears with reasoned analyses, and to adopt practical measures to deal with the remaining threat. If we do not, hysteria is likely to grow and with it the continuation of massive, ill-targeted programs that leave the most vulnerable populations still at risk. What is clear is that, while minute concentrations of lead in human blood can be measured, the lowest concentration that can be tolerated without causing any damage is a matter of debate, as is the value of efforts to reduce those concentrations still further.

Where We Were and Where We Are

The success of efforts to reduce lead exposure is measured by decreases in the concentration of lead in people's blood. Those levels have been dropping for decades, and the government could have declared victory. Instead, it kept moving the goal posts. The government-set goals, expressed as "levels of concern," have dropped sixfold over the past 20 years, from 60 micrograms of lead per deciliter of blood (mg/dl) before 1970 to 10 mg/dl in 1990.[3]

Whether blood lead levels as low as 10 mg/dl in children have any adverse effects is a major source of disagreement. As we will see, the studies that suggest the existence of such effects are marked by controversy and, possibly, fraud. In contrast, every lowering of the level of concern has the certain effect of increasing greatly the number of children who are classified as at risk from lead.

Beleaguered Homeowners

Property owners and all taxpayers are bearing the major share of the costs of solving the lead problem. Barraged by the one-sided views put forward by certain government agencies, without access to the counterpoise of more balanced studies, and in the teeth of often punitive legislation, they frequently find themselves not only

---

[3]The gram (g) is the basic unit of mass in the metric system; it is about 1/30th of an ounce. A microgram (μg) is 1/1,000,000th of a gram. A liter (l) is a unit of volume in the metric system; it is about the same as a quart. A deciliter (dl) is 1/10th of a liter or 100 milliliters (ml)—roughly half a cup. One mg per dl (1 mg/dl) is 1 part per 100 million. See U.S. Department of Housing and Urban Development, *Guidelines for the Evaluation and Control of Lead-Based Paint Hazards in Housing*, June 1995, Appendix 1-1. Cited hereafter as HUD, 1995.

FIGURE 2.1
LEVELS OF BLOOD LEAD IDENTIFIED AS LEVELS OF CONCERN

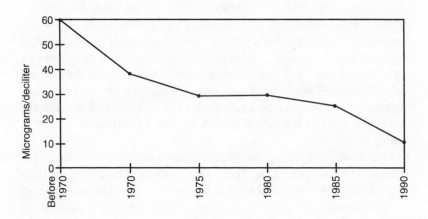

frightened but bewildered. Journalists have often fueled the hysteria by repeating unchecked assertions of toxic dangers.

Here is just a taste of the current situation: Should the owner of a home, a co-op, or a condominium or any tenant suspect the presence of lead and fear the consequences, the owner has to order and pay for an inspection. Although inspection and eventual deleading are compulsory only in public and Indian housing, disclosure protocols for private real estate transactions are increasingly demanding the appraisal of possible lead problems if the property is to be salable and the broker protected from suit.[4] An inspection usually costs between $300 and $400. If the inspector finds lead, the owner is then responsible for removing the lead or controlling access to it on an interim basis. A landlord must relocate any tenants until the work is completed. That is an expensive process, and in the end owners short of funds may not be able to hold on to their property.

There are worse scenarios. In some cases, families face health problems plus the loss of their homes and their savings. In a system

---

[4]A federal rule on disclosure of lead in housing went into effect on September 6, 1996, for owners of more than four units, and on December 6, 1996, for owners of four or fewer units. Fear of liability has already led to the widespread adoption of disclosure requirements in the real estate industry.

more punitive than supportive, parents may even be threatened with losing custody of their children. States and municipalities are beginning to require universal screening of children. In April 1993 New York mandated annual testing of blood lead levels for children under the age of seven. In Connecticut and New Jersey, testing is voluntary, but in all three states a blood lead level of 20 µg/dl or higher triggers a mandatory inspection of a house or apartment by the state or the local health department. A finding of lead levels above specified limits brings an order to remove the lead. In some states and municipalities, a homeowner with young children must abate the lead in the home or risk having the children placed in foster care.

One New York couple spent more than $4,000 on remediation of a two-bedroom apartment.[5] They were lucky. The lead levels of their two children fell below the level of concern, the children suffered no permanent neurological damage, and the medical costs were minimal. The Burkes of Allentown, Pennsylvania, were less fortunate. Finding that efforts to renovate their "dream house" had produced dangerously elevated lead levels in their two young children and unable to pay for the medical bills and the cleanup, they moved out. They then faced a Hobson's choice: they could try to sell an almost unmarketable house to cover their loan or allow the Federal Housing Administration to foreclose on the mortgage.[6]

The federal government provides no funds to cover cleanup costs in the private sector, and private-sector lenders are reluctant to support removal programs that may fail and come back to haunt the lender. The federal lead legislation of 1992 did set up a program of competitive grants, separately applied for by cities and states, to fund low-interest-rate loans for low-income housing through revolving funds. After three years of operation, the program had paid out $279 million in subsidies. But the costs of deleading make this the proverbial drop in the bucket.[7]

[5]Nick Ravo, "Lead Paint Moves Up as Housing Issue," *New York Times*, March 21, 1993.

[6]Jeanne Ponessa, "Government's Role in Cleaning Up Lead," *Governing*, August 1992, p. 20.

[7]The author would like to acknowledge her debt to HUD's Office of Lead-Based Paint Abatement and Poisoning Prevention for detailing this program.

The Department of Housing and Urban Development estimated in the early 1990s that it would take between $2 billion and $2.5 billion per year to test for and eliminate lead hazards in a half million privately owned homes occupied by families with young children. Those half million homes are about 1/100th of the 57 million privately owned units estimated to contain lead paint, and the cost estimate takes no account of medical costs.[8] Nor does it include the billions needed to clean up lead in the roughly 900,000 units of public housing occupied by families that may have children.

State programs, where they exist, are minimal or muddled. In 1991, for example, California passed legislation assessing fees on paint companies, gasoline dealers, and lead smelters to pay for screening—but the law is difficult to enforce and often disregarded and provides no money for cleanup.[9]

Early Progress

It is ironic that the emphasis on abatement of lead in housing emerged and has been escalating just as lead exposure was dropping dramatically. In fact, lead concentrations in humans have been decreasing for more than a century, at least in the industrialized world. In the United States, the rate of decrease has accelerated in the past 20 years. The Environmental Protection Agency (EPA) imposed prohibitions on lead in gasoline in the early 1970s, and levels of airborne lead fell sharply. In 1970 automobiles spewed 200,000 metric tons of lead into the air of the United States. Ten years later the level had dropped by roughly two-thirds. In 1989 it was down to 5,500 metric tons, less than 3 percent of the original figure. The decline has continued in the 1990s, although it has been less dramatic. In 1990 roughly 5,000 metric tons of lead entered the air; by 1991 and 1992 the total had dropped another 10 percent, to roughly 4.5 tons.[10] It will drop more. The Clean Air Act amendments of 1990 completely prohibited the use of lead in gasoline after December 31, 1995, a ban that has now taken effect nationwide.

---

[8] Ann Mariano, "U.S. Faces Huge Costs to Alleviate Lead Paint's Hazards," *Washington Post*, June 21, 1991, p. F1.

[9] Ponessa, p. 20.

[10] U.S. Department of Commerce, Economics and Statistics Administration, Bureau of the Census, *Statistical Abstract of the United States, 1994* (Tables no. 364 and 365).

Atmospheric emissions from other sources sank as well. In 1970 industrial processes, the second largest source after gasoline, disgorged 28,600 short tons of lead into the air, mainly from lead smelters and battery-recycling plants. By 1994 the total had dropped 90 percent, to 2.9 tons.[11]

As might be expected after those reductions, blood lead levels plummeted. From a mean of 17 µg/dl in the early 1970s, blood lead levels in children in the United States dropped to the current mean of 2.8 µg/dl. In San Francisco, an older city with widespread lead, a study done 20 years ago found that 50 percent of the children tested had levels of 20 µg/dl or more; in 1991 a repeat study showed only 1.7 percent at that level, a 30-fold decrease. The results of that study and others in Oakland, Los Angeles, and Sacramento indicate that the country has already met one of the 28 child-health goals established by the federal government for the year 2000—that blood lead levels not exceed 15 µg/dl in more than 2.5 percent of the population.[12]

What explains the dramatic change in only two decades? There was no magic. Industry responded to mounting consumer concern fueled by reports of the damaging effects of lead; new materials came on the market; and government action targeting lead in gasoline and lead in paint accelerated the decline.

One of the main sources of lead poisoning well into this century was the pewter from which common tableware, cooking utensils, and storage containers were made. (Even the seams of the ubiquitous "tin" can were often soldered with lead.) In 1972 the American Society for Testing and Materials, a trade group, issued specifications restricting lead content in pewter to 1/20th of 1 percent by weight. The industry complied voluntarily. Without government mandate, advertisements in catalogues and grocery store displays began to carry the notice "contains no lead." New products and materials were also gaining in popularity. Plastic and other lead-free materials began to substitute for "tin" cans and pewter plates, partly for reasons of cost, efficiency, and industrial design and partly as a

[11]*Economic Report of the President* (Washington: Government Printing Office, February 1996), pp. 138–39. Table 5-1, "Atmospheric Emissions of Lead by Source, 1970–94," source: Environmental Protection Agency.

[12]Edgar Schoen, "Spending Billions to Test Children for Lead Is Just a Waste of Money," *Sacramento Bee*, July 5, 1993.

response to the concern over lead. In 1973 the first amendment to the Lead-Based Poisoning Prevention Act of 1971, which applied primarily to paint in construction, prohibited lead-based paint in toys, furniture, and utensils used for food. For Congress and the government that was a relatively cost-free move: industry could be counted on to comply voluntarily and there was no need for expensive enforcement efforts. Thus, a major lowering of blood lead levels was accomplished with relative ease through a cooperative effort of the public and private sectors.

Meanwhile, copper and sometimes plastic pipes were replacing lead in piping systems and in household plumbing. Again, the reasons were mixed: copper is sturdier than the softer lead and plastic piping is easier to install and therefore cheaper.[13] Following passage of the 1986 amendments to the Safe Drinking Water Act of 1974, the Department of Housing and Urban Development banned lead from use in new plumbing and plumbing repairs in housing under its jurisdiction,[14] and regulation prohibited the use of lead as a material for solder and leaded brass on submersible pumps by the end of 1994. The four primary national building codes are judged against HUD standards, and the building industry adopted the agency's recommendations.[15]

Of all the changes in lead use, which were most important in reducing human exposure? The Centers for Disease Control and Prevention concluded that the removal of lead from gasoline and from the solder used to seal "tin" cans was the major contributor to the 70 percent decrease in blood lead levels in people ranging in age from 1 to 74 over the past quarter century.[16]

---

[13]Trade groups and unions have sometimes opposed plastic on tendentious grounds. Installing plastic piping may not be a job for the weekend handyman, but it can often be done without a plumber's license. The polybutylene that hit the market in the late 1970s, however, is alleged to have a flaw: the chlorine added to drinking water causes it to break down and the pipes to leak. A massive class-action suit, settled recently, seems to have made more money for the attorneys involved than for the homeowners. See Richard B. Schmitt, "Suits over Plastic Pipe Finally Bring Relief, Especially for Lawyers," *Wall Street Journal*, November 20, 1995, pp. A1, A5.

[14]Bruce Lippy and G. Timothy Haight, "Environmental Alert: Lead Contamination in Property," *Real Estate Accounting & Taxation* (Summer 1991): 81.

[15]Telephone conversation with HUD administrator, June 8, 1995.

[16]James Pirkle et al., "The Decline in Blood Levels in the United States," *Journal of the American Medical Association* 272 (July 27, 1994): 284.

Lead Paint

Today, the most persistent source of lead in the general environment is lead paint. Both white lead (lead carbonate, sulfate, or silicate) and colored lead (chrome yellow, red lead, gray, orange, and green) were used as pigments,[17] and a lead additive made the paint smoother and easier to spread. Almost all lead paints were oil paints, and for years leaded paint was premium paint. Lead improved the paint's opacity, making it possible to mask underlying colors and hide surface defects. Leaded paint also "chalked" easily. The surface became powdery and eroded quickly, like chalk. That was desirable because chalking kept exterior paint looking clean and new; rain rinsed away the chalky pigment, taking surface dirt with it. However, the pigment wound up as dust after the rain, mixing with the soil around the house. Inside the house, washing could bring about the same result. A child running his hand over the chalking surface and then putting it into his mouth would absorb a fair amount of lead from the dust—more, in all likelihood, than from eating a bit of peeling paint.[18] The sponges or rags used to wash the wall would also pick up lead. Unless they were washed thoroughly, they would, when dry, become a source of lead dust in the air. Breathed by children in the vicinity of an ongoing cleanup, the dust would elevate blood lead levels.

Before World War II such problems were largely unrecognized and almost all paints contained lead, although zinc and other opacifiers, such as titanium dioxide, began to replace the more expensive lead in the 1930s and 1940s.[19] In the 1950s deteriorating lead-based paint was found to be a probable cause of lead poisoning in older cities.[20] In 1955, the paint industry reacted, voluntarily adopting a standard limiting lead in paint for interior uses to 1 percent by weight. At about the same time, local jurisdictions began adopting the same standard in their codes and regulations. By 1960 the percentage of lead in paint had dropped slightly, partly as a result of

[17]HUD, 1995, pp. 11–15.

[18]David Owen, The Walls Around Us (New York: Villard Books, 1991), pp. 27–28.

[19]Irwin H. Billick and V. Eugene Gray, Lead Based Paint Poisoning Research: Review and Evaluation 1971–1977, U.S. Department of Housing and Urban Development, Office of Policy Development and Research (Washington: Government Printing Office, July 1978), p. 81. Cited hereafter as HUD, 1978.

[20]HUD, Comprehensive and Workable Plan, pp. 1–2.

the standard and partly as a result of the increasing substitution of other binders for lead. Still, lead-based paint continued to be widely available until 1978, when the Consumer Product Safety Commission finally banned the sale of lead-based paint to the construction industry and thus to consumers.[21] That ban, an appropriately targeted government action, accelerated a development already taking place, enhancing consumer safety. It was, however, one of the few benchmarks of rationality in the lead area, for regulation, fueled by consumer hysteria, quickly spun out of control, to the detriment of all concerned.

The Legislative Chronicle

Two federal laws form the basis for the regulation of lead-based paint: the Lead-Based Poisoning Prevention Act of 1971, with amendments in 1973, 1976, 1987, and 1988; and the subsequent 1992 Residential Lead-Based Paint Hazard Reduction Act. The 25-year-long debate about lead and the best ways to get rid of it has been rancorous at times and certainly prolonged, but it has yet to produce a consensus on the extent of the danger and the best protective measures.

In the debates surrounding the initial Lead-Based Poisoning Prevention Act of 1971, the House of Representatives backed a housing-oriented approach that emphasized the elimination of lead-based paint from public housing and would have given primary responsibility to HUD. Briefly, lead-painted units would be identified and the paint would be removed. Adults and children living in low-rent but private housing would be largely unaffected by the legislation, even if their housing had lead paint on the walls. The housing approach, requiring removal of lead paint without regard to whether or not children were exposed, was more costly than the health approach favored by the Senate.

The health approach called for screening of children to determine blood lead levels, identification and treatment of those with elevated

---

[21]HUD, 1978, p. 82; HUD, *Comprehensive and Workable Plan*, pp. 1–3.

It should be noted that the commission was acting under the authority of the Consumer Product Safety Act of 1972. The 1976 amendment to the 1971 act had reduced lead in paint to the level noted, but provisions for enforcement had been vague at best. Under the authority of the Consumer Product Safety Act, which had established the commission in 1972, the CPSC stepped into the breach. For an agency moving to ban lead, however, it made a signal error: it failed to ban the use of existing stocks, so contractors continued to apply lead-based paint well into the 1980s.

levels of lead, and deleading of their homes. The Senate version made the Department of Health, Education and Welfare the key agency.[22] That version had the advantage of early detection of at-risk children, which is particularly important because children's low body weights mean that ingestion of relatively small amounts of lead can have disproportionate effects. Moreover, poor children, who are often found concentrated in the lead-painted ghettos of the inner cities, are less likely to receive an adequate supply of calcium, which acts as a barrier to the absorption of lead into the bones. Poorly nourished, lead-exposed children are therefore particularly vulnerable and could be identified by screening.

Before passage of the initial federal legislation, most cities were using a health approach and directing their finite resources specifically to affected children. Even HUD originally favored that approach. The health-oriented Senate version that became law in 1971 struck a bureaucratic balance: HUD was to establish a demonstration and research program directed at the deleading of housing; HEW was to provide grants for detection and treatment of lead-based poisoning.[23] The package of amendments (1973, 1976, 1987, 1988) that followed whittled away at the primacy of HEW and made the housing approach dominant. HUD was given the mandate to embark on a "search and destroy" mission "to eliminate ... the immediate hazards of lead-based paint in all housing subject to the Act without regard to the risk factor."[24]

The 1992 legislation incorporated most of the features of the earlier legislation while adding three directives: the Occupational Safety and Health Administration was to promulgate a rule detailing protective devices for lead-exposed construction workers, the EPA was to set up model certification programs for lead removal workers, and states were to administer lead removal programs based on a federal model. The 1992 act also required that a booklet be prepared for all prospective buyers or tenants of housing built before 1978. A booklet for properties with more than four units was released in September 1996 and for other properties in December 1996.

[22]HUD 1978, p. 2.
[23]Ibid, pp. 2–3, 10.
[24]Ibid., p. 8.

Bureaucratic Paralysis and Expansion of Research

As the years went by, projections of staggering costs and the increasingly obvious difficulty of deleading the nation's entire housing stock induced bureaucratic paralysis, limiting the scope of most removal programs undertaken as a result of the 1971 act and its amendments. That may not have been all bad in that it saved taxpayer dollars while protecting inhabitants from the dangers caused by careless removal. Research did move forward, however, and over time provided the evidence necessary to shift legislation and practice from the "search and destroy" approach to a more workable containment strategy.

The research program produced improvements in the methods of determining lead content in paint and building materials. New, more accurate portable X-ray fluorescent devices and testing methods were developed. Those methods and devices have been critical in court cases over mandated lead removal, but none of them is inexpensive or useful for the average property owner.

The research program also studied barriers for reducing or eliminating risk. Biological barriers were the least promising. Lead-based paint tastes sweet, and consideration was given to a scheme to cover all lead-based paint surfaces with a bitter-tasting coating that would deter a child from eating the paint. Coatings that would prevent biological uptake of lead were also considered. Those approaches were rejected once the possibility of introducing a substance of unknown toxicity was raised and the specter of a long series of clinical trials loomed. State and local officials generally mistrusted biological barriers, and the paint companies were unwilling to shoulder the expense of testing.[25]

Attention therefore focused on the evaluation of physical and spatial barriers. Encapsulation by a new coat of paint, as was being done with asbestos, proved impracticable. In the case of asbestos, paint trapped the fibers and kept them from escaping for relatively long periods of time, but unleaded paint over lead-based paint tended to deteriorate quickly, exposing the leaded substratum. Encapsulation of lead required creating physical barriers by coating lead-based paint surfaces with materials such as wallpaper reinforced

[25]Ibid., pp. 60–62.

with fiber or vinyl-coated fabric or by applying rigid, durable barricades, generally wallboard, fiberglass, or wood. The barriers would make the paint inaccessible to children between the ages of one and six. They would also be relatively inexpensive and would cause little danger to those applying them.[26] On the downside, they required periodic maintenance: water leaks could cause deterioration, or the barrier could become dislodged. They were envisioned as, at best, a temporary solution pending eventual deleading.

Spatial barriers, as defined by the report, were the most difficult. They entailed removing and replacing the lead-based paint with a nonleaded substitute, a tedious, time-consuming, expensive, and lead-dust-producing option. Dust, easily spread around a worksite and carried on the workers' skin and clothing, is easily inhaled or ingested and presents a major hazard to workers (and bystanders). Replacement of components such as windows, doors, balustrades, and trim would be the simplest and least hazardous choice, since it would keep lead dust to a minimum. Unfortunately, it would also be the most expensive.[27] Regardless of expense, removal and replacement of components were the options most attractive to policymakers because they seemed to promise permanent solutions and permanent solutions held out the prospect of absolute safety once the offending substance, lead, was removed.

Researchers reviewed the costs and risks of various removal techniques—scraping and sanding, heat guns and infrared devices, solvent stripping. All of the removal methods were hazardous in one way or another, increasing costs and workers' risks. Scraping and sanding produced lead dust; solvents might be carcinogenic; blow torches presented a fire hazard. Electrical heat guns were somewhat safer, "but elevated blood lead still remains an occupational risk."[28] Replacing doors, windows, and frames, recommended in spite of the expense, did create some dust. The goal in terms of cost in evaluating new systems for abatement was set at $1/ft^2, although the researchers quickly admitted that many cities were using techniques that were more costly.[29]

[26]Ibid., pp. 28, 32.

[27]David E. Jacobs, "Abating Lead-Based Paint," *Journal of Property Management* 56, no. 2 (March–April 1991): 33.

[28]HUD, 1978, p. 53.

[29]Ibid., p. 39.

The 1978 HUD report painted a bleak picture of costs and difficulties. Despite efforts to decrease costs while improving the speed, safety, and ease of abatement, since 1971 the process has grown in complexity while the underlying difficulties have remained.

HUD's estimate of the cost of completely deleading the nation's 72 million housing units was staggering—between $35 billion and $41 billion, including administrative costs of from $7 billion to $12 billion. That was the cost estimated for reaching the goal of 2.0 mg lead/cm^2 of painted surface. [A milligram (mg) = 1/1,000 of a gram.] Tightening the goal by 25 percent, to 1.5 mg lead/cm^2, increased the estimated cost to between $44 billion and $51 billion. Budget constraints created a reality check, and the bureaucrats of HUD and HEW became reluctant to ask Congress for the funds that would be necessary for a major national program.

It should also be noted that the scope of the 1978 report was limited. It focused almost exclusively on interior lead-based paint as the source of lead poisoning in children. Although it sketched the problem of lead in dust and soil (exacerbated by the tendency of children to put whatever they happen to be playing with into their mouths), the emphasis was clearly on abatement in the home and, in fact, on interior walls and trim and on doors and window frames.

Such single-mindedness has characterized the crusade against lead paint. Lead, whatever its source, contributes to the problem. A well-thought-out program would surely consider as many factors as possible. But early on, as in the 1978 HUD report, that was not done. Lead-containing dust and soil were ignored. Of equal importance was the fact that major reductions in lead exposure because of changes in gasoline and tin cans resulted in significant improvements in blood lead levels. Those reductions have never been considered as reducing the risk or justifying a reconsideration of the emphasis placed on deleading housing. Nowhere is there evidence of rethinking, declaring progress, or of accepting the measured reductions in lead exposure as justifying pulling back from the single-minded pursuit of lead paint removal.

Raising the Heat and Raising the Costs

The debate over the best way to tackle the problem raged on and heated up in the years following the 1978 HUD report. In 1987 and

1988 Congress passed two additional amendments to the 1971 act in attempts to force HUD, which had become notably reluctant to incur the costs associated with imposing effective deleading requirements, to inspect and begin deleading all public housing by the end of 1995. So flawed were abatement techniques, however, according to HUD and industry representatives, that Congress was forced to suspend the agency's new lead regulations pending the development of safe abatement guidelines and to delay the start of the inspection and deleading period for several years. In recognition of the difficulties of deleading, the amendments again focused on research that might simplify the process and make it less expensive.

HUD responded by compiling a series of reports. In September 1990, it was *Lead-Based Paint: Interim Gudelines for Hazard Identification and Abatement in Public and Indian Housing*. In December 1990, the department issued the Report to Congress, *Comprehensive and Workable Plan for the Abatement of Lead-Based Paint in Privately Owned Housing*. The following year it published *The HUD Lead-Based Paint Abatement Demonstration (FHA)*.[30] It could point to those reports as evidence of its efforts to resolve the problem.

The 1990 report on privately owned housing indicates HUD's growing sophistication in dealing with lead and the beginnings of a change in emphasis from "search and destroy" to containment— that is, making lead inaccessible to children. Moreover, attention was paid to worker safety as well as the safety of residents during abatement.[31] Because lead paint was no longer in common use, concern was shifted from old and flaking interior lead paint as the primary health hazard to lead dust generated in and around the home as older houses were renovated and remodeled and as paint deteriorated with age. In addition to residents of aging housing in the inner cities, buyers of older homes who were sanding previous layers of paint to modernize their purchases found themselves at risk.

---

[30]U.S. Department of Housing and Urban Development: *Lead-Based Paint: Interim Guidelines for Hazard Identification and Abatement in Public and Indian Housing*, ILBPG REV-3, September 1990; *Comprehensive and Workable Plan for the Abatement of Lead-Based Paint in Privately Owned Housing*, December 7, 1990; *The HUD Lead-Based Paint Abatement Demonstration (FHA)*, HC-5831, August 1991.

[31]HUD, *Comprehensive and Workable Plan*, pp. 1–6.

The U.S. Public Health Service lowered the blood lead level warranting medical attention three times between 1970 and 1985. The decreased levels increased pressure on HUD, and HUD made abatement standards more rigorous. Complicating the picture was a growing awareness that lead-based paint on exterior surfaces might pose a hazard equal to that posed by lead on interior walls. Of the 57 million housing units with lead paint, 18 million had lead-based paint only on exterior surfaces as opposed to 11 million with such paint only on interior surfaces; 28 million had leaded paint on both the exterior and the interior.

Lead in the soil on the outside of a home can be tracked inside, and of course children play in the soil and can transfer dust from their hands to their mouths. Controlling exposure outside the home through removal of contaminated soil would substantially raise the costs of abatement; whether it does much good remains unresolved. On the other hand, simple hygienic precautions, such as having residents brush off their shoes on an entrance mat and insisting that children wash their hands, appear to reduce exposure to lead.

Identification of additional sources of lead resulted in more complicated abatement procedures. The Housing and Community Development Act of 1987, in amending further the Lead-Based Poisoning Prevention Act of 1971, recognized those problems but simply piled on new requirements. It directed HUD to publish testing and abatement regulations by June 1988 and to test all HUD-subsidized or HUD-rehabilitated units within five years of that date. It was another deadline that HUD would miss.[32]

Between HUD's 1978 study and publication of the interim guidelines of 1990, there was a quantum leap in federal requirements for the deleading of housing built by the federal government or renovated with its assistance. Essentially that meant public housing. In 1978 the average cost of "local abatement programs using less stringent guidelines" had been $2,100 per housing unit. In 1990 the figure rose to $7,700 for removal or $5,500 for encapsulation. The report was quick to note that "the average costs are influenced by a relatively small minority ... with exceptionally high costs" and that "more than half of all units ... can be abated for less than $2,500"[33]—

[32]Ibid., p. xix. See also Lippy and Haight, p. 82.
[33]HUD, *Comprehensive and Workable Plan*, pp. 4–22.

still a lot of money for the average homeowner if the requirements were extended to privately owned housing. Finally, the report's summary conceded that "the total cost of abatement by today's standards is thus five or six times as large as it would have been by the standards of 20 years ago."[34]

The costs rise still higher when the costs of testing are added. HUD has estimated that testing for lead paint costs $375 per unit whereas per unit testing for lead in dust costs between $340 and $1,028. Whether lead is present or not and whether abatement is required or not, testing costs can total about $1,400.

The HUD "Comprehensive and Workable Plan" of 1990 stopped short of citing the costs required for a national deleading effort— one that would cover both private and public housing—but they can be estimated. "Five or six times as large" would mean a total of roughly $250 billion, judging by the figures included in the 1978 report. Those figures were given in 1976 dollars;[35] adjusting for inflation brings the bill to perhaps $500 billion in 1990 dollars, a daunting figure even for bureaucrats and legislators.

The View from the Nineties

Given these costs, HUD had little choice but to turn toward "in-place management" of lead "as an interim procedure to protect occupants until safe, cost-effective abatement procedures could be established and implemented."[36] In-place management "focuses on removing dust and repairing nonintact paint while leaving the lead paint in place, at least temporarily."[37] Doubts were raised about the long-term cost and efficacy of such management, but it was clearly a winner in the short term. That conclusion was further supported by later HUD reports, which reflected growing concern over lead dust in the home, in soil, and as a byproduct of abatement. Disposal itself is costly—approximately $1.18 per pound or $255 per unit— adding significantly to the bill.[38]

---

[34]Ibid., p. xxviii.

[35]Billick and Gray, Tables A.2–A.5, A.8, pp. F-12–F-15, F-19.

[36]HUD, *Comprehensive and Workable Plan*, pp. 1–8.

[37]Ibid., pp. 4–23.

[38]HUD, *Lead-Based Paint Abatement Demonstration*, p. xi.

Everything indicates that removal is risky for worker and bystander, no matter the method used. A 1984–85 study conducted in Baltimore comparing "traditional" abatement practices and "modified" practices found both to be inadequate. Traditional practices include the use of open-flame burning and sanding techniques as well as the repainting of surfaces from which lead paint has been removed. Modified practices are methods that generate less dust, such as hand-held heat guns. Modified practices also emphasize the protection of workers and occupants, cleanup, and off-site disposal of debris. "By six months," the study reported, "it was clear that neither form of abatement resulted in long-term reductions of PbB [blood lead concentrations] or house dust lead levels, leaving children at continued risk."[39]

In the short term—that is, after one month—the lead levels of children living in housing where traditional abatement techniques were used were significantly higher than the levels of children living in dwellings where modified practices were used. At six months, however, children in both groups continued to have elevated lead levels not significantly different from the preabatement levels. The researchers concluded that continued exposure to lead dust was the operative factor.[40]

The study may have been less important for its comparison of traditional and modified practices than for its conclusions about the significance of lead dust: "At pre, post, and six months postabatement, children's PbBs [blood leads] were significantly correlated with floor and windowsill PbD [lead dust] in their homes." Lead paint was not removed from most window components "and window wells remained reservoirs of very high levels of lead dust of PbD during the entire study."[41] In other words, the leaded paint itself was less important than the dust released through friction and deterioration.

A 1990 HUD demonstration project to evaluate the hazards and effectiveness of 11 methods in the HUD guidelines had already led

[39]Mark R. Farfel and J. Julian Chisholm Jr., "Health and Environmental Outcomes of Traditional and Modified Practices for Abatement of Residential Lead-Based Paint," *American Journal of Public Health* 80, no. 10 (October 1990): 1240.

[40]Ibid., pp. 1242–43.

[41]Ibid., p. 1243. The study did have flaws. The sample was small (151 children); testing by health care providers was inconsistent and inadequate.

to similar conclusions. Eight of the eleven techniques, used under optimal conditions, resulted in residents having high exposure to lead. Aaron Sussell, who headed the team evaluating a lead removal project for the National Institute for Occupational Safety and Health, noted that the demonstration project "does not represent what is going on out there in the private sector," where contractors often cut corners to minimize costs and win competitive bids.[42] Thus, what is hazardous under optimal conditions will become more so in everyday practice.

Sussell focused on the importance of authorized training programs and certification of contractors to minimize risks but acknowledged that regulatory pressures, while leveling the playing field for contractors scrupulous about protecting their workers, could force abatement costs even higher, with unfortunate effects on housing:

> All the economics are working against . . . a landlord or a homeowner or an apartment owner . . . They're being socked with a huge bill, and some of them are saying "I'm not going to pay it, I'm just going to tear it down." So more and more low income housing is getting torn down.[43]

By 1992 the evidence that removal raised the risk for workers and occupants, especially children, and that a wholesale effort to remove lead could increase the deficit in low-income housing, particularly in rental housing, persuaded legislators to favor in-place management of lead. In that year Congress passed legislation embracing that approach.

Title X of the Residential Lead-Based Paint Hazard Reduction Act of 1992

Title X of the Residential Lead-Based Paint Hazard Reduction Act of 1992 codified changes that were already in progress. Rather than insisting on the removal of all lead-based paint from all surfaces, exterior and interior, the statute drew a clear line between an imminent hazard, such as lead-contaminated dust and soil or flaking and accessible paint, and a latent hazard, meaning intact lead paint on

---

[42]R. Blake Smith, "Building a New Lead Standard," *Occupational Health and Safety* 62, no. 2 (February 1993): 35–36.

[43]Ibid., p. 38.

surfaces inaccessible to a child's mouth.[44] The latter could now be tolerated; deteriorating surfaces could be covered with material such as an adhesive-backed vinyl that would bond to the deteriorating paint; relatively permanent enclosure with plywood or wallboard was also a possibility. Removal was no longer a mandate.

Reflecting a new sense of pragmatism, the legislation established a series of treatment levels based on the degree of federal involvement ranging from public housing to property purchased with the assistance of the FHA, the Veterans Administration, and the Farmers Home Administration. Removal was required only in public and Indian housing and then only during renovation and rehabilitation. In addition, the legislation phased in the dates on which requirements would become effective, allowing time for the expansion of existing abatement companies or the establishment of new firms, thus avoiding the creation of demand for nonexistent services, something that had been a problem in the past with asbestos.

In addition, the statute directed the Environmental Protection Agency to set up model programs for the training and certification of contractors, workers, supervisors, inspectors, and risk assessors working with lead-based paint hazards. Originally projected for the spring of 1993, then the fall of 1995, the rule has been issued for public comment and is now in the final stages of drafting. According to one HUD administrator, it should be "out in months." The states will then have two years from the effective date of the EPA rule to comply.

The EPA's delay in setting forth a rule would have imposed a delay on grants to the states: the statute stipulated that states must have in place certification programs based on the federal guidelines before they could spend more than 10 percent of the grant money earmarked for abatement by Title X. To resolve the problem, HUD, acting on the rationale that it knew what the EPA would eventually do, created a pathway for the grant money that it already had at its disposal.

---

[44]John D. Graham and Joshua T. Cohen, *Risk in Perspective,* Harvard Center for Risk Analysis 1, no. 5 (November 1993). Graham and Cohen list lead-based paint hazards as defined by the statute: lead-contaminated dust or soil, deteriorated or accessible paint, and paint on surfaces subject to friction or impact. Window frames and doors would be examples of such surfaces.

Accordingly, to obtain a grant, a state must either have a state-certified program that HUD believes is satisfactory or must *commit* to developing such legislation. Once committed, the state, in order to receive funds, must implement legislation on training and certification—that is, pass the legislation and implement the regulations needed to put it into effect. There is an additional bypass: local jurisdictions can receive grants directly, even if state legislation has not been passed and implemented, *if* the jurisdiction assures HUD that those doing inspections and abatements have been trained and certified in states with programs approved by HUD. Approximately 20 states, covering roughly 45 percent of the U.S. population, now have certification programs up and running and can spend more than 10 percent of grant money despite the lag in issuing the final rule. The delay is a prime example of the burden placed on the states when they are called upon to comply with yet-to-be-published federal rules before they can fully fund their programs.

By the time Title X was passed, there was general anxiety about where the lead program was going. The oft-amended and oft-ignored original prevention act of 1971 combined with an unwieldy mix of state and local regulations to escalate both anxiety and cost. Therefore, many in the real estate and lead industries, as well as buyers and sellers of homes, greeted the 1992 act with a sense of relief. It had become clear that the nation simply could not afford to spend roughly $500 billion to delead the interior and exterior of the 57 million homes built before 1980 that still contained lead-based paint.[45] And that was the low estimate. According to the Environmental Defense Fund, simply removing lead in the 24 million homes most in need of abatement would cost $240 billion.[46] The taxpayers, it was assumed, would pick up the bill.

It should be noted, however, that, although the passage of Title X signaled a more sensible and realistic basic philosophy about solving the lead problem, the legislation has some worrisome aspects. Previously HUD had been able to require inspection and eventual deleading of public housing only. Title X expanded HUD's authority by authorizing the agency to provide grants to state and local governments to implement "innovative" lead hazard control

[45]Ibid.

[46]Jonathan Adler, "Is Lead a Heavy Threat?" *Regulation* 15, no. 4 (Fall 1992): 13.

programs in low-income private housing. That was on the positive side. On the negative side, the legislation also required HUD, together with the EPA, to develop regulations on disclosure of lead-based paint hazards for real estate transactions.

For any residential property built before 1978, the seller, the seller's agent, or the landlord must supply a pamphlet outlining the hazards of lead-based paint and inform the buyer or tenant of any known lead-based paint or known lead evaluation report. The prospective buyer or tenant must have 10 days in which to inspect the property before becoming obligated to purchase or lease. Contracts of sale must contain an addendum, signed by the buyer, warning against the dangers of lead-based paint.[47] Failure to comply subjects sellers, landlords, and agents to both civil and criminal penalties, a frightening prospect. Originally scheduled to go into effect in October 1994 but often delayed, the rule finally appeared in the *Federal Register* on March 6, 1996. The effective date was September 6, 1996, for owners of more than four dwelling units; for owners of four or fewer units, the effective date is December 6, 1996.[48]

The proposed rule ignores the property condition disclosure forms, currently mandated in 14 states, which routinely note the possibility of lead-based paint. Several other states, in accordance with case law or consumer protection acts, also require disclosure.[49] Moreover, the educational efforts of state and federal governments and of trade associations, to say nothing of the exchange of information among the homebuying and home-renting public, have greatly raised awareness of lead as a potential threat. The rule, in other words, provides yet another example of administrative overkill and constitutes a questionable intrusion of the federal government into private contract negotiations.

The costs added by the legislation should also be of concern. Even a requirement as seemingly innocuous as a disclosure statement complicates a real estate transaction. Without giving a basis for the figure, one HUD official estimated that the rule would add about $6 to the cost of renting an apartment or buying a home. Nationwide,

[47]Ravo, p. 6.

[48]*Federal Register* 61, no. 45, March 6, 1996, pp. 9064–88.

[49]Mary Star-Hood, "Knowledge vs. Suspicion," *Real Estate Today*, October 1993, p. 10. See also HUD's 1995 Guidelines, as noted.

however, the cost for the estimated 9 million leasing transactions and 3 million sales transactions could run about $75 million annually. Brokers and agents worried about potential liability may believe that the requirement represents cheap protection, and perhaps it does. It will be especially welcome if it helps to hold down the skyrocketing cost of errors and omissions insurance.

Nevertheless, establishing one more layer of bureaucracy to cover an issue currently dealt with competently by the private sector burdens the housing industry with an additional regulation, imposes costs on all parties to a property transaction, and needlessly diverts homebuyer dollars. The vaunted goal of "protecting consumers"— who are usually quite capable of protecting themselves—becomes a shield for protection against the plaintiff's bar. The $6 might be better used to fund a private effort to reform the tort system.

The 1995 Guidelines, the Most Recent HUD Report

HUD released its most recent report, *Guidelines for the Evaluation and Control of Lead-Based Paint Hazards in Housing,* in June 1995. The guidelines devote additional attention to worker health and safety and to testing for lead with nearly total disregard for expense.[50]

Occupational Health and Safety

The 1995 guidelines place new emphasis on the role of the Occupational Safety and Health Administration, an understandable development given the growth of the market for contracting, testing, and control and the concomitant growth in the number of workers required to deal with lead. For many years there was a disparity between OSHA requirements for lead-exposed workers in general

[50]U.S. Department of Housing and Urban Development, *Guidelines for the Evaluation and Control of Lead-Based Paint Hazards in Housing* (June 1995), chap. 9, pp. 7–8. The guidelines replace the *Interim Guidelines for Hazard Identification and Abatement in Public and Indian Housing,* issued by HUD in 1990. The risk assessment protocol for these units issued in 1992 remains in place. The 1995 guidelines were actually written by the National Center for Lead Safe Housing under contract to HUD. The National Center is a nonprofit organization that oversees projects in a number of cities. It has strong ties with the Enterprise Foundation and the Alliance to End Childhood Lead Poisoning. It has received $5 million from the Ginnie Mae Foundation and support from HUD, EPA, and private foundations.

industry and for those in construction.[51] In 1978 OSHA set the allowable exposure levels for construction workers four times higher than for other workers, and OSHA regulations that required medical monitoring, removal of overexposed workers for medical reasons, and specific protective measures against lead did not reach to the construction industry. Only in 1990 did OSHA begin to develop a comprehensive standard regulating lead exposure in construction. Since there was as yet no final rule, Title X required that OSHA issue an interim rule.

For those working to remove lead from public or private housing, there are provisions for protective equipment, elaborate decontamination procedures, and lengthy medical surveillance. In addition to measuring the blood lead levels of employees who will be exposed on any one day to levels of lead equal to or greater than 30 $\mu g/m^3$ in the air, the employer must make available ongoing biological monitoring. Finally, the employer is required to make medical examinations "available at least annually for any employee who had a blood lead level equal to or greater than 40 $\mu g/dl$ any time during the past 12 months." An employee "medically removed from the job due to exposure to lead" must be examined for elevated levels of lead in the blood and possible adverse effects. A second and even a third opinion must be made available.[52]

Finally, "medical-removal protection benefits" must be provided "for up to 18 months, or as long as the job continues, each time an employee is removed." In other words, normal earnings and seniority are to be maintained during removal.[53]

The guidelines, however, seem blithely unaware of expense. Certainly, the chapter dealing with "Worker Protection" never mentions dollars and cents. After all, someone else, presumably the employer, is going to pay the bill. And the employer is not likely to be concerned if he is working on federally subsidized housing. The taxpayer will pay. But the small contractor or the homeowner, confronted with the bill and unable to shift the burden to the public, may consider filing for bankruptcy.

[51]HUD, *Guidelines*, pp. 9-7–9-8.
[52]Ibid., pp. 9-26–9-27.
[53]Ibid., p. 9–28.

Testing and Its Discontents

How does the owner or contractor know lead is present? Is it present in paint in concentrations greater than 2 mg/cm², the reduction of which is one of the usual goals of removal activities? Such simple questions have no simple answers.

X-ray fluorescence analysis (XRF) is the technique most commonly used to detect lead in housing. Hand-held detectors use radioactivity to stimulate fluorescent X-ray production by lead, which the machine detects and measures. Unfortunately, the machines cost between $8,000 and $10,000 and are difficult to maintain. They are also inaccurate at low lead levels—that is, below 2.0 mg/cm².[54] Because the machines contain radioactive isotopes emitting X-rays and gamma radiation, precautions are necessary to protect the operator and those around him.[55] Depending on the size of the house, the cost of on-site XRF testing runs between $400 and $1,000. If the general home inspection preceding a sale turns up evidence of lead, that specialized fee will usually be added to the inspector's fee, pushing up costs.

An X-ray technique similar to XRF but used on paint samples taken to a laboratory is more accurate and has lower detection limits but is more costly, between $4 and $10 per sample tested. It is also destructive, requiring repainting and repair of the areas tested.[56] The cost may sound low, but enumerating the roughly 30 "commonly encountered interior painted components that should be tested" makes it clear that the bill is likely to be high.[57] A second laboratory method, atomic absorption testing, is highly accurate but costs between $15 and $40 per sample. It detects lead by comparing minuscule weight differences between lead and nonlead paints. Although the method is useful in confirming inconclusive XRF tests, its accuracy depends on careful sampling, meaning that it is vulnerable to inclusions of substrata in the sample.

A less arduous approach involves spot testing with sodium sulfide. If the lead concentration exceeds 0.5 percent or 5 mg/g, a

[54]Stephanie Pollack, "Solving the Lead Dilemma," *Technology Review* 92, no. 7 (October 1989): 26–27.

[55]HUD, *Guidelines*, p. 7-7.

[56]Jacobs, pp. 32–33.

[57]HUD, *Guidelines*, pp. 7–10.

solution painted on a small cut in the surface will turn black or dark gray. The test is highly subjective, and HUD refuses to allow it.[58]

A related problem is the reliability of the testing laboratories on whose analytical results all procedures depend. Incorrect data are likely to result in needless exposure of workers or a failure to remove lead as specified.[59] The guidelines note that laboratories that analyze samples of lead in dust and soil will now be required to be accredited through the EPA's National Lead Laboratory Accreditation Program and will be able to list themselves as "EPA recognized."[60] At the same time, accreditation or licensing costs money and is likely to raise lab fees, the cost to contractors, and ultimately the price paid by consumers. Even in the absence of licensing, a reliable lab is likely to gain a following and to profit. A lab that becomes known for its sloppy work will lose customers and eventually its entire business. In the interim, it may harm workers and those who depend on the removal. Nevertheless, the tradeoff is worth noting.

On the retail front, hardware stores have begun to respond to the anxieties of homeowners by stocking home lead detectors. They are inexpensive but close to worthless, revealing the presence of lead without providing a means of evaluating concentration or risk.

The Costless Universe of the Guidelines

The grubby subject of money rarely, if ever, raises its head in the guidelines. Earlier HUD studies had at least supplied figures, increasingly alarming figures, covering the costs of dealing with lead. The agency now adopts a posture best characterized as "coy." The volume notes that Title X accepts "interim controls" designed to reduce exposure to lead temporarily; "abatement" has been clarified and restricted "to mean the elimination of 'lead-based paint hazards,' not necessarily all lead-based paint."[61] Because elimination can include encapsulation and enclosure, a homeowner or a landlord has a degree of flexibility. However, the statutory requirements for public and Indian housing, enacted in 1987, remain unchanged: inspection of all pre-1978 construction and removal of all lead-based

[58]Pollack, p. 27. See also HUD, *Guidelines*, p. 5–35.

[59]Smith, pp. 35, 36.

[60]HUD, *Guidelines*, p. 1–11.

[61]Ibid., p. xxii.

paint when the unit is rehabilitated.[62] The rigidity of the mandate for federally subsidized housing contrasts sharply with the more moderate tone of the guidelines, and removal imposes a heavy financial burden on HUD and on the taxpayer.

The guidelines do provide much needed clarification and amplification of terms and procedures that have become confused by time and repetition. The report devotes an entire chapter to "Interim Controls," carefully distinguishing them from "Abatement." At the same time, it notes the evolution of the terms "encapsulation" and "enclosure," often seen as synonyms in previous literature on lead. Encapsulation is a barrier achieved by "using a liquid-applied coating . . . or an adhesively bonded covering material. . . . The primary means of attachment for an encapsulant is bonding of the product to the surface (either by itself or through the use of an adhesive)."[63] Certain paints; liquid coatings reinforced with cloth, mat, or fibers; and materials made to adhere with an adhesive, such as vinyl floor tile, all qualify as encapsulants.

As a class of barriers, encapsulants were relatively new, and the development of a protocol governing their testing was an elaborate process supported in particular by the state of Massachusetts which, in 1990, convened a Lead Abatement Technology Task Force to identify the properties desired in an encapsulant. The task force included representatives of the EPA (which provided some financial support), HUD, and universities, as well as pediatricians, lead inspectors, toxicologists, and coating technologists. A draft of the task force report was circulated nationally and became part of the impetus behind the establishment of a subcommittee on encapsulants by the American Society of Testing and Materials. Representatives from Massachusetts served, of course, on that subcommittee. When it became apparent that the subcommittee would agree on specific testing procedures for encapsulants that were acceptable to

[62]Citing a dollar amount for the first and perhaps the only time, the guidelines note that Title X decrees that "any residential construction job receiving more than $25,000 per dwelling unit in Federal funds is required to have lead-based paint hazards abated. If $5,000 to $25,000 per dwelling unit in Federal funding is received, either abatement or interim controls must be implemented." Those who doubt the subsidies flowing to housing should contemplate the projected budgetary disaster.

[63]HUD, *Guidelines*, p. 13-5.

the state, Massachusetts adopted that protocol. The National Institute of Testing and Standards has since published three guides based on the protocol: the first covers "reinforced" encapsulants, the second covers "non-reinforced," and the third deals with selection and use. In addition, a recent report outlines the capacity of encapsulants, which is generally high, to prevent lead from leaching to the surface. Whatever the continuing controversy over lead, companies can now refer to a national protocol for the manufacture of these liquid coatings.[64]

The guidelines list encapsulation as "less costly and more timesaving than some other techniques" but fault it for requiring periodic monitoring and maintenance since the lead remains.[65] The exact meaning of "less costly" is left to the imagination.

In contrast, enclosures are "durable, rigid construction materials that are mechanically fastened to the substrate" and can be expected to last at least 20 years.[66] Those are listed under the general heading of "Abatement," meaning measures designed to remove the lead or to make it permanently inaccessible. In dealing with abatement, the guidelines discuss in detail interior surface enclosure materials, such as wood paneling and drywall, as well as the interior building components suitable for enclosures, methods of removal, and requirements for waste disposal. There are photographs of workers engaged in removal, illustrations of proper tools, and a diagram of a worker installing new tile. Here as elsewhere in the guidelines, there are step-by-step summaries on "How to Do It," plus endless reproductions of necessary forms. All that is lacking is an itemization of probable costs.

Controlling lead often involves all three methods: encapsulation, enclosure, and removal. The goal, however, is always the same, to meet the HUD standards for lead-based paint dust after abatement. The standards vary according to the surface and refer to units of lead loading: 100 µg of lead per square foot on floors; [67] 55 µg/ft²

---

[64]Telephone conversation with a representative of the Massachusetts Childhood Lead Poisoning Prevention Program, July 22, 1996. Telephone conversation with the National Institute of Testing and Standards, July 23, 1996.

[65]HUD, *Guidelines*, p. 3–7.

[66]Ibid., p. 12-10.

[67]Jacobs, p. 33.

on windowsills; 800 μg/ft² in window wells.[68] If components are replaced, the guidelines suggest that the replacements be energy efficient. The cost of the components is never in question.

Ironically, the summary at the end of chapter 11, "Interim Controls," includes the admonition, "Pay contractor and clearance examiner."[69] "With what?" the reader is tempted to ask.

In fact, the government eludes the question of cost-benefit analysis by creating, in effect, unfunded mandates. For example, under Title X, homeowners may find it necessary to abate the lead in their homes in order to sell them, but they will generally be given little or no assistance in doing so. HUD simply assumes that lead is a ubiquitous menace to be eliminated regardless of the cost. To read the guidelines is to be transported back 40 years to a time when lead, like polio, was indeed a menace. We won the war on polio. Perhaps it is time to declare a truce in the war on lead.

Flawed Research and Weak Policy Foundations

Although the guidelines highlight HUD's role, it is important to emphasize that Title X makes the EPA a far more visible and powerful player in the lead controversy. Given that the EPA has shown itself to be one of the agencies fueling the lead hysteria, that exacerbates the problems.

In 1991, even as legislative proposals were becoming more reasonable, certain agencies in the executive branch were setting an opposite course, most notably the HHS and the EPA. In October 1991, Dr. James Mason, assistant secretary for health at HHS, announced that the CDC, an HHS agency, was formally lowering the level of concern from 25 μg to 10 μg per deciliter of blood. The reduction caused the number of children "at risk" to soar from 400,000 to 4.5 million, a more than 10-fold increase, and an analyst estimated that the cost of litigation and regulation would be somewhere between $200 billion and more than $500 billion.[70]

---

[68]Ralph Ray II, Environmental Services Coordinator, Alameda County, California, Lead Poisoning Prevention Program, electronic transmission directed to the author, August 31, 1994.

[69]HUD, *Guidelines*, p. 12-6.

[70]Warren Brookes, "Science Overdosed on Lead?" *Washington Times*, October 23, 1991.

A year later, Edgar Schoen, a California physician who has emerged as a persistent and well-informed critic of many aspects of the federal program directed at lead, decried the CDC's "epidemic by edict," estimating that the number of "asymptomatic 'affected' children had zoomed from about 300,000 nationwide to between three and four million."[71] In an article published the following year, he elaborated on the problem. The $974 million estimated by the 1991 CDC Strategic Plan to Eliminate Childhood Lead Poisoning over a five-year period was a "gross underestimate."[72] At $10 to $75 per test, "the annual cost of the laboratory phase alone would be $160 million to $1.2 billion." The inclusive program necessary, which would entail tracking, counseling, abatement, treatment, and follow-up, "would carry a multibillion dollar annual price tag. Meanwhile, critical health care needs of our children are being ignored or underfunded."[73]

Schoen draws attention to "faulty assumptions" about costs:

> For example, Pb abatement for a typical dwelling was assumed [by the CDC] to cost $2,000; Needleman [a proponent of lead's harms, see below] had earlier estimated $5,000, and the actual amount required to delead the average inner-city home in a Baltimore program is $20,000. In contrast to the CDC estimate of $974 million for a total Pb testing, treatment, and abatement program, Needleman estimated the cost of Pb abatement alone to be $10 billion, and a trade paper recently estimated the potential Pb abatement market to be $600 billion.[74]

"Faulty assumptions" seems charitable. It is reasonable to suggest that the CDC itself must have been aware of the costs involved and that its estimate represented a deliberate attempt to "soft-pedal" the expense.

---

[71]Edgar J. Schoen, "Lead Toxicity in the 21st Century: Will We Still Be Treating It?" Letter to the editor, *Pediatrics* 90, no. 3 (September 1992): 481. See also Edgar J. Schoen, "Spending Billions to Test Children," *Sacramento Bee*, July 6, 1993.

[72]Edgar J. Schoen, "Childhood Lead Poisoning: Definitions and Priorities," *Pediatrics* 91 (February 1993): 504–5.

[73]Edgar J. Schoen, "AAP Lead-Screening Recommendation Ill-Advised," *AAP News* 9, no. 11 (November 1993).

[74]Schoen, "Childhood Lead Poisoning," p. 505.

The controversy swirling around the figures cited, the putative need for universal screening, and the lead "epidemic" reveal an alarming play of politics as well as the potential for disaster when policy is built on shaky foundations. For starters, the research on which Mason and the CDC had based the decision was suspect, as became evident in a long, bitter research dispute.

Needleman's Research

The research debate over lead boiled up in 1979 when the *New England Journal of Medicine* published a study by Herbert Needleman, a professor of child psychiatry and pediatrics, and his associates at the University of Pittsburgh, that purported to show that children with relatively high, although not toxic, levels of lead had measurably lower IQs and performed less well in the classroom. The study compared 58 elementary school children in Massachusetts with "high" lead levels to 100 children with "low" levels and found that the former performed less well on a battery of tests. The behavioral assessments of the teachers involved correlated with the test results: they found children with relatively high levels of lead less organized, more easily frustrated, and lower in "overall functioning." The lead levels in the children were determined primarily by analyses for lead in baby teeth, which presents a problem as to whether those seldom-used measurements can be used to make estimates of blood lead levels.

In any case, Needleman and his associates never clearly defined what they meant by "high" or "low." They did conclude that the "permissible exposure levels of lead for children" should be reexamined.[75] At the time, the CDC had set a blood lead level of 30 μg/dl as the tolerable threshold.

Two years later, in 1981, Professor Claire Ernhart of the Departments of Psychiatry and Reproductive Biology, Case Western Reserve University, and her colleagues challenged Needleman's findings, pointing to "serious methodological flaws." Ernhart

[75]Herbert L. Needleman et al., "Deficits in Psychologic and Classroom Performance of Children with Elevated Dentine Lead Levels," *New England Journal of Medicine* 300, no. 13 (March 29, 1979): 689–95. A graph in the article, Figure 1, p. 690, gives the "Cumulative Frequency Distribution of Dentine Lead Concentrations" of 3,221 specimens; but the text, as noted, disregards vital definitions.

asserted that Needleman had not controlled adequately for "confounding variables," such as parental neglect, inadequate nutrition, or poor schools, that might explain the disparity in IQ scores. Needleman's multiple comparisons between lead levels and various measures of behavior and intelligence meant that a few would be statistically significant "merely by chance." Ernhart's own work indicated that IQ would be affected only at the highest levels of exposure, "just below what would be considered toxic."[76]

EPA's Expert Panel's Review of Needleman's Research

The challenge by Ernhart et al. might have gone unnoticed had the EPA's Office of Research and Development not instituted a review of the health effects of lead exposure as a prelude to revising air quality standards for lead. At the same time, the EPA's Office of Policy Analysis and Evaluation, which had funded some of Needleman's work, was pushing for a complete phasedown of lead in gasoline. To settle the potentially embarrassing Needleman-Ernhart controversy, the agency convened an expert panel on pediatric neurobehavioral evaluation in the spring of 1983 to look into their work.[77] The investigation and its aftermath read like a suspense novel and reveal a good deal about the flaws in the government's use of science.

The expert panel found Needleman's methods less than straightforward and his results inconclusive. Specifically, it concluded that "the study results, as reported in the Needleman et al. (1979) paper, neither support nor refute the hypothesis that low or moderate levels of Pb exposure lead to cognitive or other behavioral impairments in children."[78]

The panel was disbanded, and the actions of the EPA speak clearly about its regard for the panel's analysis: the agency proceeded to use Needleman's conclusions as part of the "scientific" basis for the revised air lead standards promulgated in 1986.[79]

---

[76]Claire Ernhart, Beth Landa, and Norman B. Schell, "Subclinical Levels of Lead and Developmental Deficit—A Multivariate Follow-up Reassessment," *Pediatrics* 67, no. 6 (June 1981): 911–19.

[77]See also Claire B. Ernhart, Sandra Scarr, and David F. Geneson, "On Being a Whistleblower," *Ethics and Behavior* 3, no. 1 (1993): 75.

[78]Ibid., p. 76, citing Environmental Protection Agency, 1983, p. 38.

[79]Joseph Palca, "Get-the-Lead-Out Guru Challenged," *Science* 253 (August 23, 1991): 843.

More Criticism of Needleman's Work

In May 1991 Professor Ernhart and her associate, Sandra Scarr, sent a report outlining their problems with Needleman's research to the federal Office of Scientific Integrity at the National Institutes of Health, which, in turn, asked the University of Pittsburgh to investigate the charges.[80] A University Inquiry Panel found itself unable to exclude research misconduct or misrepresentation and recommended that the university open an investigation. A second panel, the University Hearing Board, concluded in May 1992 that there had been "deliberate misrepresentation of the procedures actually used in the conduct of the study as reported in 1979 and thereafter" and that "Dr. Needleman was deliberately misleading in the published accounts of the procedures used in the 1979 study." The hearing board, however, cleared Needleman of the most damning charge, "scientific misconduct."[81]

As a result of objections raised by Needleman, the university adopted the report only six months later, in October 1992; it was finally released in April 1993. Even with no charge of "scientific misconduct," the university report is a stinging criticism of the investigator and his work. It has made no difference to the EPA and its supporters in its drive to reduce lead exposures.

The Office of Research Integrity, the successor to the Office of Scientific Integrity, accepted the report of the Hearing Board as "timely, thorough, objective, and competently conducted." It also agreed with a major criticism, "that the details of the method and criteria for the provisional selection of high- and low-lead subjects were inaccurately and incompletely reported . . . and that the sequence of statements about these procedures reveals 'a pattern of errors, omissions, contradictions, and incomplete information from the original publication to the present.'"[82]

Essentially, the ORI said Needleman was a sloppy scientist but that he was not dishonest. Such criticism of a scientist's work is

[80]"Lead Researcher Under Investigation," ed. Richard Stone, "Science Scope," in *Science* 294 (December 13, 1991): 1575.

[81]Confidential: Needleman Hearing Board Final Report, May 20, 1992, pp. i–ii. Photocopy in the possession of the author.

[82]ORI Oversight Report: University of Pittsburgh: ORI 91-27, n.d., pp. 3, 5. Photocopy in the possession of the author.

uncommon; for most scientists it would surely mean a diminution of support. Apparently the criticism has not hurt Needleman.

The ORI sidestepped the question of "deliberate misrepresentation," noting only that the university had made such a finding. Essentially, however, it confirmed the earlier verdict of the University Hearing Board, and it concurred that there had been no "scientific misconduct,"[83] a much more serious charge.[84]

The controversy had begun in scientific journals and in the courts well before the official inquiries and it continues to rage, doing great damage not only to the image of science but to the public purse. The University Hearing Board, probably considering Needleman's "deliberate misrepresentation," observed that his finding "certainly should not have been a basis for federal policy."[85] Others were less kind, finding gross misrepresentation, misconduct, and error. Yet Needleman's research, neither blessed nor rejected by the ORI, was in fact incorporated into EPA policy.[86] It has since been used by the CDC as a basis for their recommendations, thereby setting the stage for a widespread "lead scare" programmed to rival the "asbestos panic" of the past decade.

Some Specifics about Needleman's Research: Criticisms and Retorts

Needleman's study has shown itself vulnerable to a number of criticisms. The exposure levels were relatively high: 35 µg/dl in the high-lead group, 25 µg/dl in the low-lead group, as estimated from the measurements in teeth. By today's standards, those levels would be very high and rarely seen. Methodological issues remain a concern. The size of the study group kept changing. Originally 2,000 children were to participate, but winnowing reduced the sample to 524 and then to 270. In the process, Needleman may have thrown out data that would have been necessary if the findings in the study group were to represent what was going on in the entire population of 2,000 children. Moreover, to maximize the possible lead effect,

[83]Ibid, pp. 3–7.

[84]The definition of "misconduct" is a thorny issue in the scientific community, involving, among other factors, the question of intent. See Ernhart, Scarr, and Geneson, "On Being a Whistleblower," pp. 87–89.

[85]"Confidential: Needleman Hearing Board Final Report," p. 41.

[86]ORI Oversight Report, ORI 91-27, p. 2 n. 2.

he analyzed only those with lead levels in the highest 10 percent and lowest 10 percent of his sample.[87]

Eventually Needleman was able to obtain "a modest but statistically significant 4 point IQ difference between high and low groups," but he had excluded 254 of the 524 subjects before IQ testing, leaving 270. A finding that 112 more children were ineligible resulted in a sample size of 158 subjects, 58 "high lead" and 100 "low lead." As critics have pointed out, "When the actual analysis is performed on less than one third of the original sample it is very hard to be sure that some bias has not crept in."[88] The extensive manipulations of the sample itself also make the study vulnerable to criticism.

Even more important may have been Needleman's cavalier treatment of confounding variables. Factors such as socioeconomic status, maternal IQ, parental education, and violence in the household can be as important as or more important than lead in determining the intelligence of a child. Although Needleman collected data on the families, he seems to have used it selectively. "Critics suggested that employing all the relevant confounders would weaken the apparent lead effect still further."[89]

Finally, the vaunted re-analysis of Needleman's data undertaken by Joel Schwartz when he was at the EPA Office of Policy Analysis is fatally flawed. Although Schwartz later claimed that he had included all 270 children,[90] he admitted in a discussion with Ernhart that he had used data from only about 210,[91] opening the door to speculation about the selection of children to include in the analysis.

Evidently nettled by critics, Needleman has continued to defend his work stoutly. In a 1994 letter to the editor of the *New England Journal of Medicine*, he admits that the 1979 paper contains two "errors

[87]Harvey M. Sapolsky and Sanford L. Weiner, "The Science and Politics of Environmental Lead Poisoning," September 1993. Incomplete draft in the possession of the author, pp. 4–5.

[88]Ibid., pp. 4–5. The authors cite Pocock and Ashby (1985) on the bias created by downsizing the sample. Telephone conversation with Sanford Weiner, September 9, 1994.

[89]Ibid., citing Marshall (1983), Pocock and Ashby (1985), and Smith (1985), p. 5.

[90]National Research Council, *Measuring Lead Exposure in Infants, Children, and Other Sensitive Populations* (Washington: National Academy Press, 1993). Schwartz was a member of the council.

[91]Claire Ernhart, notes taken at the meeting sponsored by the Alliance to End Childhood Lead Poisoning in May 1984 and in the possession of the author.

in reporting," but he says they had no effect on the analysis of the data or the conclusions drawn.[92] Critics disagree. In a letter submitted to the editor of the same journal, Ernhart pointed out that Needleman had "ignored the request that he correct erroneous counts of cases in the tails of the distributions [a statistical flaw]." She also said he did not comment on other identified flaws, including "(a) representativeness of the sample, (b) exclusion criteria which shifted at least 3 times, (c) unequal numbers in two groups, and (d) differences in age."[93]

Sanford Weiner and Harvey Sapolsky, scholars in the field, also submitted a letter for publication in 1994. They noted that the ORI request that Needleman correct the scientific literature "remains unfulfilled." In particular, Needleman had failed to discuss discrepancies between two graphs published in 1982 and 1987. The "1987 version . . . purports to represent the same data, though the medians and the tails of the curves have been altered." More disturbing yet, "The 1987 graph has been widely reprinted . . . , but ORI could not reproduce it from Needleman's data."[94]

In the third letter submitted, Schoen avers that the Needleman letter "is just another example of Needleman's pattern of misrepresentation." He also takes issue with the graph, noting that "he omits mention of a third, significantly different graphic depiction of the same data which has been widely used to promote his viewpoint of neurobehavioral damage due to low lead levels, and which appeared in the 1991 Centers for Disease Control and Prevention (CDC) influential publication on childhood lead poisoning."[95] In other words, by misrepresenting his data, Needleman has managed to frame the policy debate in such a way as to vindicate his own claims, raising costs and anxiety in almost equal measure.

Needleman has, of course, found defenders inside and outside the EPA. His frequent coauthor, Dr. David Bellinger of Children's

[92]H. L. Needleman, "Correction: 'Lead and Cognitive Performance in Children'." *New England Journal of Medicine* 331 (1994): 616–17.

[93]Claire B. Ernhart, personal communication. Photocopy in the possession of the author.

[94]Sapolsky and Weiner, photocopy in the possession of the author.

[95]Edgar B. Schoen, to *New England Journal of Medicine*, December 1994. Photocopy in the possession of the author. It is worth noting that the *Journal* published none of the letters.

Hospital in Boston and the Harvard Medical School, has claimed that there is no substance to Scarr's charge that Needleman manipulated the data until he got the results he wanted.[96] Psychologist Lester Grant of the EPA declared that the debate was no longer of interest, since "We now have a decade of additional research that confirms lead effects on IQ and behavioral development at much lower levels" than those under discussion.[97]

The assertions made by the EPA and other government officials should be viewed with caution. The assistant secretary of health at HHS, Dr. James Mason, cited 18 "sophisticated studies" from abroad justifying concern about lead and claimed that federal policy had taken those studies, as well as Needleman's work, into account when setting policy. Fundamentally, the cited reports fail to support the government's reduction of "safe" exposure levels to 10 μg/dl; none showed statistical correlations between such low-level lead exposure and IQ levels.[98]

The director of a lead study in England, Marjorie Smith, has gone further, asserting that 10 μg/dl, the goal of the EPA, is "'unrealistically low'" and can only cause anxiety for parents.[99] Summing up his review of the literature, Weiner claims that studies showing adverse health effects at levels below 25 μg/dl are hard to find.

Nature, one of the world's most respected science journals, published a scathing indictment of Bellinger in which Weiner and biophysicist Gay Goodman demolished Bellinger's analysis of 13 well-known studies from several countries on IQ and lead in blood and teeth, three of which he had coauthored, that he said provide "strong support . . . for the view that even low lead levels produce IQ deficits." Although widely circulated, the figures in his graphs "do not accurately represent the [data presented in the] primary sources and thus may provide inappropriate policy guidelines." Since "lead

[96]Bellinger and Needleman have collaborated in establishing the Alliance to End Childhood Lead Poisoning.

[97]Palca, p. 844.

[98]Adler, p. 14. Among the studies cited by Mason was that by Dr. Marjorie Smith, discussed in the text paragraph that follows, whose research explicitly contravened his contentions.

[99]Palca, p. 844.

exposure and IQ scores are both correlated with socioeconomic variables, these parameters have to be taken into account when estimating the effect of lead on IQ." Bellinger, however, failed to consider them. While claiming to plot mean adjusted IQ scores, he actually plotted raw, unadjusted data, a significant misstep since "confounding covariates were found to account for half of the apparent effect."

Even for the studies in which the data were plotted accurately, the grouping raised "serious methodological issues." In summary, so flawed was Bellinger's presentation of the research that it should not be used as the basis for regulation. "Moreover, the actual lack of consistency across the studies suggests that the policy options being considered require further examination."[100]

How Are Risks to Be Estimated?

Lead is poisonous at high levels (certainly at levels higher than 30 μg/dl). How risky is it at lower levels? Does risk decrease linearly with dose? Does it decrease more rapidly at lower doses so that a sublinear model might be closer to the truth? Could there be a level below which lead is nontoxic?

After reviewing 16 studies, Joshua T. Cohen concludes:

> The shape of the lead dose-response relationship is highly uncertain, especially at blood lead concentrations below 15 to 20 μg/dl. Biochemical mechanisms make it possible that the dose-response relationship has no threshold but do not prove that no threshold exists. Epidemiological evidence is far from conclusive.[101]

To confuse the issue, "It is also possible that while there is no strict effect threshold, the lead dose-response function is sublinear with a smaller impact on IQ at lower blood lead levels than at higher

---

[100]Sanford W. Weiner and Gay Goodman, "Lead Risks," *Nature* 352 (August 1, 1991): 385. The letter, published in abridged form, refers to Bellinger's paper in *Research in Infant Assessment*, ed. N. Paul (White Plains, N.Y.: March of Dimes Birth Defects Foundation, 1989), pp. 73–97.

Dr. Goodman supplied an unabridged copy of the letter, cited in conjunction with the published version, and corrected a typographical error in the published version. Photocopy of the unabridged letter in the possession of the author.

[101]Joshua T. Cohen, "Evidence Documenting the Relationship Between Blood Lead Concentrations and IQ," Ph.D. dissertation, Harvard University (1994), pp. 2B.3: 2B-20–2B-23.

blood lead levels." According to Cohen's analysis, the jury is still out about effects at low levels.

Stuart Pocock, Marjorie Smith, and Peter Baghurst, British and Australian researchers, reviewed 26 epidemiologic studies from Australia, Eastern and Western Europe, the United Kingdom, and the United States.[102] They concluded that five prospective studies showed "no association of cord blood lead or antenatal maternal blood lead with subsequent IQ. Blood lead at around age 2 had a small and significant inverse association [that is, higher lead levels were associated with lower Iqs]. . . ." Fourteen cross-sectional studies of children's blood lead "showed a significant inverse association overall, but showed more variation in their results and their ability to allow for confounders." Although "the estimated magnitude was somewhat smaller," the seven cross-sectional studies of tooth lead in children "were more consistent in finding an inverse association."

Pocock, Smith, and Baghurst leave open the possibility that there is no completely safe level: "A threshold below which there is negligible influence cannot currently be determined." Because a threshold cannot be demonstrated, the possibility exists that the lowest exposure can cause an adverse effect. At the same time, the fundamental question about whether a linear model (with its relatively high risk) or a sublinear model (with its lower risk) best fits the data remains unresolved.

Pocock, Smith, and Baghurst sum up their review: "While low level lead exposure may cause a small IQ deficit [perhaps 1 or 2 points], other explanations need considering: are the published studies representative; is there adequate allowance for confounders; are there selection biases in recruiting and following children; and do children of lower IQ adopt behavior which makes them more prone to lead uptake (reverse causality)?" It is just those "other explanations" that the EPA, Needleman, and the shrill chorus of his allies tend to neglect. They are, however, critical to isolating and determining the effects of lead, if any.

Pocock, Smith, and Baghurst counsel a prudent balancing of the costs of detecting and reducing these current lead levels with the

[102]Stuart J. Pocock, Marjorie Smith, and Peter Baghurst, "Environmental Lead and Children's Intelligence," *British Medical Journal* 309 (November 5, 1994): 1189. Quotations in the three text paragraphs that follow are from this article.

costs of reducing "other important social detriments that impede children's development." That type of cost-benefit analysis has been sorely lacking in the politicized debate about lead in the United States for the past two decades.

A recent report from Costa Rica provides information about lead and IQ in a developing country. The study enrolled 184 healthy 12- to 23-month-old children in a community-based effort to measure blood levels while evaluating family and developmental information that might influence the results. The children were first evaluated as infants and toddlers, at which time the mean blood level was 11 μg/dl, ranging from 5.4 to 37.0 μg/dl. All children were reevaluated when they were five years old, using a battery of physical and psychological tests.

The results? "Blood lead levels in infancy did not predict any of the developmental outcome measures. Thus, among a group of healthy toddlers in a developing country, no ill effects on development of low blood lead levels were observed."[103]

Should finite resources be diverted from such concerns as nutrition and safety and better schools to an expensive campaign whose results are open to question?

At least two agencies emphatically answer, "Yes."

The Politics of Hysteria

HHS has opted for universal screening of children to determine blood lead levels, and EPA officials have consistently advocated that more be done to reduce lead exposures. Decreasing blood lead levels indicate that it is time to consider alternative approaches, targeting tests to children most at risk and determining the most important sources of lead exposure, but HHS and the EPA, responding to some bureaucratic imperative, continue along the roads they chose years ago. Those choices are being challenged, however, by scientists and physicians who see other investments in health as having far more benefits.

HHS and Universal Screening

In 1991, HHS, through the CDC, recommended that virtually all children be screened for lead. Commenting on this proposal, Dr.

---

[103]Abraham W. Wolf, Elias Jimenez, and Betsy Lozoff, "No Evidence of Developmental Ill Effects of Low-Level Lead Exposure in a Developing Country," *Developmental and Behavioral Pediatrics* 15, no. 4 (August 1994): 224.

Birt Harvey asserted in the February 1994 issue of *Pediatrics* that the disadvantages of universal screening outweighed the advantages. The cost, the disruption of the family, and the diversion of resources from more cost-effective projects represented "an unjustified burden to society and to individuals." As an alternative, he recommended selective blood lead screening which would target children most at risk and lead to prompt intervention.[104]

Sadly, the costs are escalating just as the need for testing has diminished. The 1991 CDC proposal envisioned testing annually up to 16 million children under age six at a cost of at least $10 billion over the next few years.[105] CDC seems to have assumed that parents, pediatricians, and tax-funded public health officials would absorb the cost.

Some policymakers evidently felt that the proposal fell short of the mark. While they could do no more than recommend universal screening, they could mandate that screening be offered in federal health programs, and in 1992, the HHS Health Care Financing Administration did just that. HCFA issued a regulation that required that blood lead testing be offered to all Medicaid-eligible children aged 6 to 12 months and again at 24 months, except in "lead-free communities." In October 1993, HCFA lifted the exemption, producing a mandate that all Medicaid-eligible children, regardless of risk, be offered testing twice during their first two years of life.[106] The directive is an unfunded mandate that imposes heavy burdens on the states.

The militant insistence on screening has puzzled many physicians, especially on the West Coast, who have yet to see a lead-poisoned child. At one meeting of the American Academy of Pediatrics, members from the eight western states agreed unanimously that "targeted," as opposed to "universal," testing was desirable. The state of California's delegation submitted a resolution calling on the AAP

[104]Birt Harvey, "Commentary: Should Blood Lead Screening Recommendations Be Revised?" *Pediatrics* 93, no. 2 (February 1994): 203. Harvey cites a study by Gellert et al. which determined that the case-finding cost for the blood lead test itself was $310 per child for those with blood lead levels greater than 10 µg/dl and $19,139 per child for those with blood lead levels greater than 25 µg/dl. He also notes that nine states now require screening of some or all children under six.

[105]Schoen, "Spending Billions."

[106]State of Alaska Epidemiology, "Bulletin," No. 14, June 28, 1994.

"to rescind its current policy recommending universal blood lead screening." It had no effect. The AAP Council on Scientific Affairs in its report maintained its endorsement of universal testing. One physician commented: "Apparently it [the Council] had been tweaked by several government agencies urging the status quo."[107]

The Washington State delegation to the AAP then passed a resolution asking the American Medical Association's House of Delegates to curtail passage and/or distribution of the Council report. A letter explaining the action noted: "We in the state of Washington are convinced that we can far better use our limited resources ... than in pursuing [sic] universal blood lead testing. ... We are convinced AMA should be leading and not dragging its feet on this particular issue."[108]

The physicians of the western United States are far from alone. Researchers in the broader scientific community also oppose the CDC insistence, backed by the EPA, on universal screening. In a paper prepared for the Lead Tech Conference of October 1994, Claire B. Ernhart, the outspoken critic of unfounded belief in an "epidemic" of childhood lead poisoning, noted that blood lead levels are low and declining.[109] What indeed is the point of suggesting universal screening to detect lead levels so low that their effect, if any, is uncertain? In addition to the problems posed by testing, the costs of abatement are high, and "Abatement has not been linked to changes in cognitive test scores or other clinical outcomes."[110]

The disadvantages, she concludes, outweigh the advantages, given "the costs of universal screening in terms of money, the time of care providers, discomfort to children and the anxiety to the parents." Targeted screening of children with blood levels above 25

[107]William O. Robertson, AMA Delegate, Washington State Medical Association, to Robert Burnet, attaching Washington State Delegation's Resolution I-94 (November 14, 1994), pp. 1, 2.

[108]Ibid., p. 2.

[109]For purposes of treatment, children with measurable levels of exposure fall into five classes: minimal or Class I, 9 mg/dl or lower; low or Class II, 10–19 mg/dl; moderate or Class III, 20–44 mg/dl; severe lead poisoning or Class IV, 45–69 mg/dl; Class V, 70 or more mg/dl, a level almost always requiring hospitalization and chelation.

[110]Claire B. Ernhart, "Does Universal Screening for Lead Meet Accepted Criteria for a Screening Program?" Paper prepared for the Lead Tech Conference, October 17–19, 1994, pp. 1–6.

µg/dl, about 0.5 percent of the population according to the most recent National Health and Nutrition Evaluation Survey (NHANES) survey, "could be beneficial" and much less costly.[111] The benefits of concentrating on children at high risk, mainly those in the inner cities, older public housing, or those living near active lead smelters or battery recycling plants, would outweigh the costs.

Studies outside the United States have reached the same conclusion. An international assessment of low-level blood lead effects, sponsored by the Commission of the European Communities and the EPA, declared:

> Despite the wealth of data, and including data from experimental studies with animals, it is still not possible to conclude with any certainty that lead at low levels is affecting the performances or behavior of children.

The study did not recommend the mass screening of European children.[112]

Even the CDC appears to be having second thoughts. At a meeting of the CDC Advisory Committee in February 1995, the difficulties of implementing blood screening for all children were acknowledged. But there was a general reluctance to retreat from the previously announced position.[113] In particular, Needleman and Rosen "emphasized that the goal of universal screening should not be abandoned to sustain credibility." Abandonment might signal to the public that "lead poisoning is no longer important." In other words, manipulation of the public constitutes an acceptable tactic.[114]

Of the eight recommendations finally agreed upon, the following three seem the most significant:

> 1) There is a group of children for which screening is unnecessary because blood levels are so low.

> 3) The boundary between the low risk group and all other risk groups should be based, if possible, on the NHANES

---

[111]Ibid., pp. 6–8.

[112]Schoen, "Spending Billions."

[113]"Draft-Confidential," CDC Advisory Committee Meeting, February 15–16, 1995. Personal communication. Photocopy in the possession of the author. Quotations are from that unpaginated document.

[114]Ibid.

[National Health and Nutritional Examination Survey] III data which defines low risk as a 4% prevalence of elevated blood lead levels above 10 μg/dl.

7) Several members of the committee felt that the public would interpret the new guidelines as a retreat from former recommendations and the net impact would be to reduce public funds. . . . It was suggested that the new set of recommendations be couched properly to emphasize that the lead problem is not yet over. . . .

Although the recommendations suggest a more practical approach, they underline the CDC partiality for Needleman's views and its willingness to keep the public in the dark. Evidently, those who are paying for the CDC cannot be trusted with the truth. The final paragraph underlines this position:

The Advisory Committee was generally reluctant to retreat from their universal screening policy because of the concern that the lead problem would be de-emphasized in the public arena; but, in recognition of the necessity to allocate limited resources properly the above recommendations to CDC were generally supported.[115]

Despite the committee's general support for universal screening, CDC has made no public announcement. As Ernhart noted in July 1995, "Last we heard, CDC was still thinking about backing down on universal screening."[116]

The EPA: Willful Ignorance and Political Interplay

Like the press and HHS, the EPA has consistently plunged ahead, generally ignoring criticism. Its supporters assert that "The scientific debate over lead's toxicity is over, and it is pointless and distracting to delay action further."[117] Given the plethora of conflicting studies and inconclusive reports, that is patently tendentious.

[115]Ibid.

[116]Claire Ernhart, "Common Sense about Lead," July 1995. Personal communication. Photocopy in the possession of the author.

[117]"Summary of HHS Review of Needleman Study: Final Report by the Office of Research Integrity," flyer distributed at the May 1994 conference of the Alliance to End Childhood Lead Poisoning. Personal communication. Photocopy in the possession of the author.

Carol Browner, current administrator of the agency, declared in a keynote speech to a preparatory meeting for the 1995 "Fourth World Conference on Women" that lead-poisoned children were flocking to the nation's hospitals.[118] The remark, although untrue, showed political savvy. The conference focused on "Women and the Environment," and the women who attended were in the main devout environmentalists who saw danger lurking in the air and the water and thought that government should expand to meet the challenge.

The most notable political pressures at work in the conference are not hard to find. In addition to environmentalists and commentators who claim repeatedly that the United States is polluting not only the nation but the world, certain businesses benefit as well from widespread fear. The lead abatement industry, for example, has a powerful interest in maintaining the theory of a lead "pandemic" that can have disastrous consequences for the next generation. Grants for lead removal, of course, are likely to have profitable consequences for those doing the work. In a complex interplay, the EPA feeds into those interests to bolster its own image as a protector, even at the expense of truth.

Alameda County, California, provides an illustration. In the late 1980s Lynn Goldman, then employed by the Department of Health Services in California, conducted a survey of 500 children in six census tracts in Oakland, using fingerstick blood collection. About 67 percent of the examined children had blood lead levels of 10 μg/ dl or higher. That was no surprise really because the fingerstick method is notorious for false positives: a smudge of lead-contaminated dust can elevate the reading. Evidently mindful of the methodological problem, Dr. Goldman and her colleagues then conducted a second survey using venipuncture, which is far more reliable. The results were striking: fully 75 percent of the fingerstick measurements were misleadingly high. One-quarter of those who tested

[118]Carol M. Browner, keynote speaker, at "Women Thinking Globally, Acting Locally," Official U.S. Preparatory Meeting for the United Nations Fourth World Conference on Women, Oakland, California, November 15, 1994. The publication accompanying the conference outlined the workshops but did not carry any reference to Browner's speech. Several requests made to the EPA for a copy of the text were unsuccessful.

122

lower on repeat with venipuncture were below the CDC cutoff point of 10 µg/dl.

An interim report to the California legislature in 1989 reviewed the discrepancies in the data, noting the false-positive rate of over 50 percent. A later submission to the *Mortality and Morbidity Weekly Report (MMWR)*, however, muddied the waters. It alluded to the "possibility of sample contamination" by asserting that the children's hands were washed "vigorously" before obtaining the fingerstick samples and stated that "a confirmatory venous blood sample was obtained from 74 percent of the Oakland children" whose fingerstick tests had shown levels above 15 µg/dl. The results of testing the "confirmatory" sample were not given, however. Finally, it simply declared a prevalence figure of 67 percent for blood lead levels greater than 10 µg/dl in the city of Oakland.[119] Alameda County then used the 67 percent figure to buttress two applications for lead abatement grants. The CDC funded the first; HUD, the second, for $4.4 million, in December 1992. The grants will not only pay for abatement but will also cover the salaries of those running the lead abatement program.

Accused by Schoen of a "serious omission" in the report sent to the *MMWR*, Goldman retorted: "This was not a 'serious omission' but one of many results from our study that didn't fit within the content of a brief report." The justification seems specious at best: Dr. Schoen noted that a 37-word explanation "would fit neatly into a brief publication." In addition, Dr. Goldman claimed that she and her colleagues ". . . never have tried to apply these rates beyond the boundaries of the study neighborhoods." Whether she or they did or not, Alameda County certainly did in its two applications for federal funds, where the 67 percent figure was cited to prove the existence of a serious problem.[120] Dr. Goldman, incidentally, was appointed to a senior position at the EPA.

Other interests cloud the issue. Home builders who no longer paint with lead or install lead plumbing consider lead a problem of the past and have no reason to enter the scientific arena or to oppose

[119]M. Haan et al., "Blood Lead Levels among Children in High-Risk Areas—California, 1987–1990," *MMWR* 41, no. 17 (May 1, 1992): 292.

[120]Lynn Goldman, "Lead Screening: To the Editor," and Edgar Schoen, "In Reply," *Pediatrics* 91, no. 4 (April 1993): 854–55.

programs for removal. The real estate community, to shield itself from suit, is likely to second any and all efforts to detect lead in used housing. Consumers, who pay the bill for abatement either directly or through taxes, have few champions.

Interlocking Directorates

As the presence of Dr. Needleman on the CDC committee illustrates, the very scientists who have "discovered" or "reported" the lead problem are advisers to the government. That makes sense, of course. Who is better able to advise than researchers in the field? But the skeptics are noticeably absent from advisory and decisionmaking bodies. The result is that interlocking directorates of government and private organizations have generally adopted uncritically the results of Needleman's research despite its flaws. One physician offered a scathing critique:

> The "passionate commitment" to universal testing—in the face of epidemiologic data on the one hand and the need for cost accountability on the other—is scientism at its worst. A brief glance at the "inbreeding" [sic] in the advisory committees to government with their heavy representation from the Environmental Defense Fund, the Natural Resources Defense Council and the Alliance to End Childhood Lead Poisoning proves disconcerting. Doesn't it seem a tad inappropriate for the "Chair" of the CDC's advisory council who serves simultaneously as the AAP's Environmental Health Care Committee Chair . . . to receive the Alliance's "Public Awareness Award . . . ?"[121]

Even a casual observer is likely to conclude that it is more than "a tad inappropriate."

A more pointed attack comes from Dr. Schoen. After noting, "Evidence is continually accumulating to show that much of the data upon which the 1991 CDC report were based are faulty," he continues:

> The members and consultants of the Advisory Committee on Childhood Lead Poisoning Prevention, who were responsible for the 1991 CDC report, were dominated by a biased

---

[121]William O. Robertson, to Linda Bresolin, director, Office of Women's and Minority Health, American Medical Association, September 7, 1994, pp. 1–2.

group of investigators and professionals ... who, like Dr. Needleman, had a long history of commitment to low-lead-damage as a *cause célébre*.

The list that follows includes Dr. J. Rosen, Lynn Goldman, and David Bellinger.[122] The scenario scarcely inspires confidence in the supposedly "scientific" and "dispassionate" analyses of the EPA.

A recent analysis notes a flagrant example: Ellen Silbergeld, a toxicologist at the University of Maryland, chairs the EPA's National Policy Committee on Lead and serves as a board member of the alliance. She has proposed taxing lead by the pound to pay for abatement, a proposal that "left the lead industry fuming and the lead-abatement industry cheering."[123]

The same committee members who write articles or give interviews highlighting the lead "epidemic" are to some extent "preaching to the choir," reinforcing a message that their colleagues already believe. Often it is their articles or letters that are published in the scientific journals, to the detriment of those holding more temperate views. Their testimony has crowded out the moderates in congressional hearings. The bias in hearings before Democratic Congresses is understandable because of that party's interest in big government. Hearings before the Republican Congress might redress the balance, but few have been held, and none has caught the attention of the media. In any case, prophecies of doom find a receptive audience in the popular media, proving the theory that bad news sells better than good.

A 1995 article by Jane E. Brody in the *New York Times* illustrates the credulity of the journalistic community and makes clear the problem of interlocking directorates.[124] Brody cites not only Rosen but also Needleman's frequent coauthor, Bellinger, who is quoted as saying, "We infer from these findings that lead affects aspects of neuropsychological development that are not measured by IQ tests. . . . a child [who] has trouble carrying out fine motor skills . . . might have trouble taking tests in school because he has to concentrate so

[122]Edgar Schoen, Letter to the author, December 13, 1994, p. 2.

[123]Ellen Ruppel Shell, "An Element of Doubt," *Atlantic Monthly*, December 1995, p. 38.

[124]Jane E. Brody, "Despite Reductions in Exposure, Lead Remains Danger to Children," *New York Times*, March 21, 1995.

hard on the act of writing. . . ." In other words, the IQ tests are unable to measure an effect, but that is unimportant. It is quite clear, to Bellinger at least, that an effect must and does exist. Brody also lionizes Needleman, never once suggesting that there are doubts about the statistical validity of his work. She notes, without comment, Joel Schwartz's claim that even 2 µg/dl of lead can produce harmful effects. Schwartz, formerly at the EPA, and now at Harvard, reanalyzed Needleman's lead studies, concluding that his results and conclusions were correct. (For the record, both Ellen Silbergeld and Joel Schwartz have received "genius awards" from the MacArthur Foundation.)

In contrast, Brody dismissed Ernhart as a supporter of and advocate for the lead industry. She gave short shrift to the review of 26 epidemiologic studies that concluded that there was still much "uncertainty" concerning lead's effects. Dr. James W. Sayre of St. Mary's Hospital in Rochester, New York, is cited toward the end of the article as suggesting that the resources devoted to lead abatement might better be used in improving the health of pregnant women, vaccinating children, and increasing enrollments in Head Start.

The last word, however, goes to Dr. Rosen, who claims that "skepticism about the value of controlling lead exposure" is "politically and economically motivated." Such a charge is unwarranted—certainly it was unsupported by her article. But Brody evidently accepted it at face value.

A 1995 Progress Report on the Lead Problem

Any status report on finding solutions to the lead problem must be filled with contradictions. Deleaded gasoline, copper pipes, and tin cans have removed the major threats to human health. Blood lead levels in children have dropped to a mean well below the 10 µg/dl declared by the CDC to be the level of concern. In general, the population of the United States has never been better protected from lead.

Federal government agencies, particularly HUD, the EPA, and the CDC, still act as though they were in the middle of a full-scale war. Instead of acknowledging the victories achieved, they keep arguing for broad-based testing and abatement. If lead is to be removed, whether at the direction of the federal, state, or local government, legislation and subsidies should be targeted to the inner cities where houses and apartment buildings still constitute a reservoir of lead.

Instead, the agencies have often become an intrusive presence, squandering resources in the process. The actions of the EPA in Triumph, Idaho, are directed at lead from an old lead and silver mine and not at lead paint, but they illuminate the single-minded pursuit of a less-than-reasonable policy.

There appears to be little risk from lead in Triumph. Lead levels in blood and urine tests are normal, indeed well below those in large cities. All but one retest of the town's well failed to show a high lead content. Armed with such data, the residents, all 46 of them, have vowed to keep "backhoes and bureaucrats" from taking charge of their town. Angry at the intrusion of the government, they have vowed to defend their homes, now made almost unsalable by the EPA report. Despite strong and organized opposition, the EPA is refusing to back down. One resident was quoted as saying, "In the end ... the fight boils down to a 'very American principle'— the right to choose, and accept the consequences."[125] That "very American principle" seems unknown to the EPA.

The EPA and HUD are, to some extent, caught in a dilemma. Unable to deal with findings that run counter to deeply held beliefs, they are unable to announce that the worst has truly passed. Only talk of a lead "pandemic" can sustain their credo, the subsidies they make available to firms in the private sector, the research grants they award, and their jobs.

Cost: A Reality Check

HUD appropriations for the prevention of lead poisoning doubled from fiscal year 1992 ($47.7 million) to fiscal year 1993 ($100 million). In fiscal year 1994, they reached $150 million. During those years, the department awarded 56 grants to states, cities, and counties. As a result of the budget stalemate, a projected budget of $100 million for fiscal year 1995 shrank to $15 million, barely enough to cover technical assistance and research; no grants were awarded. In fiscal year 1996, appropriations rebounded to $65 million, of which roughly $50 million was to be awarded beyond the Beltway for the

---

[125]Tony Horwitz, "For These Residents, EPA Cleanup Ruling Means Paradise Lost," *Wall Street Journal*, September 21, 1993, pp. A1, A14.

reduction of lead hazards. For fiscal year 1997, projected appropriations totaled $60 million. As the budget summary indicates, the ebb and flow of concern about lead has had its counterpart in the HUD budget.

Fortunately for taxpayers and property owners, HUD's more relaxed 1990 interim guidelines covering "management in place" or "lead safe housing" have succeeded in substantially reducing the cost per unit treated, in some cases by as much as half—that is, from $7,700 to $3,900 or less. The guidelines of individual states, however, supersede the federal guidelines and, if more strict, may limit cost savings.[126] Advocacy groups are now seeking to bring pressure to bear on several state governments to set reasonable, affordable standards for housing that is "lead safe" rather than "lead free." The funding available for the work may hold the key to keeping expenditures in check. Otherwise, as the cost per unit goes down, the number of units may well increase so that the funds available are used.

States and Cities as Laboratories

Grants flow from HUD, EPA, and HHS for major state, city, and county programs, but each administrative entity varies its implementation according to its own statutes and regulations, the age of the housing stock, the extent of its inner cities, and even the type and extent of bare soil. States and cities focus on rental properties, where they can impose requirements on owners; owners increasingly bear the costs as insurers refuse to underwrite properties without excluding liability for lead.

Massachusetts

With an inventory of older housing loaded with lead, Massachusetts has reacted to the problem with Draconian severity.[127] Its landmark 1971 legislation, the first in the country, has undergone several revisions; overall its statute and regulations remain the strictest in the nation. In 1987, after 16 years of mitigation efforts, complaints

---

[126]The author again acknowledges the help of HUD's Office of Lead-Based Paint Abatement and Poisoning Prevention for its discussion of Title X.

[127]The state's Childhood Lead Poisoning Prevention Program contributed heavily to this report (telephone conversations, March 4, 1996). See also Skip Schloming and Alfred Singer, "Lead Poisoning: Is There a Thief Somewhere?" *Small Property Owner* 1, no. 4 (January 1996): 6.

about continuing accessibility to lead and sloppy work practices by lead abatement workers brought about a major revision.

Prior to that time, the regulations had simply recommended that a family move out while deleading was in process. The revision made it mandatory. Double plastic was to be taped over floors and furniture while workers replaced windows, moldings, and doors or "dry scraped" them down to the bare wood—creating clouds of lead dust in the process. (Machine sanding was forbidden.) After wrapping and sealing debris for disposal, all surfaces were to be vacuumed with a HEPA (High-Efficiency Particle Accumulator) vacuum cleaner and washed twice with a high-phosphate detergent. Dust wipes would then be used to determine the level of leftover dust. Once all surfaces were smooth and easily cleaned, the family could move back in—that is, if return were possible. Given the cost of cleanup, tenants might find that the owner was no longer in business or, given the fear of lingering lead dust, tenants might decide to relocate permanently.

A 1993 legislative change was followed by a shift in regulations. Property owners and unlicensed agents—carpenters or even friends—could perform low-risk deleading, defined as encapsulation, removing doors, shutters, and all interior coverings, such as paneling and wallboard, and the capping of baseboards. Removal of vinyl siding on the exterior was also a "low-risk" activity. Moreover, a family could remain in residence during the performance of low-risk work as long as they stayed out of the work area.[128]

The 1993 legislation also created interim controls as a temporary alternative to full deleading. "Temporary" in that case meant "good for up to two years," provided that the unit were recertified after one year. The HUD interim controls are more flexible, requiring only that the interim controls be inspected and the repairs maintained, but Massachusetts marches to its own drummer.

The state has no registry of children with high levels of lead, but it has instituted universal screening, requiring insurance companies to provide it as a benefit. Pediatricians in private practice and at clinics must test all children under the age of six and report the results to the Department of Public Health. The results for children

---

[128]The regulation has a "catch-22": most deleading has both high-risk and low-risk components, and the high-risk work may well force eviction.

with lead levels of 25 µg/dl or higher are reported to a state lab. In fiscal year 1995, 1,200 children were newly confirmed as having 20 µg/dl or higher through a venous test. Case management services are available to children with lead levels of 20 µg/dl or more, and roughly 900 children identified in previous years are still receiving services.

Lawsuits have proliferated, but, as a result of the revision, a lead lawsuit can now be brought *only* on behalf of a child considered lead poisoned as defined by state regulations—that is, having a blood lead level of 25 or more µg/dl. Prior to the change, parents could bring suit for a child with any lead level.

As a result of the revisions, a new owner, instead of being immediately liable for the cleanup, can now use a 90-day "exemption" that gives him time to have the work done. Unless a child living in the unit is identified as "poisoned," triggering full abatement, the owner may opt to deal with lead on an interim basis and to receive a letter of interim control issued by private lead inspectors licensed by the state agency. Two years after the institution of the interim controls, the owner must proceed to full abatement using licensed deleaders. Once their work has been completed, he can expect a letter of full compliance from the state agency for poisoning prevention.[129]

Paying for the work still constitutes a heavy burden. Based on income tax claims, one estimate cites $5,000 per "average" unit; clearly the cost can go much higher. Massachusetts, Boston, and Cambridge have received HUD grants totaling roughly $25 million since 1993, but that covers only a small part of the work. Funds that flow through the state cover administrative expenses, laboratory services, inspections, and social services, not deleading.[130]

As might be expected, loan programs have proliferated. The Massachusetts Housing Finance Authority, under its "Get the Lead Out" program, offers some loans at zero percent interest; on others, the interest is deferred. In addition to outright grants, the state also offers a tax credit of $1,500 per unit, an increase from the first offer of $1,000 in 1987. Given that costs per unit can easily reach five

[129]Licensing is a lengthy and therefore a costly process. Private providers supply the necessary training, which is followed by an examination and an apprenticeship with a master lead inspector who will supervise the trainee's first inspections.

[130]As a remedy the state has established a health education trust funded through a surcharge on professional licenses. In its first year, 1995, it received $1.5 million.

times that figure, the aid is better than nothing, but it leaves major shortfalls.

Indeed the expense and the liability have led many landlords to refuse quietly to rent to families with children—doing so openly would be a violation of state and federal law—or to abandon the property, thus constricting the housing stock. Their finances severely depleted or totally wiped out, landlords and homeowners may postpone needed repairs, exacerbating the condition of already marginal housing.

Ironically, the state's focus on lead in paint means that children are likely to be exposed to lead from soil or other nonpaint sources even after deleading. The dust-generating removal process itself poses risks. "One study found that 37 percent of children in the study had blood levels so high from deleading that they needed chelation [medical treatment with a chemical that removes lead from the body]. . . ."[131] In many cases, hygiene and education in the form of a mat in front of the door and frequent hand washing, especially before meals, would have proven equally effective in controlling the lead.

The Baltimore Experiments

Of the $279 million in 56 grants to states, cities, and counties made in fiscal years 1992 through 1994, Baltimore has garnered roughly $12 million for its Lead Abatement Action Project.[132] Over a seven- to eight-year period, the project's managers hope to create a pool of 1,000 "lead-safe" houses at a cost of roughly $7,000 to $10,000 per unit. Full-blown abatement could nearly double those figures. HUD will subsidize the entire cost for homeowners and 80 percent for landlords. The generous subsidies are designed to induce participation, mitigate hazards for children, and preserve the rental housing stock.

How long will the intervention last? That question constitutes a major component of the initiative. Every six months children's blood lead levels are checked by means of venipuncture, and dust wipes are taken to measure environmental lead levels. The concern is

[131]Schloming and Singer, p. 6.

[132]Telephone conversations with a representative of the HUD Office of Lead-Based Paint and Poisoning Prevention and with a Baltimore manager of the action project, February 29, 1996.

always that removal techniques may prove faulty and that lead in ambient air (auto and industrial emissions), from lead-laden soil tracked into the house by children and animals, from water, even from dust in crevices that escaped the cleaning may raise blood lead levels once more, requiring additional attention.

Two studies are in progress at the Kennedy Krieger Institute, a children's hospital affiliated with Johns Hopkins University.[133] The first, sponsored by the EPA, emphasizes repair and maintenance. Seventy-five rowhouses have been divided into categories, depending on the amount of work done on each. In Level I, for $1,650 the project tries to make the existing lead in a house safe. In Level II, for $3,500 certain components, such as the upper window sash, are replaced. In addition, the window well may be capped with aluminum while aluminum window channels take the place of wood. In Level III, for $7,500 units are given full-blown replacement of all leaded components. Half of Level II and Level III units are vacant during the work; half are occupied. The process is less arbitrary than it sounds, since the project managers determine the amount of time and money to be spent in each case.

The object once again is to determine how long the interventions will last before components start to break down. How much is being spent on the program? In addition to the abatement workers, the project must pay administrative and research costs, pushing the total above half a million dollars.

There are administrative snags in the HUD and EPA programs. Despite the high levels of funding, one official noted that the two agencies "don't share information very well," a comment suggesting that operations supported by public funds should be more open in communication.

The National Institute of Environmental Health Sciences of the National Institutes of Health is sponsoring the second study. Known colloquially as the "TLC Program" (Toxicity of Lead Children), it consists of a double blind analysis of 300 children contacted through three Maryland clinics who have blood lead levels between 20 and 44 μg/dl. Half are given the drug succimer orally to chelate the lead out of the body. The second group is given a placebo. Intervention is carried out in all homes to reduce the lead hazard and the program

---

[133]Telephone conversation with a study manager, February 29, 1996.

covers all costs, except for a $350 application fee, whether the unit is owner or tenant occupied. The fee is still high and may discourage people from applying.

The objective in that study is to determine whether those receiving the drug will ultimately show an IQ higher by one or two points and to determine the health effects. Screening begins at 10 to 33 months with venipuncture testing and continues for four years, or until the child is enrolled in school.

It seems reasonable to question the wisdom of such a program. Venipuncture can scarcely be pleasant for an infant or toddler, and double blind tests raise ethical questions. The report, when and if it is published, should prove intriguing.

Philadelphia

A third city in the northeastern "lead belt," Philadelphia, received $6 million from HUD to control lead in 485 houses.[134] At $12,000 per house, that seems particularly high. An administrator, however, noted that this is a demonstration project and that such projects are "always more expensive." Extensive follow-ups—at 6, 10, 18, and 25 months—complete with visual inspections and dust wipes undoubtedly add to the cost.

Litigation and Liability

The mere presence of lead, whether intact or deteriorating, inspires fear in tenants, landlords, and homeowners. The effort to find a scapegoat has led to an explosion in lawsuits that may eventually rival the litigation surrounding asbestos. The actual and potential liability threatens a serious constriction of housing stock.

In 1994 in Massachusetts, a court "awarded damages to a family whose child had a blood lead level of zero simply because lead paint was present in the home."[135] It would be difficult to find a verdict that would inspire more fear in those who rent apartments and houses.

In Maryland, where much of the housing stock dates from World War II or earlier, 2,200 children were reported in 1995 as having blood lead levels high enough to warrant evaluation. In the summer of 1993, landlords faced with skyrocketing jury verdicts banded

[134]Telephone conversation with a Philadelphia administrator, February 29, 1996.
[135]Shell, p. 36.

together with "reasonable" health advocates who found the tort system slow and flawed to promote passage of a statute governing liability. After 18 months spent developing rules, the statute took effect at the end of February 1996.[136]

The law covers all pre-1950 rental housing, some 160,000 units in the Baltimore area alone. Under its provisions a landlord must register each unit annually, unless he can prove that it is lead free. There are then two possibilities for treatment. Under full-risk reduction, vacant units will be abated and cleaned with a HEPA vacuum cleaner and a high-phosphate detergent. After a visual inspection, for which the owner pays, a certificate will be issued that effectively indemnifies the owner and limits his liability to $17,000 per unit. Equally important, insurers in Maryland must waive a lead exclusion in the policy if it contains one and provide coverage up to that amount.

The majority of units remain occupied and undergo a modified risk reduction. After a visual inspection, peeling and flaking paint is removed and structural problems that could lead to deteriorating paint, such as a leaking roof, are corrected. All windowsills and walls are made smooth and cleanable, as are kitchen and bath work surfaces.

Tenants must be notified by registered mail of the projected risk reduction and offered $17,000 for uninsured medical bills and for relocation if they wish to leave. Provided an inspector signs off on the work after completion, the landlord will have reached a safe harbor, for that amount will be covered by insurance.

One large property management company has been carrying out in-place maintenance since 1994 for $400 to $600 per unit, a figure that contrasts favorably with the $7,000 per unit often cited for risk reduction subsidized by HUD. The comparison suggests that the need to control cost has provided a powerful spur to efficiency in the private sector.

Philadelphia has been less fortunate. Ninety-five percent of its housing consists of residential units built before 1978, meaning that 350,000 to 400,000 of its residential units probably harbor lead. The city now has a case load of 6,000 children reported to have blood lead levels high enough—20 µg/dl or above—to warrant medical and environmental evaluation.

[136]Alfred Singer, "Maryland Lead Law Update," *Small Property Owner*, forthcoming.

Faced with an unresponsive state legislature, the Philadelphia City Council in June 1995 passed two ordinances directed at lead.[137] The first is a real estate disclosure form mirroring the federal requirement soon to go into effect. Philadelphia's ordinance became effective on October 18, 1995. A companion ordinance, promoted by a tenant action group, was billed as a protection for tenants who, it was alleged, were being evicted for a variety of reasons following an inspection that had found lead. Since all landlords must have a license in order to rent, the ordinance works by suspending the license of an owner who fails to comply with orders by the city to remediate or remove lead once a city inspection has found lead in the unit. Without a license, the owner is unable to go to court to file for eviction. The process seems convoluted, but many tenants evidently preferred to live with the lead, at least for a short period of time, rather than face the hazards of eviction.

Meanwhile, owners are losing their liability insurance. Insurance companies are phasing themselves out of coverage; remaining policies now routinely include exclusion clauses for lead. The state insurance commissioner, according to one source, has done nothing, leaving owners vulnerable to suit.

Who Will Pay?

Litigation is, in fact, the engine driving much of the debate centered on lead. To remove all lead from the approximately 60 million private residences in the United States would cost $30 billion. Adding in commercial and industrial structures, plus the expense of cleaning up the dust, could push the total above $500 billion. If the government is unwilling to subsidize such a sum and if homeowners cannot be induced to spend the thousands necessary to remove lead,[138] then landlords can be driven to do so by suit. Suits may result in covert discrimination against children or end in bankruptcy and abandonment, but those considerations are downplayed or brushed aside.

Advocates are explicit on this point. The Alliance to End Childhood Lead Poisoning has no expectation that the owners of private

---

[137]Telephone conversation with the Philadelphia administrator, February 27, 1996.

[138]Until 1995, Massachusetts homeowners were under a state mandate to delead; but few did so. Shell, p. 36.

homes will delead their properties. Don Ryan, the executive director of the Alliance, asserts: "We're focusing on rental units where the other force at play here is the tort system. . . . The idea is that renters will sue landlords who fail to comply with the lead laws—and they will."[139]

The advocates have in some measure succeeded. The costs of managing lead impose a heavy burden on the homebuyer and the property owner in particular and the taxpayer in general. Indeed, certain of Title X's rules and provisions, in conjunction with state regulations, ensure escalating costs, especially for first-time buyers and young renters. That is the group least able to afford costly abatement or the higher rents generated by passing on the cost of dealing with lead or by constricting the number of rental properties. Their resources are generally minimal, so a rise in costs can quickly become an intolerable expense.

A Legal Overview

Many analysts have expected suits for harm caused by lead-based paint to overwhelm, in number and dollar amount of damages, suits alleging harm from asbestos. In contrast to the large and distant companies manufacturing asbestos, which were thought to have "deep pockets," the property owner is usually an identifiable person; normally he is close at hand; his supposed wealth makes him fair game for tenants who fear they have been injured. Laws barring discrimination against families with children, the very population the owner might most hope to avoid, leave him teetering between Scylla and Charybdis. If he avoids prospective tenants with children, he risks a discrimination suit. If he rents to them or even to adults but fails to remove the paint, tenants may sue for personal injury. If he lacks funds or is unable to obtain funds from a bank reluctant to loan on a contaminated building, he is still liable.

Should he turn to his insurance company for help, he may again run into a brick wall. Many policies contain exclusion clauses for lead, enabling insurance companies to divest themselves of all legal obligation to intercede.

---

[139]Ibid.

Landlords are often relatively poor with few resources other than their run-down inner city buildings. Ironically, not being wealthy may be their best defense. A successful suit may net little.

The manufacturers of lead paint have furnished a more inviting target. Even that has proved illusory, since many firms manufactured a nearly identical product for more than 50 years, and it is difficult to pin a particular paint job on a particular paint manufacturer.

Pressed to find a villain, lawyers have turned to the manufacturers of lead pigment. A lengthy case in New York State, yet to be resolved, cites as defendants the manufacturers, Atlantic Richfield Company, the Glidden Company, NL Industries, Inc., Sherwin Williams Company, and a trade group, the Lead Industries Association. The suit began with a 1989 complaint alleging that the defendants had known for years from their own studies that lead-based paint was hazardous to children. Nevertheless, they continued to manufacture and sell it for interior surfaces, which made them liable to charges of fraud and misrepresentations of safety.

In December 1991, a trial court dismissed New York City's negligence and strict liability claims on the grounds that they were "time-barred"—the city had known about lead's dangers for 30 years. At the same time, the court allowed the fraud/misrepresentation and restitution claims to proceed.

Two years later a New York appeals court affirmed the lower court ruling, allowing the city and two city agencies to proceed with the claims of fraud/misrepresentation and restitution. In addition, the New York Supreme Court Appellate Division said the defendants, including the Lead Industries Association, may be held jointly and severally liable to the city under the theory that there was collaboration among the paint makers and their trade group to conceal the hazard.

Three years later the case is still in the pleading stages and bids fair to rival *Jarvis v. Jarvis* in Dickens's *Bleak House* in length and complexity. Three judges have been involved: the first retired; the second resigned; the third was appointed late in 1995. At issue is the characterization of fraud, whether it requires reliance on a manufacturer's representations, and the bearing of that characterization on the statute of limitations.[140] Optimists speak of a decision in the summer or autumn of 1996; realists believe that a resolution is years away. In the meantime, the costs mount.

Large-scale lawsuits against paint companies in Boston, Philadelphia, and other cities in Pennsylvania have been largely unsuccessful. The legal and technical grounds were weak; unable to find a particular harm from a particular source, judges were dismissive.[141] In short, the owner of the property is generally left holding the bag, but the bag may be empty.

A statistical analysis of verdicts in lead litigation throughout the United States over the past five years suggests the scope of the problem. There were some 50 cases, involving 57 children with verdicts ranging from defense verdicts (the largest number) to a single verdict of $10 million. Excluding the two highest plaintiff's verdicts, both reached in the Bronx in New York City, a jurisdiction known for very high personal injury awards, the median award was $50,000, the mean $566,107. Again excluding the Bronx, roughly half of the verdicts awarded $50,000 or less; 20 percent fell between $500,000 and more than $1 million.[142]

The commentary accompanying the analysis suggests the risks for a property owner: "... where a lead case goes to trial, there is approximately a 50 percent chance of an outright defense verdict or a negligible plaintiff's verdict. By the same token, once juries reach a verdict for the plaintiff, there is a one-in-five chance of a significant award of $500,000 or more." Few private citizens have the resources to cover such sums.[143]

If the tenants lack means, however, a nonprofit group or a public-interest law firm or members of the plaintiffs' bar can often be counted on to step into the breach. The landlord has no such recourse and may well prefer to quit the rental business altogether rather than face unlimited liability and financial ruin.[144]

---

[140]*New York v. Lead Industries Association*, NY Sup Ct App Div 1st Dept, No. 48289, May 13, 1993. See "Lead Paint," *Toxics Law Reporter* (Washington: The Bureau of National Affairs, Inc., June 16, 1993), p. 43. Telephone conversation with the Lead Industries Association, April 5, 1996.

[141]Weiner and Sapolsky, pp. 26–28.

[142]Mintz et al., "Lead Litigation Verdicts: A Statistical Analysis," p. 1.

[143]Ibid., p. 2.

[144]The tax implications of lead abatement are far from clear. Should the cost of removal be expensed or capitalized? The ongoing debate does little to set the mind of the landlord and the investor at ease. See Lippy and Haight, p. 79.

To make matters worse, tenants may receive the tacit or open backing of state governments. Early in 1993, the attorney general's office in Massachusetts was formulating "fill-in-the-blank" lawsuits for tenants to use against their landlords. Designed to guide tenants suspecting the presence of lead paint through the complaint process, the draft forms outlined the steps to take. The first letter to a landlord was to ask for inspection—the second, to demand that any lead found be abated. Finally, the office supplied two sample suits to be used if the landlord failed to comply.[145]

The real estate community accused the attorney general's office of promoting lawsuits, and the office insisted that the forms, which were being revised, would simply help tenants "in navigating their way through the courts, which many people find intimidating." The spokesman for the Massachusetts Public Interest Group was more forthright: "We should applaud any effort on the attorney general's part to educate tenants on their existing rights. . . . We hope that the attorney general stands by the existing pro-consumer law."[146]

Others have been less politic. Late in 1993, the *Washington Times* of Washington, D.C., carried an advertisement headlined, "Lead Paint Hurts Children." It continued: "If Your Child Has Been Exposed to Lead Paint You Should Consult an Attorney," and ended with the assurance that "meritorious cases" would be accepted on the basis of a contingency fee. If there were no recovery, there would be no charge.[147]

Lenders and Risk

As if the vulturous tactics of the plaintiffs' bar were inadequate, the increasing reluctance of lenders to underwrite commercial loans on properties harboring environmental hazards like lead has facilitated the slide toward abandonment. Risks include cleanup costs, which could depress the value of the property serving as collateral for the loan, the threat to the financial soundness of the borrower and thus the increased potential for default, and the possibility of third-party suits for personal injury and property damage. As a

---

[145]Matt Carroll, "Landlords Try to Nix Generic Lead Paint Suits," *Boston Sunday Globe*, April 11, 1993, p. A17.

[146]Ibid., pp. A17, A20.

[147]*Washington Times*, December 13, 1993, p. A5.

practical matter, it has become impossible to insure such risks. Institutional lenders, who underwrite three-quarters of the loans for commercial real estate, are nervous about exposing themselves to costs that could exceed the amount of the loan.[148]

Superfund, technically the Comprehensive Environmental Response, Compensation and Liability Act of 1980 or CERCLA, exacerbates the problem. The imposition of unlimited liability on present property owners and retroactively on previous owners thought to have caused or contributed to environmental contamination has increased the reluctance of lenders to underwrite loans on "contaminated property."

If a landlord who wants to sell is unable to find a buyer, the lender may find himself owning worthless property. Worse, he may be subject to suit. As a result, the specter of liability continues to discourage institutional lending, not only on commercial construction but also on the aging rental stock most in need of funds for rehabilitation.

Risk in Perspective

Given the extraordinary costs, the increasing burden on taxpayers, the burdens imposed on homeowners, buyers, sellers, and landlords, the effects on the housing stock, and the uncertainty surrounding the effects of lead at scarcely detectable levels, it behooves the public, the regulatory agencies, and Congress to take a more rational look at the situation. As noted throughout this chapter, blood lead levels have been plummeting. The best evidence, at least from the West Coast, suggests that one of the federal child-health goals for the year 2000, that blood lead levels not exceed 15 μg/dl in more than 2.5 percent of the population, has not only been met but bettered.[149]

Phase 1 of the Third National Health and Nutrition Examination Survey, covering 1988 to 1991, supplies dramatic evidence of declining lead levels. A sample of 13,000 persons aged one year or older showed an overall geometric mean blood lead level for the U.S. population of 2.8 μg/dl, about one-quarter of the 10 μg/dl set by the CDC as a level of concern in 1991. Residents of the Northeast, with its older housing stock, had higher levels. Blood lead levels

---

[148]Paul Katcher, "Lenders' Liability for Environmental Hazards," *Real Estate Review* 20, no. 3 (Fall 1990): 72–73.

[149]Schoen, "Spending Billions."

were higher for blacks than for whites and for central-city residents than for non-central-city residents. Socioeconomic indicators, such as low income and limited education, correlated with higher blood lead levels.

Over approximately a 10-year period, from the time of the NHANES II survey conducted in 1976–80, the percentage of children with lead levels in excess of 15 μg/dl and 25 μg/dl had fallen from 53 and 9.3 percent, respectively, to 2.7 and 0.5 percent. On the basis of NHANES III, 1.7 million of the nation's children between one and five years of age (8.9 percent) had lead levels of 10 μg/dl or greater. The percentage may not be considered ideal, but it is obviously a vast improvement.

The report concluded that "the low overall mean blood lead levels demonstrate a major public health success in primary prevention efforts" but that minority children from low-income families living in cities were still a cause for concern. To reduce lead exposure, "Strategies to identify the most vulnerable risk groups are necessary."[150] That advice is consistent with goals of targeting the population most at risk, finding those children, fixing those houses, and educating parents to minimize risk.

There is some irony here. The National Center for Health Statistics administers NHANES, and it concludes that strategies are necessary to identify the most vulnerable groups. NCHS is part of the CDC, and the CDC, which has favored universal screening, is playing a coy game by not releasing its latest report on the desirability of such screening. High blood lead levels are a symptom of poverty. When children in the suburbs experience a sudden rise in blood lead level, it is generally the result of renovation or remodeling. Once the work is done, the level returns to normal. Children in the inner cities face a far bleaker prospect. In old and deteriorating housing, chipping and peeling lead paint present a hazard, but removal of the lead may do little to reduce the incidence of symptomatic lead poisoning.

---

[150]Debra J. Brody et al.,"Blood Lead Levels in the US Population, Phase 1 of the Third National Health and Nutrition Examination Survey," *Journal of the American Medical Association* 272, no. 4 (July 27, 1994): 277. The survey is directed by the National Center for Health Statistics, Centers for Disease Control and Prevention. See also "Recommendations Re: Lead Screening, Resolution I-94," Washington State Delegation, American Medical Association House of Delegates (November 5, 1994), p. 2.

In fact, the dust created constitutes a far greater menace since the minute particles are easily transferred from hand to mouth.

Of equal or perhaps greater importance is the fact that decades of leaded gasoline have left a residue of dust-laden soil. Picked up on toys and fingers by children playing outdoors, it is tracked into the home and becomes part of the household environment. Such relatively inexpensive and easily implemented steps as covering bare soil with plants or cement, installing sandboxes in play areas and mats in front of doors, and insisting on frequent hand washing would greatly mitigate the problem for those most threatened. As often noted, the Japanese live in a far more polluted environment but their emphasis on hygiene has largely protected them from environmental hazards, including lead.

Ongoing Battles

The numbers cited are witness to the fact that lead is no longer a universal public health menace. The major sources of accessible lead have largely vanished: lead has disappeared from gas, from tin cans, and from paint; industrial emissions have fallen sharply. Except in the inner cities, two decades of abatement efforts have removed lead from the reach of children. Though problems remain in marginal housing and particularly in areas with a residue of lead-laden dust in the soil, the time has come to take stock, recognize the gains made, and target needed resources to the dwellings and occupants who are most in need.

Instead, recent publications reveal all too clearly an ongoing campaign on the part of federal agencies and their advocates to preach the dangers of lead and the importance of spending vast sums to achieve the Utopian goal of a lead-free society, whatever the cost.

The Needleman Saga: Update

Clearly Needleman has not backed down on lead. In a paper published by the *Journal of the American Medical Association* early in 1996, he claims that he and his colleagues have demonstrated a correlation between bone lead levels in 301 grade school boys and delinquency. After testing the group at age 7 and again at age 11, the researchers assert that "High-lead subjects were more likely to obtain worse scores on all items of the CBCL [Child Behavior Checklist] during the 4-year period of observation. High bone lead levels were associated with an increased risk of exceeding the clinical score (T>70) for attention, aggression, and delinquency."[151] As in their 1979 study, the researchers emphasize reporting by teachers, and once again they never clearly define "high" and "low" lead levels. The more recent study, however, includes the reactions of parents and self-reporting by the subjects.

At least one analyst has found the study deeply flawed, doubting that the testing method can produce reliable results when it measures only small amounts of lead.[152] More important problems are revealed in the paper's discussion of the control of confounding variables. The study claims to have evaluated covariates including maternal intelligence, socioeconomic status, and quality of child rearing, factors known to affect behavior. Yet the authors assert that "adjusting for nine covariates did not substantially alter the strength of the association,"[153] a surprising claim.

The omission of parental supervision and discipline and parental criminality as covariates was notable as well, since those factors are known to contribute to delinquency. Failure to control for those important influences suggests that the results are far from certain. Nor did the paper mention reverse causality—that is, that children whose behavior is problematic to begin with may engage in activities that increase their risk of lead exposure.

Finally, the most striking finding, that the lead measure was *positively* and significantly related to IQ, receives no mention in the abstract. The body of the paper clarifies the issue. The researchers assert, "The positive association between bone lead and IQ that we encountered was limited to African-American subjects."[154] The import of this "positive association" explains its omission from the abstract.

Eighteen years after his first report of an adverse effect of lead levels of 30 or so μg/dl on intelligence and after 18 years of controversy, Needleman's 1996 paper reports no such association. Moreover, it says that there is an association between higher lead levels

---

[151]Herbert L. Needleman et al., "Bone Lead Levels and Delinquent Behavior," *Journal of the American Medical Association* 275, no. 5 (February 7, 1996): 363.

[152]Personal communication with the author from an expert who requested anonymity.

[153]Needleman et al., p. 368.

[154]Ibid.

and higher IQs in African-American boys. Quite clearly, the 1996 report is a contradiction of the thrust of Needleman's earlier findings and should fuel criticism or questioning of the earlier reports. That would be the case for any scientific finding, even for those that have not been besmirched by documented charges of sloppiness, or been called "deliberately misleading" (University Hearing Board at the University of Pittsburgh), or been tarnished by investigations of possible "scientific misconduct." Yet there has been no change in the federal programs directed against lead, even though their scientific underpinnings, long suspect, have been undermined by the same researchers who first erected them.

Predictably, the popular press found further evidence of lead's damaging effects in the 1996 paper. Jane Brody of the *New York Times*, in a lengthy report entitled "Aggressiveness and Delinquency in Boys Is Linked to Lead in Bones,"[155] stated that the study had been conducted among more than 800 Pittsburgh boys. That is incorrect; the actual sample size was 301, reduced to 212 before the analysis was completed. She then echoed the assertion by Needleman et al. that consideration of family and social factors had little effect on the results. She also missed the positive correlation noted in the body of the article between lead and intelligence.

Brody then cited the 50-year-old findings of Randy K. Byers, who linked "acute" lead poisoning to aggressive behavior. It seems never to have occurred to her that 50 years ago "acute" lead poisoning surely meant much higher levels of lead and more radical effects. Brody also cited an undated study by Dr. Deborah Denno, a sociologist, who found that lead was a strong predictor of delinquency among African-American males and females aged 1 to 22. At no time did she suggest the possibility of countervailing views.

"Lead causes children to be more aggressive," said the *Washington Times*.[156] Lee Bowman, the author, picked up the line that adjustment for "other factors known to influence delinquency, such as poverty and whether both parents were present in the home," had no effect on scores showing "worsening behavioral problems." Following a

[155]Jane E. Brody, "Aggressiveness and Delinquency in Boys Is Linked to Lead in Bones," *New York Times*, February 7, 1996, p. C9.

[156]Lee Bowman, "Lead Causes Children to Be More Aggressive," *Washington Times*, February 7, 1996, p. A8.

brief history of lead, he, too, noted, "A few other studies had suggested the possibility of long-term behavioral problems associated with lead." Which studies? The question remained unanswered. Nor did he note any one of the studies suggesting that lead at very low levels has a minimal and perhaps a zero effect.

Bowman did cite Needleman's contention that spending $30 billion would wipe out the threat of lead from old housing and that society is at fault for having balked at spending such a sum. "'But I can't imagine what the benefits might be from wiping it out—it would be so strong as to be remarkable." The need is unclear, the benefits are unspecified; but the demand is insistent.

Not to be outdone, the *Washington Post* ran an Associated Press syndicated news story datelined Chicago and headlined, "Study Links Lead Levels in Bones to Delinquency."[157] One scientist, Kim Dietrich of the University of Cincinnati, was quoted in the story; the quote was laudatory. (It should be noted that the University of Cincinnati has been a focal point of lead analysis funded by the EPA.) The AP author noted that "The researchers attempted to adjust for other known links to delinquent behavior" but failed to note the results of the "attempt." Professor Needleman was, however, quoted in support of his own efforts.

Reading those three articles makes clear the pattern of reporting on lead in newspapers of general circulation. First there is a "scare headline," then comes a brief report of the study in question from a point of view favorable to the researchers, complete with citations of studies supportive of that view. Statistical niceties, such as adjustment for covariates, merit no more than a brief reference, while Needleman is cited at length. The failure to find the high lead–low IQ correlation, which has been the recurring theme of Needleman's work, is not mentioned.

In that reporting, as elsewhere, the focus is always on the one damning finding. No attempt is made to place the new finding in context.

The *New York Times* also quotes Needleman as he faults society for having failed to devote the billions supposedly needed to eradicate the scourge. Without access to contradictory appraisals, the

---

[157]"Study Links Lead Levels in Bones to Delinquency," *Washington Post*, February 7, 1996, p. A3.

general public will insist on "getting the lead out." Reasoned debate and rational assessment of needs and costs become difficult if not impossible for policymakers, and the property owner/taxpayer is left to bear the burden.

The Task Force Report: Instant Replay

In the 1992 Residential Lead-Based Paint Hazard Reduction Act, Congress directed the secretary of HUD, in consultation with the EPA administrator, to create a task force to make recommendations on reducing the lead-based paint hazard. The two agencies supplied financial and technical support; in fact, Ronald Morony, then acting director of HUD's Office of Lead-Based Paint Abatement and Poisoning Prevention, was a member. The recently released report of the task force indicates that the official line has changed very little.[158] Lead is still the deadly enemy, to be wiped out whatever the cost.

An introductory note claims that the task force "is composed of individuals representing a broad range of organizations and institutions."[159] Technically that is true, as a count of the number of organizations and institutions taking part demonstrates. In fact, however, a brief survey of the roster of participants suggests a roundup of the usual suspects. Walter Farr, Executive Director of the National Center for Lead-Safe Housing, has strong ties with HUD and the EPA. The National Center, under contract with HUD, wrote the 1995 guidelines discussed earlier in this chapter and is under contract with the EPA to develop a curriculum for risk assessment training. Among others participants are: Don Ryan, executive director, Alliance to End Childhood Lead Poisoning; Ellen Silbergeld, professor of Epidemiology and Toxicology, University of Maryland Medical School; and Stephanie Pollack, senior attorney, Conservation Law Foundation.[160] Silbergeld has proposed taxing lead by the pound to pay for national abatement efforts; Pollack, who serves as a consultant for the board of directors of Ryan's Alliance, also serves on the

---

[158]Task Force on Lead-Based Paint Hazard Reduction and Financing. *Putting the Pieces Together: Controlling Lead Hazards in the Nation's Housing, Summary.* The summary is undated. Copies of the summary and final report are available through the National Lead Information Center's Clearinghouse at 1-800-424-LEAD and through HUDUSER at 1-800-245-2691.

[159]Task Force, *Summary*, p. ii.

[160]Ibid., pp. v, vi.

national CDC lead committee.[161] In short, the task force provides another example of interlocking directorates.

The task force has fulfilled its mission, that of making recommendations on the reduction of lead-based paint hazards, but its overview of the problem is one-sided and problematic. In discussing lead hazards, it declares that "recent research indicates that relatively low blood lead levels (that is, levels that until recently were not thought to be problematic) can produce significant nervous system effects."[162] Whose research? The reader is entitled to a reference. The statement ignores completely the research, outlined in preceding pages, indicating that putative reductions in IQ of one or two points cannot be definitively attributed to lead. Moreover, as expected, there is no discussion whatsoever of the relative benefits of cleaning up lead paint versus investing in better schools or other measures to improve the intellectual performance of children.

The summary ignores the good news of phase I of the NHANES third survey, that the overall geometric mean blood lead level for the U.S. population is now 2.8 µg/dl. Instead it reports, "Of the 20 million young children under age six, an estimated 1.7 million (almost 9 percent) have blood lead levels at or above the 'level of concern' [that is, 10 µg/dl] established by the Centers for Disease Control and Prevention.[163] In fact, it never reports that the "level of concern" is 10 µg/dl or that the figure represents a sixfold drop from levels acceptable as recently as the 1960s. The summary does note that children who live in poverty are much more likely to have elevated blood lead levels.[164] It is also scrupulous in underlining Title X's distinction between the mere presence of lead-based paint, which is not necessarily dangerous, and deteriorating paint and lead-contaminated dust and bare soil. "The majority of this lead-based paint is not presently dangerous," it notes. Nevertheless, "The Task Force's best estimate is that 5 million to 15 million housing units contain lead *hazards*" [emphasis in original] and "over a more extended period of time, a substantial portion of these hazardous units will house children under the age of six at some point as

---

[161]Shell, pp. 36, 38.
[162]Task Force, *Summary*, p. 3.
[163]Ibid.
[164]Ibid.

families move."[165] In other words, the specter of a nationwide lead epidemic is alive and well.

The task force is indeed acutely aware of the risks posed by deteriorating housing and the need to target resources to those units most in need of work. It notes the danger of noncompliance, further deterioration, or abandonment posed by standards so stringent that owners are unable to meet them.[166] Its solution? "A significant investment of private and public financial resources," an assertion that calls to mind Needleman's discomforting figure of $30 billion.

While acknowledging that there are no simple solutions, as well as the need to tailor strategies to fit different situations, the task force goes on to make sweeping recommendations that would have nationwide effects. Arguably the most important are the adoption of benchmark standards for maintenance and control of lead-based paint hazards for rental housing and the provision of public financing for the control of lead-based paint hazards in economically distressed housing. For the latter, "Public financing is essential. . . . By contrast, in other contexts, the task force relies on market mechanisms."[167] Considering that the recommendations include a wholesale modification of the liability and insurance systems, that concept of market mechanisms seems disingenuous in the extreme.

Only in reading the "Summary of Recommendations" do the extent and cost of the proposed controls become clear. "Recommendation 4-1" on supportive federal actions declares that "HUD, EPA, and other federal agencies should endorse the benchmark standards and urge that they be implemented by lenders, liability insurers, private organizations and trade associations, state legislatures, local jurisdictions, the courts, and property owners." A more intrusive proposal would be difficult to imagine. Under that rubric comes the note that the "CDC should sustain and encourage universal blood screening" to ensure identification and treatment.[168] The criticism leveled at universal screening, that it wastes money and needlessly traumatizes children, seems to have bounced off a brick wall.

[165]Ibid., p. 4.
[166]Ibid., p. 8.
[167]Ibid., p. 11.
[168]Ibid., p. 17.

More recommendations prescribe actions that state and local governments should take to implement the benchmark maintenance and hazard control standards. Those include "Creating New State and Local Subsidy Programs," "Requiring That Health Care Programs Cover Medical and Relocation Costs," and "Creating a Last Resort Fund," to say nothing of "Providing for Prompt Injunctive Action for Noncompliance." The private sector is far from forgotten. "Owners of pre-1978 rental housing should voluntarily revise their operations and maintenance practices" to incorporate the benchmark standards.[169]

There are to be dramatic revisions in lending, liability, and insurance systems as states act to clarify liability for noncompliance or to establish defenses for those who comply. Those revisions would include jawboning the insurance companies as state legislatures adopt "the Task Force's system of insurance and liability recommendations, including liability limitations for complying owners and an optional, no-fault alternative to the tort system for owners and occupants of housing in compliance with the standards of maintenance and hazard control." At the same time, "The Task Force recommends that bank examiners include loans, services, investments, and entrepreneurial activities related to LBP [lead-based paint] hazard evaluation and control when measuring lender performance in meeting community credit needs under the Community Reinvestment Act."[170]

The overlords of the former Eastern European Communist countries must wonder where they missed the boat. From the springboard of a hotly disputed environmental risk—lead paint—the task force has jumped to proposing (centrally directed) changes in insurance, the tort system, the banking system, and practically every aspect of public and commercial life. Where it can, it proposes installing bank examiners as Big Brother to monitor performance.

Considering that the task force asserts that it is providing a "comprehensive, health-protective, *cost-effective*, and feasible approach to solving *the most significant environmental health hazard facing America's children*" (emphasis added), the summary is singularly indifferent to costs. It mentions actual dollar figures only once, estimating that

[169]Ibid., pp. 18, 20–21.
[170]Ibid., pp. 19–21.

the cost of complying with "essential maintenance practices" for lower-priority units, that is, those built between 1950 and 1978, would range "from $100 to $200 per unit per year." Higher-priority units—those built before 1950, which are thought to contain more lead-based paint and paint with higher concentrations of lead— would cost double that amount in large multifamily properties and from about $250 to $350 for single rental units."[171] Those sums are laughably low. Even the experienced property management company in Baltimore cited above figures on $400 to $600 per unit.

In a society that has become environmentally cleaner and safer over the past few decades, lead is surely far from "the most significant health hazard facing America's children." Poverty, crime, and illiteracy with all their attendant ills pose a greater menace to health. Thus the task force's insistence on the need to create public awareness sounds an ironic note. At the beginning of the summary, it emphasizes the need for "Public awareness initiatives to better inform all affected parties" and the Recommendations outlined in chapter 10 focus on educating the public—that is, parents and property owners—concerning the hazards of lead-based paint. Given the legislative focus on disclosure, coupled with EPA insistence on lead dangers and the concern with "getting the word out" in the private sector, greater public awareness seems scarcely to merit such attention. Public pronouncements have already frightened the general public, spurred the expenditure of billions of dollars to produce questionable benefits, and enriched the plaintiffs' bar, a cost out of all proportion to the extent of the problem remaining.

A More Modest Proposal

The 1995 EPA report, *Review of Studies Addressing Lead Abatement Effectiveness*, prepared by the Battelle Memorial Institute, undercuts the elaborate scaffolding of benchmark standards and regulatory network by casting doubt on the efficacy of long-advocated removal and control procedures.[172] Education and hygiene, it suggests, may be of equal importance in reducing blood lead levels in children.

---

[171]Ibid., pp. 2, 14.

[172]Battelle Memorial Institute and the Environmental Protection Agency, *Review of Studies Addressing Lead Abatement Effectiveness, Final Report* (EPA 747-R-95-006: July 14, 1995).

150

The simplicity and cost-effectiveness of such an approach perhaps explain the EPA's reluctance to make the report readily available. Although the report was released on July 24, 1995, obtaining a copy from the agency has proved difficult. Photocopies are now circulating and the report has become a sample of "gray-literature," like the *samizdat* toward the end of the Soviet empire.

The "Introduction" defines carefully an "intervention" as ranging "from the in-home education of parents regarding the danger of a young child's hand-to-mouth activity to the abatement of lead-based paint. Interventions include activities that attempt to remove or isolate a source of lead exposure, as well as activities that attempt to reduce a child's lead exposure by modifying parental or child behavior patterns."[173]

The report summarizes 16 studies from 1981 to 1994 that deal with the abatement of lead-based paint, elevated dust lead, and elevated soil lead. All emphasized the hand-to-mouth pathway and targeted the child's home. "Ten of the 16 studies focused on the abatement of lead-based paint as a primary form of intervention, five studies focused on dust or educational intervention, and one study focused on soil abatement." Although blood lead is used as the primary measure, the report is quick to admit the difficulty of assessing health benefits "because many such benefits are subtle and, as such, are complicated and costly to measure directly."[174]

The report finds that lead hazard intervention induced declines in blood lead concentrations *"at least for children with blood-lead levels above 20 µg/dL"* [emphasis in original].[175] For children with blood-lead levels at or below that figure, that is, the majority of children in the U.S. population, *"Information is especially lacking on the effectiveness of interventions. . . . Also missing is data on effectiveness beyond one year after intervention and on the efficacy achieved by trying to prevent elevated blood-lead concentrations before they occur"* [emphasis in original].[176]

It is scarcely a surprise to learn that certain abatement methods—such as dry scraping, which produces dust—result in elevated blood

[173]Ibid., p. i.
[174]Ibid.
[175]Ibid., p. ii.
[176]Ibid., p. iii.

levels. There is, however, a startling admission: that information is lacking that would "identify a particular intervention strategy as markedly more effective than others." Even more striking is the finding that "declines in blood-lead levels after in-home educational efforts were observed in the same range as the other efforts."[177] Hand washing is essential for children.

The introductory "Discussion" emphasizes an often slighted concern, the multiple areas of exposure for children. As the report notes,

> It is important to recognize that childhood lead exposure stems from a number of media (e.g., paint, soil, interior house dust, exterior dust) across a range of environments (e.g., child's residence, school, playground, friends' residence). Unless an intervention targets all the sources of a child's lead exposure, therefore, even an intervention that fully abates the targeted source will not produce a 100% decline in the child's blood-lead concentration. If other sources of lead remain unaffected ... lead exposure may continue and the child's blood-lead level concentration may remain elevated.[178]

In other words, intervention may mitigate exposure and reduce blood levels, but the expenditure of vast sums and the creation of a pyramid of regulations will never create a lead-free environment.

The study is notable for its discussion of storage of lead in bone, an issue rarely outlined in the literature. Lead is found in a number of organ systems in the body but particularly in bone, which can act as a reservoir. If blood lead levels drop, the body, in an attempt to restore equilibrium, may transfer lead from the bone to the blood. The lead so mobilized "will maintain higher blood-lead levels than would be expected based on the reduced lead uptake from environmental sources." If significantly higher levels are maintained by transfer from bone reservoirs for six months or more, "the effectiveness of the lead hazard intervention could be seriously underestimated."[179] The appraisal serves as a valuable caution for the evaluation of blood lead levels.

[177]Ibid.
[178]Ibid.
[179]Ibid., p. 11.

Abstracts of the 16 studies reviewed in the Battelle Memorial Institute–EPA report are included in its Appendix A. The "Conclusions" following three of the abstracts deserve special mention because they illustrate the difficulty and the complexity of abating lead.

> Baltimore Traditional/Modified Paint Abatement Study: Despite the implementation of improved practices, modified abatements, like traditional abatements, did not result in any long-term reductions of levels of lead in house dust or the blood of children with elevated pre-abatement PbB levels. . . . the activities further elevated blood lead concentrations.[180]

> Boston Retrospective Paint Abatement Study: Deleading may often produce a significant, transient elevation of PbB in many children. It is most dangerous if accomplished with . . . torches, sanding, or dry scraping.[181]

> Boston 3-City Soil Abatement Project: . . . a reduction of 2060 ppm in lead-contaminated soil around homes is associated with a modest decline in blood-lead levels. The magnitude of reduction . . . observed, however, suggests that lead-contaminated soil abatement is not likely to be a useful clinical intervention for the majority of urban children in the United States with low-level lead exposure.[182]

The Boston soil study was part of a $15 million "Three Cities Study" in Boston, Baltimore, and Cincinnati. Despite expenditures as high as $4,000 per unit in Cincinnati and $6,000 per unit in Boston, the study showed no correlation between lead in dust and lead in blood in Baltimore and Cincinnati and only a mild correlation in Boston, where blood lead levels dropped by 1 μg/dl.

Researchers concluded that soil abatement "is not likely to be a useful clinical intervention." In contrast, the EPA claimed that cleaning up heavily contaminated soil "will measurably reduce blood lead," giving property owners peace of mind.[183] The EPA finally

---

[180]Ibid., p. A-8.

[181]Ibid., p. A-10.

[182]Ibid., p. A-24.

[183]Richard Stone, "EPA Lead Study Under Diverse Attack," in "Science Scope," *Science* 262 (October 15, 1993): 323. See also Sanford Weiner, "Notes from the Lead Policy Roundtable at the American Industrial Hygiene Association Meeting," May 1994. Photocopy in the possession of the author.

released the four-volume study report in 1996 after nearly 10 years of taxpayer-funded work.[184]

Collecting data and analyzing results can take a long time, which could be part of the reason for the delay in completing the Three Cities Study. On the other hand, the results were well enough known in 1993 for *Science* to run a news article about them.[185] I have not made the effort to dig out the evidence, whatever there is, for the EPA delay in releasing the report, but it seems that the agency "sat on" the results for almost three years. Taxpayers paid for the study, and they are entitled to prompt release of the results. The results were not promptly released. One can only speculate that the EPA would have been quicker to release the study had the results shown that soil removal would make a major difference in lead exposure.

So where are we with lead abatement? It is clearly an expensive business; it can clearly be a risky business for workers and others; and benefits from current practice are far from clear.

The "Summary of Scientific Evidence" in the 1995 EPA report outlines the problem, stating that although

> the studies suggest that both "in-place management" and "'source isolation or removal" methods were at least partially effective. . . . There was no definitive evidence in the litera-ture that one of these categories of methods was more effica-cious than the other. Source isolation or removal methods often had an accompanying risk of at least short-term eleva-tion of residents' blood-lead levels.[186]

---

[184]Urban Soil Lead Abatement Demonstration Project, *EPA Integrated Report*, vol. 1, EPA/600P-93/001aF (April 1996), p. 1-1. Congress authorized the research in 1986 under the Superfund Amendments and Reauthorization Act; work began in December of that year.

[185]See also Michael Weitzman et al., "Lead-Contaminated Soil Abatement and Urban Children's Blood Lead Levels," *Journal of the American Medical Association* 269, no. 13 (April 7, 1993): 1647–53. The researchers noted that the study had been sent to the EPA in July 1992; by inference, it contained large parts of the Boston study. Although the setting was given simply as "urban neighborhoods," the original cohort was the same for both reports, 154 children, as was the bracketing of blood lead levels, from 7 µg/dl to 24 µg/dl. The authors noted that the EPA had yet to review the study officially "and no official endorsement should be inferred." It seems to have taken four years for the "official review" and for the incorporation of the study into the EPA's final report, a long time even by EPA standards.

[186]Battelle Memorial Institute and EPA, p. 54.

Yet Title X decrees in-place management to be insufficient for federally assisted housing and mandates wholesale abatement. The budgetary consequences and the possible health consequences for the residents are profoundly disturbing.

The "Summary" of Scientific Evidence echoes and emphasizes the problem of multiple sources outlined in the introductory "Discussion": "There is evidence that lead-based paint abatement, by itself, may not be fully effective because of the potential recontamination from unabated sources."[187] Whether dealing with private or public housing, it is vital to recognize that lead will always be present.

Good, even revolutionary, news comes from one study of dust and three educational studies. The "Seattle Track-In Study" used the simplest of methods "to determine the extent to which low cost dust-control measures successfully lowered household dust-lead loading." The abatement procedures consisted of "a vacuum cleaner with an agitator bar in normal cleaning, removal of shoes at the entrance to the residence, and the installation of walk-off mats."[188] Dust lead levels fell dramatically, leading to the conclusion that "controlling external soil and dust track-in by removing shoes and/or using a walk-off mat reduced the lead exposure from house dust."[189] The lack of blood measurements, however, made it difficult to assess the effectiveness of the intervention.

The three educational intervention studies hold yet more promise. Two assessments in Milwaukee, Wisconsin, and one in Granite City, Illinois, used in-place management. The results detailed below may have astonished the analysts.

> In-home educational visits emphasized proper housecleaning methods to reduce dust-lead levels, improved hygiene habits to reduce hand-to-mouth lead exposure, and educated families on proper nutrition to reduce the health effects of elevated body-lead levels. The Granite City Educational Intervention Study ... found a 32% drop in mean blood-lead level ... (a drop from 15 μg/dL, on average). Both the Milwaukee Retrospective Educational Intervention Study ... and Milwaukee Prospective Educational Intervention Study

[187]Ibid., p. 56.
[188]Ibid., p. 37.
[189]Ibid., p. 38.

... reported 18% declines in blood-lead concentrations following in-home educational visits.[190]

The fact that the Granite City study had no control group makes
the effectiveness of the intervention difficult to assess. The two Milwaukee studies, however, included control groups, and the "declines
following educational intervention for these studies were significantly greater than declines observed in control children."[191]

The studies supply the supporting evidence for the note in the
Executive Summary: "Declines in blood-lead levels after in-home
educational efforts were observed in the same range as the other
interventions."[192] Critics will undoubtedly emphasize the conclusions to the Milwaukee Prospective Educational Intervention Study,
which note that "blood-lead concentrations usually remained above
10 µg/dL," even though the results "seem to imply that educational
intervention does appear to reduce blood-lead levels."[193]

"Seem to imply" and "appear to reduce" sound like efforts to
back out of a very tight corner. If mats, housecleaning, and hand
washing can sharply reduce children's blood lead levels without
the adverse side effects of abatement, policymakers should at least
suggest that they be tried extensively. To insist on expensive and
intrusive programs that may do little good and much harm seems
a costly exercise in delusion.

Conclusion

Endless and endlessly expensive studies finally produce only puzzlement. In trying to fathom the irrational insistence on the dangers
of lead and the necessity of banishing it, only one charitable explanation presents itself. Those who insist on lead's dangers have convinced themselves so completely that they are warding off a threat
to coming generations that they are willing to misrepresent the facts.
Motives, however, become irrelevant, considering the costs imposed.
Before government pours additional millions or even billions into
lead abatement, before homebuyers shoulder extra financial burdens, and before the rental housing stock shrinks further, perhaps

[190]Ibid., p. 63.
[191]Ibid.
[192]Ibid., p. iii.
[193]Ibid., p. A-41.

it is time to undertake a long-overdue reassessment of the premises on which HUD, the EPA, HHS, and Congress base their pronouncements and proposals. Rather than spending millions on universal screening, policymakers should insist on targeted testing to identify that small segment of the population most at risk and should do their best to educate parents and children on hygiene. Such an approach would free the resources needed to attend to the real and pressing needs of children for nutrition, medical care, and safety. It might even allow researchers to pursue more pressing issues than the politics of lead.

Appendix: Lead in Water

As if lead paint on the walls, lead dust in the soil, and lead particles in the air were insufficient cause for concern, the EPA early in 1993 added lead in water. A broad survey of municipal water systems found that drinking water in 819 municipal systems, roughly one-fifth of the country's largest cities, had "excessive" levels of lead. High-risk homes, that is, older properties, were the primary target of the survey; and the agency was quick to point out that the levels in the average home were lower. The 819 systems served about 30 million people, however, and many people were shocked that the hazard could be so widespread.[194]

Newspaper accounts often listed precautionary procedures, such as letting tap water run for 15 to 30 seconds before using it and avoiding the use of hot water directly from the tap. As usual, they generally failed to note that lead is a diminishing problem, at least in the United States. Although many older municipal water systems still contain lead service lines, copper has virtually replaced lead in the home. Lead solder, which contained only minute amounts of lead in any case, was banned in 1986.[195] The lead in today's water comes mainly from acidic corrosion of the pipes: the softer and more acidic the water, the more lead there will be.[196]

[194]Matthew L. Wald, "High Levels of Lead Found in Water Servicing 30 Million," *New York Times*, May 12, 1993, p. A7.

[195]Holly A. Heyser, "Cities Warned about Lead," *San Jose Mercury News*, May 12, 1993, p. 5B.

[196]Hannah Holmes with Bill Breen, "Getting the Lead Out," *Garbage* (November/December 1993): 26.

Given the much diminished presence of lead in the environment, a wholesale rush to test all domestic water, as well as the blood lead levels of all children, may well constitute another overreaction. As indicated, blood lead levels in the United States have been dropping steadily: in the 1960s, average blood lead levels were above 20 μg/dl; in the 1970s, they were still above the federal action level of 10 μg/dl. Today the average is below 5 μg/dl.[197] Those living in municipalities highlighted by the EPA survey may wish to be more cautious, but they should note that the tightening of the standard in 1992 has influenced the popular view of the results. According to the old standard, 50 parts or more per billion of lead would be cause for alarm; the new standard is less than 15 parts per billion.[198]

For those with water readings above that figure, testing is relatively quick, easy, and cheap. Many water districts test for free; but the number of inspection firms and certified labs has been growing, so commercial testing is relatively inexpensive. Those wishing to do it themselves can send samples through the mail and receive results. Filters and bottled water are readily available if the levels seem above acceptable limits. Of all the "domestic hazards," lead in drinking water, if it is truly a hazard, may be the simplest and cheapest to control.

[197]Jonathan H. Adler, "Letters to the Editor," *Garbage* (November/December 1993): 7.
[198]Wald, p. A7.

3. Asbestos: Shadow from the Past

Unlike radon, which is generally seen as an issue of concern for homebuyers, asbestos is seen primarily as a problem for commercial and public buildings. Office complexes, high-rise apartment houses, shopping malls, and schools have long been the focus of concern and the locus of expenditures for asbestos management or removal. Nevertheless, the problem of asbestos in homes is widespread,[1] creating an expensive dilemma for buyers and sellers who, like building owners and school administrators, must decide between management in place and removal, often on the basis of flawed information about risk.

Radon gas and asbestos minerals share certain similarities. As in the case of radon-related cancers, cancers that may be caused by asbestos develop 20 to 40 years after exposure, which greatly complicates the establishment of a causal relationship. As with radon, it is impossible to determine the exact levels and duration of exposure that can be harmful. There is, however, an important distinction. Although asbestos, like radon, occurs naturally, whatever hazard it creates is usually man-made. Natural outcroppings of asbestos-bearing rocks, occurring for the most part in California and the northeastern United States, may pose a risk since weathering can allow fibers to escape. Generally, however, mining and processing release fibers into the air where they can be inhaled. In the past, miners and insulation workers were highly exposed; today, members of the general population can be exposed to much lower levels from sources as diverse as worn asbestos pads in friction devices, such as brakes and clutches, and fibers released from the "friable" or easily crumbled asbestos found in some buildings.

---

[1]A popular magazine listed "18 areas of concern around the home," beginning with shingles on the roof and ending with debris in the basement. *Sunset*, September 1988, pp. 84–88.

The Environmental Protection Agency has entered the regulatory dance, claiming that the imposition of federal standards can eliminate local threats to health, no matter how small—if they exist at all—and refusing steadfastly to consider the expense involved and the fear evoked.

In considering the costs imposed on the homebuying public by government policy, it is useful to study the hysteria surrounding both radon gas and the several minerals grouped under the category of "asbestos." In each case, the EPA has manned the barricades to protect the general public from threats inflated out of all proportion to the actual risks involved. In the case of asbestos, the agency has overreacted, on the basis of questionable or limited evidence, and has fueled waves of near-panic that it has then tried halfheartedly to calm. On the other hand, confronted with public apathy about radon, the EPA has actively sought to raise public alarm.

The different responses to the two threats illustrate the role played by culture in the acceptance of risk. As an artifact of nature, radon falls in the category of "acts of God," against which there can be little or no recrimination. Asbestos is viewed in a more sinister light. Rationally, it can be regarded as a useful substance that was too much used before its harmful properties were discovered. Once its harmfulness was established, workers sued the suppliers of asbestos to recover for damages to their health and survivors of deceased workers sued for compensation. The useful, indeed lifesaving, properties of asbestos that led to its widespread use have been forgotten, and it is now often viewed as a creation of the "industrial complex," which milks consumers for profit at high cost to their health and welfare.

With regard to housing, the most direct effect of the wide publicity about the risks from asbestos has become concern that asbestos-containing materials (ACM) in homes, apartments, and other buildings pose risks to occupants and workers. Building on and fueling that concern, the EPA has expended millions of taxpayers' dollars and caused the expenditure of even more money in the private sector. Yet the agency seems not to have based its policies on dispassionate assessments of scientific research. Instead of providing a rational source of information, its bureaucracy appears eager to accommodate congressional demands for absolute safety, scare stories in the media, and the outcry from professional environmentalists and consumer "advocates" whose zeal for protection is matched only by their disregard for the nation's and the homeowner's pocketbooks. And, of course, each increase in the EPA's asbestos program has meant more staff, more money, and more power for the agency.

Asbestos: A Definition

"Asbestos" can be any of a family of six naturally occurring fibrous inorganic minerals found in certain rock formations. Ironically, the "state rock" of ecologically conscious California, serpentine, contains chrysotile asbestos, and fibers of the mineral are to be found in outdoor air. Chrysotile, or "white asbestos," is the most common and predominant fiber type, accounting for 90 to 95 percent of the asbestos used in U.S. buildings.[2] The remaining varieties, although less important industrially, appear most often in pipe and boiler insulation, particularly crocidolite, or "blue" asbestos, mined in parts of Africa and Western Australia, and amosite, or "brown" asbestos, mined in South Africa. Studies of asbestos in occupational and nonoccupational settings have led to a growing consensus among scientists that the "white" fiber is much less harmful than the fibers that are "blue" or "brown," often called "amphibole fibers."

The risk of disease from accumulated exposure to asbestos depends not only on duration and level of exposure but especially on the length and width of the fibers, which influence the depth of their penetration into the lung. The "white" fibers of chrysotile are curly, often short (less than 5 microns—5 millionths of a meter—in length), and very thin; and they penetrate less deeply into the lung than the other fiber types. Moreover, chrysotile is more soluble in aqueous solutions, like those found in the human cell, than the amphibole varieties, and it tends to deteriorate more rapidly. "Tends to" is an important qualification, since many chrysotile fibers have been found in the lungs of asbestos workers long after last exposure.

In contrast, the amphibole fibers of "blue" and "brown" asbestos are relatively long and needle shaped, often longer than 5 microns and with diameters as small as 0.1 μm. Their needlelike shape makes it easier for them to penetrate deep into the lung tissue, and this in turn seems to affect the readiness with which fibers can be removed

[2]Brooke T. Mossman, "Asbestos," photocopy in the possession of the author, undated, and Energy and Environmental Policy Center, Harvard University, "Harvard's Energy and Environmental Policy Center Finds Fear of Asbestos in Buildings Out of Proportion to Public Health Risk" (Cambridge, Mass.: August 9, 1989).

by the lymph system or by the "muco-ciliary escalator," which also removes particles from the lung.[3]

A recent authoritative paper in *Science* presents "the amphibole hypothesis" in detail. The authors of the paper argue, convincingly, that the long, needlelike fibers "are the major cause of mesothelioma in asbestos workers" and that they are associated with the majority of asbestos-related lung cancers. Nearly all experts accept sharp differences in the levels of risk associated with different fibers. For instance, European regulatory bodies, judging chrysotile to be less hazardous than the other fiber types, allow greater exposure to it in the workplace. Federal policy in the United States fails to draw such distinctions,[4] and the widespread use of the all-encompassing term "asbestos" has blurred the differences. As a result, the complex question of appropriate responses to a possible threat has slipped from sight to be replaced, in many cases, by panic.[5]

Why Use Asbestos?

The fire-retarding properties of asbestos have been recognized for centuries. In classical Greece, asbestos fibers pulverized out of rock, twisted into a wick, and doused with oil were used for lamps, such as that held by Calimachus's statue of Athena. The fibers would "burn" without being destroyed, hence the derivation of the word "asbestos" from a Greek word meaning "unquenchable." Centuries

[3]Malcolm Ross, "A Survey of Asbestos-Related Disease in Trades and Mining Occupations and in Factory and Mining Communities as a Means of Predicting Health Risks of Nonoccupational Exposure to Fibrous Minerals," in *Definitions for Asbestos and Other Health-Related Silicates*, ed. Benjamin Levadie, American Society for Testing and Materials, Special Technical Publication 834, Philadelphia, 1984, pp. 51–104. The mucous membrane lining the lungs serves as a protective shield, trapping foreign particles and expelling them by means of the rhythmical beating of the cilia, which are hairlike extensions of the cells' surfaces. The macrophages, the "housekeeping cells," which simply "eat" invaders, also play a role, although they have difficulty consuming fibers longer than 10 mm and can evidently be overwhelmed by the sheer numbers of the invading army. Taken as a whole, however, the body has an impressive line of defenses, protections rarely if ever mentioned in the press or the government literature.

[4]B. T. Mossman et al., "Asbestos: Scientific Developments and Implications for Public Policy," *Science* 47, no. 4940, January 19, 1990, p. 296. The authors note, "Unlike most other countries, particularly in the European community, which have more stringent requirements for regulation and importation of amphiboles, federal policy in the United States does not differentiate between different types of asbestos."

162

later Charlemagne amazed guests by throwing a tablecloth woven of asbestos fibers into the fire and then retrieving it intact. Widespread use of asbestos, however, had to await the Industrial Revolution of the 19th century, with its need for insulation against high temperatures.[6] Virtually indestructible, asbestos insulates against noise as well as heat, resists friction and chemicals, and can repel water. It has high tensile strength and is relatively inexpensive compared with man-made materials.

During the first half of the 20th century, asbestos was mined widely in the United States and abroad and industrial use expanded. The mining, milling, shipbuilding, and manufacturing industries found uses for asbestos. It became part of cement construction materials, such as cement pipe, roofing, and siding shingles. The automobile industry incorporated asbestos into friction devices such as brake linings and clutch pads. Jointing compounds, gaskets, and coatings and sealants often contained asbestos.[7]

Asbestos-containing materials were often spray-applied on the structural steel members of multistory office buildings as fireproofing material. Sprayed applications of asbestos replaced

[5]R. Murray, "Asbestos: A Chronology of Its Origins and Health Effects," *British Journal of Industrial Medicine* 47 (1990): 362. According to Murray, dimensions may be more important than type. He draws attention to a 1972 study indicating "that the carcinogenic potency, certainly in experimental animals, depended on the length and diameter of the fibre. *Any fibre with a length greater than five microns and a diameter less than three microns could induce cancer if the fibre had sufficient durability and therefore residence time in the lung.*" [Emphasis added.] He also refers to studies carried out between 1975 and 1978 in Cappadocia, an area of the central mountainous Anatolian plateau of Turkey, where mesothelioma has long been endemic. In the village studied, there was no asbestos in the soil: "This showed clearly that any fibre, whatever its origin, with appropriate dimensions and durability could cause mesothelioma" (p. 364).

Later research revealed the culprit to be erionite, a form of zeolite occurring as fine needles that easily penetrate lung tissues. Exposure begins at birth, for the inhabitants of the plateau use volcanic ash deposits or tuffs as building material for their homes, occasionally grinding the tuffs for stucco pastes and whitewashes.

See also Malcolm Ross et al., "Health Effects of Mineral Dusts Other Than Asbestos," *Health Effects of Mineral Dusts, Reviews in Mineralogy* 28 (Washington: Mineralogical Society of America, n.d.): 397–8.

[6]Michael J. Bennett, *The Asbestos Racket* (Bellevue, Wash.: Free Enterprise Press, 1991), pp. 89, 90; Susan McGrath, "Danger Is Less from Asbestos if Left Undisturbed," *Daily*, Harrisburg, Pa., September 16, 1991, no page.

[7]Detailed lists of the uses of asbestos are given by Mossman et al., p. 295; *Sunset*, pp. 84–87; "Home Notebook," *Dallas Morning News*, September 13, 1991.

cumbersome and expensive concrete encasements in the construction of high-rise office buildings. (The application of asbestos kept steel beams from twisting in the heat of a fire, which improved structural integrity, reduced mortality, and made it easier to rebuild.) Before 1978 the decorative plasters of homes and apartment buildings often contained asbestos. An easily identifiable remnant of that era is the "cottage cheese" ceiling, with or without glitter, so-called because of its rough, pebbly texture. Buyers found it aesthetically pleasing; builders hailed its noise-insulating qualities (although those were minimal). In reality, the troweled ceiling made construction cheaper and easier, substituting for careful and expensive sanding and multiple coats of paint; the addition of asbestos made the plaster easier to spread.

Asbestos-containing insulation for thermal systems, manufactured from 1920 to 1972, included pipe and boiler wrap as well as flue and exhaust coverings. "The white stuff" encasing the arms of the coal-fired furnaces that often heated American homes in the earlier part of this century contained asbestos. It formed part of the cement sheets and millboard used to protect the floor and walls around wood-burning stoves. Door gaskets in furnaces, ovens, and wood and coal stoves also contained asbestos.

Over several decades asbestos appeared in many other guises in homes and factories. Vinyl floor tiles often contained asbestos because it increased resistance to wear and tear and prevented cracking. Sheet vinyl and its backing could contain asbestos, as could some patching compounds, adhesives, and mastics. To deaden sound, asbestos became an element of acoustical ceilings. Until the mid-1970s, freestanding ovens and dishwashers were often wrapped in insulating blankets or sheets that contained asbestos. Older freezers and water heaters may still have asbestos in the insulating blanket inside the metal cover. It appeared in ironing board pads, barbecue gloves, and even in hair dryers. In other words, when it came to construction and home appliances, asbestos was everywhere.

Appliances are relatively short-lived and the new models are asbestos free. But American houses and public buildings are solidly constructed and durable, so the asbestos used in building them is omnipresent. Contrary to widespread fears, the mere existence of ACM in proximity to humans does not necessarily pose a risk. An assessment of the risk must take into account the material used and its state of repair, but primarily the likelihood of asbestos fibers being released into the air where they can be breathed. Those appraisals are too often neglected.

Perhaps as important as the failure to distinguish among fibers has been the failure to categorize asbestos materials used in buildings in terms of their composition. Asbestos-containing plasters were applied in liquid slurries, mixtures of water and fine particles of cement, plaster of Paris, or clay that acted as a binder. Plasters age, become brittle, and may release the fibers embedded in them; they can also be damaged by impact. Much of the concern about ACM in buildings has centered on such plasters. In plasterboard or wall-board, fibers were embedded in a solid material by using a binder, such as plastic, cement, or gypsum, which entrapped the fibers, producing something hard and dense. It is unlikely that asbestos fibers present in those three types of material will become airborne, and they present very little risk of exposure.

The EPA found that 85 to 92 percent of asbestos end-product uses have effectively immobilized the asbestos fibers by mixing them into a strong binding material (e.g., cement).[8] Unless they are old or substantially damaged, especially by moisture, those materials release few fibers into the air. In other words, the mere presence of asbestos does not necessarily pose a risk.

In its many guidance documents, the EPA draws attention to damaged ACM that are "friable"—that is, easily crumbled and likely to release asbestos fibers. After many careful studies there is now general agreement that there is no relationship between the presence of damaged ACM and concentrations of fibers in the air. In one study, to be described later, the concentrations of airborne fibers in buildings with undamaged and damaged ACM were essentially equal to and *essentially the same as* concentrations in outside air. One of the principal arguments between the EPA, whose actions caused school boards to spend millions of dollars to remove ACM, and former manufacturers of such materials, who were sued by school boards to recover their costs, turned on the appropriate indicator of exposure. The EPA argued that the mere presence of friable material

[8]Frank B. Cross, "Asbestos in Schools: A Remonstrance against Panic," *Columbia Journal of Environmental Law* 11 (1986): 75. Cross cites the Office of Toxic Substances, Environmental Protection Agency, "Sprayed Asbestos-Containing Materials in Buildings: A Guidance Document," pp. 1-1 to 1-2, March 1978.

(or material that might become friable) indicated potential exposure; the manufacturers argued that measurements of airborne fibers were the critical factor in estimating exposure. With the passage of time and the accumulation of measurements, the manufacturers' view largely prevailed, but only after millions had been spent on removal and billions contested in lawsuits.

Asbestos in Wartime

The widespread use of asbestos-containing building materials during the post-World War II building boom and the problems it has created, especially for insulation workers, have largely overshadowed the wartime importance of asbestos in reducing risk. During World War II, paints, plasters, and fire retardants containing asbestos delayed or prevented that most dreaded of naval disasters, fire. Battle damage often produced potentially devastating conflagrations. The process of applying the materials to protect against such disasters exposed some 4 million shipyard workers, who often labored in cramped quarters with little ventilation, to dangerous levels of asbestos. In other words, there was a net tradeoff: the asbestos that saved the lives of seamen jeopardized the lives of those who built their ships.[9]

Health and Asbestos

Recognition of the health problems associated with asbestos was slow in coming. At the turn of the century, asbestos had been shown to cause asbestosis, a pulmonary fibrosis that stiffens the lungs, impairs breathing, and eventually causes disability and death.[10] Shortly after World War II, however, reports on other dangers of occupational exposure began to appear with increasing frequency. In 1960 a British study of South African miners established a connection between crocidolite (blue) asbestos and mesothelioma, a rare and fatal cancer attacking the lining of the lung and abdominal cavities, in asbestos miners, in those who lived near the mines, and in those who transported the material.[11]

[9]Bennett, p. 133.

[10]Mossman et al., p. 295. See also R. Murray, "Asbestos: A Chronology of Its Origins and Health Effects," *British Journal of Industrial Medicine* 47 (1990): 362.

[11]Mossman, "Asbestos"; Mossman et al., p. 296; Murray, p. 363.

In 1955 Sir Richard Doll, the British epidemiologist, established the role of asbestos in causing lung cancer, noting that the average risk among men employed for 20 or more years in places where they were very heavily exposed to asbestos dust was 10 times that of the general population. He also concluded that the risk was decreasing as working conditions improved. He did not mention smoking as a contributor to that risk, even though his earlier work had demonstrated the smoking-lung cancer link.[12]

In the 1960s a U.S. scientist, Irving J. Selikoff, confirmed that exposure to asbestos increased lung cancer rates, especially among smokers. He made no distinction among the types of fibers, and others followed his lead. U.S. studies on insulation workers (including shipyard workers) exposed to all three types of asbestos—white, brown, and blue—indicted all fibers indiscriminately.[13]

In 1964 Selikoff chaired a symposium at the New York Academy of Sciences that highlighted the incidence of asbestos-related disease, including mesothelioma, in a group of New Jersey shipyard insulators. The meeting captured the attention of the media and resulted in what one analyst termed "a pandemic of mediagenic disease."[14]

By 1973 Selikoff had tracked down many of the asbestos workers in a refrigeration workers union and established that their death rate was 50 percent greater than that of average white males. Three diseases strongly linked to asbestos accounted in large part for the above-average death rate: asbestosis, which is frequently fatal and has no cause other than asbestos; mesothelioma, which is invariably fatal; and lung cancer, which is very often fatal. Although Selikoff's studies emphasized repeatedly that smoking increased the risks from asbestos 80 to 90 times, the media and the government generally ignored that link. Selikoff himself evidently found it advantageous

[12]Murray, p. 363.

[13]"Amosite, crocidolite, and chrysotile were almost universally used aboard ships during World War II, amosite for high-temperature boilers and pipes, crocidolite for packings exposed to acids or salt-water, and chrysotile for low-temperature and electric insulation." See Ross, p. 58.

Since those workers had generally been exposed to all three types of asbestos during their working lives, establishing distinctions among fibers might have been of little importance to the workers themselves. It would, however, have clarified the later policy debates, underscoring the need to distinguish among degrees and types of risk.

[14]Murray, p. 363.

to keep the spotlight on asbestos as the culprit. He could then indict the entire industry for exploiting its workers while implying that other researchers were no more than hired hands of the large companies.[15]

A 1979 study by Selikoff and E. C. Hammond provides a careful assessment of the link between smoking and asbestos exposure. As cited by Cossette,[16] the two researchers reported that, with regard to asbestosis alone, "mortality for men who smoked a pack or more a day was 2.8 times higher than the asbestosis mortality for men who had not smoked regularly." In other words, there was a nearly threefold smoking-related increase in mortality from a disease that has no cause other than asbestos. Selikoff and Hammond also "reported the following data: the death rates for lung cancer (per 100,000 man-years, standardized for age) were 11.3 for men who neither worked with asbestos nor smoked cigarettes, 58.4 for men who worked with asbestos but did not smoke, 122.6 for cigarette smokers who had not worked with asbestos, and *601.6 for those unfortunate enough to have had both exposures.*"[17]

According to this analysis, asbestos exposure causes a 5-fold increase in lung cancer; smoking causes an 11-fold increase; and the combination causes a 55-fold increase. This is a near-perfect example of synergism where the risk from two exposures—in this case smoking and asbestos—is the product of multiplying together the two individual risks. In other studies of asbestos, the risks have been still larger and still synergistic: about 8-fold from asbestos, 10-fold from smoking, and 80-fold from the combination.

As study followed study, it became increasingly clear that "the synergism that exists between asbestos exposure and cigarette smoking may depend on the type of asbestos involved."[18] That connection was never made, or was ignored, by Selikoff and the EPA.

[15]Bennett, pp. 52, 101–02.

[16]Marcel Cossette, "Defining Asbestos Particulates for Monitoring Purposes," *Definitions for Asbestos and Other Health-Related Silicates,* pp. 5–50.

[17]I. J. Selikoff and E. C. Hammond, "Asbestos and Smoking," *Journal of the American Medical Association* 242 (1979): 458–59. Cited in Cossette, p. 39.

[18]W. Weiss and P. A. Theodos, "Pulmonary Disease among Asbestos Workers in Relation to Smoking and Type of Exposure," *Journal of Occupational Medicine* 20, no. 5 (May 1978): 341–45. Cited in Cossette, p. 40.

During the late 1970s, Selikoff estimated that over the next decade 40,000 excess deaths a year would be attributable to asbestos. He was unable to justify the projections, however, and reduced the estimate, first to 20,000, then to 12,000, and finally, in 1983, to 8,200.[19]

The reduction followed on the heels of a meeting about the risks of asbestos at the world-famous Cold Spring Harbor Laboratory on Long Island, New York, in 1980.[20] Scientists who had studied asbestos-related mortality presented a number of estimates for the then current asbestos-related mortality rate, which ranged from 1 to 3 percent of total cancer mortality, or between 4,000 and 12,000 asbestos-related deaths annually. In a consensus statement, the participants at the 1980 meeting agreed that the lower estimate of 4,000 deaths annually was more likely correct. Making additional corrections for smoking and using a different method, Malcolm Ross of the U.S. Geological Survey estimated an average 522 to 587 yearly asbestos-related deaths,[21] but those low estimates do not account for underreporting of asbestos-related deaths in national mortality statistics.

While the estimates fell, the public remembered—and the EPA fanned the memory—that asbestos had killed and would kill thousands of men as the workers exposed in the 1940s developed asbestos-related diseases in the 1980s, 1990s, and later. Often lost to memory was the fact that "lung cancers were almost exclusively reported in heavy smokers,"[22] and public reports placed relatively little stress on smoking as a contributing factor.

---

[19]Bennett, p. 52.

[20]*Quantification of Occupational Cancer*, Banbury Report no. 9, eds. R. Peto and M. Schneiderman (Cold Spring Harbor, N.Y.: Cold Spring Harbor Press, 1981).

[21]Ross, "A Survey of Asbestos-Related Disease in Trades and Mining Occupations," pp. 86–89, 96–97.

The estimate was based on two appraisals. In the first, "utilizing the mortality pattern of excess disease in 17,800 North American asbestos insulation workers and the incidence of mesothelioma in 1972 given by a pathology review panel, the author estimate[ed] that 587 individuals died in that year because of exposure to asbestos." The second took "the reported number of asbestosis deaths given in *Vital Statistics of the United States* and again utilizing the mortality data of the North American insulation workers, the author estimat[ed] that the average yearly asbestos-related mortality in the United States during the period 1967 through 1977 was 522 deaths." The figures are remarkably similar.

[22]Mossman, "Asbestos."

Selikoff's failure to distinguish among fibers proved particularly unfortunate for the development of rational policy, for the EPA came to rely heavily on his assertions, making no distinctions among fiber types and downplaying the synergistic interactions between asbestos and smoking. Equally unfortunate was the continuing focus in the media, particularly in the *New Yorker*, on asbestos, rather than smoking, as the prime cause of lung disease, even though many of the shipyard workers, the subjects of Selikoff's original studies, had been heavy smokers of unfiltered cigarettes. One critic went so far as to ascribe the bias to the zeitgeist of the 1960s and 1970s, which "disdained caveats, such as the influence of smoking on asbestos-related diseases, as 'sell-outs' to capitalist interests when 'everyone knew' cancer was a by-product of industrial civilization."[23]

Federal Response

As part of its startup in 1971 the Occupational Health and Safety Administration (OSHA) adopted already-established voluntary standards for exposure to many workplace risks, including asbestos. Two years later the EPA prohibited the spraying of asbestos-containing materials for insulation, fire protection, and soundproofing. Two years after that it prohibited asbestos in pipe covering, on the grounds that the material could be crumbled easily after it dried. In 1977 the Consumer Product Safety Commission banned patching compounds containing asbestos and artificial fireplace ash and embers containing respirable asbestos. At no time during those years did the EPA or the CPSC present a coherent quantitative analysis of the risks involved and the potential benefits to be gained. In other words, the cost-benefit analysis was generally ignored.

The "Estimates Document" and Its Aftermath

In 1978 the U.S. Department of Health, Education, and Welfare launched a major campaign to promote public awareness of asbestos, especially among those who had worked in the shipyards during World War II. Then-secretary Joseph Califano, during an April press conference, asserted that 8 million to 11 million workers had been exposed since the start of the war. In September, in conjunction with a major speech before the National Conference on Occupational

[23]Bennett, pp. 52–54, 101–9. See, in particular, pp. 102–3.

Health and Safety of the American Federation of Labor/Congress of Industrial Organizations (AFL-CIO), Califano poured oil on the flames by releasing a mimeographed "draft summary" reporting on nine occupational carcinogens that, taken together, might account for anywhere from 20 to 38 percent of cancers occurring over the coming decades. In its single most shocking extrapolation, the report estimated asbestos-related deaths over the next three decades at 2,000,000, or 17 percent of all cancer deaths, or 50,000 per year. The prediction was loosely based on Selikoff's studies.[24]

The draft summary report listed the National Cancer Institute and the National Institute of Environmental Health Sciences as authors, meaning that it cloaked those responsible in anonymity. In a more detailed version of the paper that appeared four days later, the number of carcinogens had shrunk to six, but they were still held responsible for as much as 38 percent of American cancer and asbestos was still very much in evidence. The time period had also become rather vague. The National Institute for Occupational Safety and Health had joined the list of "authors," and an alphabetized list of nine "contributors" had suddenly materialized. "The alphabetized list of names meant that no individual among them was taking responsibility for the data in the paper," so the nine were effectively shielded from the critical storm that was to come.[25]

No other scientists had reviewed the paper, nor had it been published in a scientific journal. It applied risk calculations derived from the highest exposures to those who had not experienced those exposures and thus arrived at estimates wildly exceeding prior projections of cancer attributable to occupation. Nevertheless, once Califano had used the figures to alarm a national conference of the AFL-CIO, worried delegates and uncritical reporters ensured their spread here and abroad.[26]

The scientific community derided the "Estimates Document" for its gross errors. John Weisburger of the Dana Institute for Cancer Prevention declared: "This document would never had [*sic*] seen

[24]Tom Reynolds, "Asbestos-Linked Cancer Rates Up Less Than Predicted," *Journal of the American Cancer Institute* 84, no. 8 (April 15, 1992): 560. Bennett, pp. 224–25. See also Ross, "A Survey of Asbestos-Related Disease," p. 84.

[25]Edith Efron, *The Apocalyptics* (New York: Simon and Schuster, 1984), p. 439.

[26]Ibid., pp. 437–42.

the light of day if it were ever carefully inspected." In 1981 Sir Richard Doll, in collaboration with Richard Peto, also of Oxford, published a study that dismissed the estimates because the risks for all workers, whatever the dose and duration of their exposure, had been estimated from the disease rates observed in the relatively few who had been most heavily exposed for many years.[27] Disregard of both dose and duration was "indefensible," producing risk estimates "more than 10 times too large." So grossly in error were the government's figures "that no arguments based even loosely on them should be taken seriously."

Within three years of release of the draft summary, evidence for cancer risk from occupational exposure was analyzed by a blue-ribbon group of epidemiologists and statisticians. The book from their conference, mentioned previously,[28] demolished the inflated claims of asbestos-related cancers. Edited by Richard Peto, the long-time collaborator of Sir Richard Doll, and Marvin Schneiderman, the book reports 4,000 cancer cases annually as the best estimate for the toll from occupational exposure to asbestos. That is, indeed, a far cry from the 50,000 figure in the "estimates document."

Schneiderman's appearance as editor of the conference proceedings appears to have been a break from his campaign to picture asbestos as a terrible health risk. He had contributed to the draft summary paper, after retiring from the National Cancer Institute, where he had been associate director of field studies and statistics; and he became the EPA's sole scientific counsel during its 1986–1989 efforts to ban asbestos entirely.

Focus on the Schools

Accurately reported information about the death toll from occupational exposure to asbestos translated naturally into concern about risks from asbestos exposure in the general environment and from ACM inside buildings. Early in the 1980s, reports of asbestos in a number of public schools began to appear, frightening parents and

[27]R. Doll and R. Peto, "The Causes of Cancer: Quantitative Estimates of Avoidable Risk of Cancer in the United States Today," *Journal of the National Cancer Institute* 66 (1981): 1193–1308. See also chapters 2 and 3, Office of Technology Assessment, *Technologies for Determining Cancer Risks from the Environment* (Washington: Government Printing Office, 1981, OTA-138).

[28]*Quantification of Occupational Cancer.*

administrators. In response, in 1982 the EPA issued its rule on asbestos, requiring public and private elementary and secondary schools to inspect for asbestos. The rule required no action other than inspection and reporting of the inspection results to school employees and parents. Predictably, employees and parents demanded removal of the ACM.

In support of its 1982 rule, the EPA reported that high levels of asbestos had been found in schoolrooms in a school district that was subsequently identified as Houston, Texas. The method used by the EPA contractor to estimate those high levels was immediately challenged by experts in measuring levels of airborne contamination; in fact, it is no longer used. In the years that followed, the EPA, without reporting any additional data, dropped its estimates of the concentrations of asbestos in schoolrooms by a factor of 10, but its estimates still remained far higher than those based on actual measurements of asbestos in schoolroom air.[29]

In any case, the EPA claim that "exposure to asbestos in school buildings poses a significant hazard to public health"[30] was demonstrably untrue, even at that time. Studies inside and outside the EPA had already shown that the removal process, with its very high contribution of exposures to asbestos from ripping out ACM, risked the health of abatement workers while providing negligible benefits for the building occupants who would move back in after removal was completed. Removal operations actually increased ambient levels of airborne fibers. Moreover, as the published research mounted during the 1980s, it became increasingly clear that "asbestos levels in buildings, including schools, are barely detectable and over one thousand times lower than the occupational levels found to be harmful."[31] Richard Doll, who originally demonstrated that occupational

[29]Michael Gough, "Uncle Sam Flunks Asbestos Control in Schools," *Issues in Science and Technology* 4 (Spring 1988): 81–85.

[30]Bennett, p. 148. See also Richard Wilson et al., "Asbestos in New York City Public School Buildings," *Regulatory Toxicology and Pharmacology* 20 (1994): 163. The authors note that the 1982 "Yellow Book" was the second in a series of seven EPA "guidance documents" issued from 1979 to 1990 that focused on the management of asbestos in schools. For ease of reference, they are often referred to by the color of the cover. "Yellow 1982b" asserted that health risk was to be gauged by visual inspection and "exposure assessment." The document also detailed the inadequacy of air monitoring, a claim repeated in later documents.

[31]Cross, pp. 81–82. Cross cites the relevant studies in his notes.

exposure to asbestos increased lung cancer rates, stated that the risk to building occupants from exposure to asbestos was minimal, comparable to that associated with smoking half a cigarette in a lifetime.[32]

The EPA rule actually constituted a political gambit designed to shift responsibility for asbestos control from the federal government, which had essentially created the problem through heavy-handed rulemaking, to local officials. People living in the school districts were to shoulder the costs of abatement. Money was the issue. William Ruckelshaus, two-time EPA administrator, admitted in an interview: "That's what the fight is all about. Who's going to pay for it."[33] The EPA had ignited the fire but was offering neither water nor sand to put it out.

The agency never had the authority to order a "contaminated" school district to take action. It required only inspection and notification of parents, relying on the parents to pressure local school boards to remove the asbestos and paying for the removal. Had it mandated asbestos removal, the federal government would have had to underwrite the costs. Energizing the parents to pressure local boards to take action would not only force the local populace—those who, the EPA asserted, would benefit from the removal—to pay the bill but might in the process also force cost-benefit analysis and other efforts to contain the staggering cost of removal. The local districts, in other words, would have pockets far less deep than those of the federal government.[34] Moreover, removal of ACM from schools was expected to lead to its removal from all public buildings without a federal mandate to require it.

Growing Controversy

In part as a response to pressure from constituents, in part to support EPA policy, in part because of widely reported overzealous "rip-outs," in 1986 Congress passed unanimously the Asbestos Hazard Emergency Response Act (AHERA), which required inspection of public and private schools for asbestos-containing material by the spring of 1988, the development of management plans for its control

---

[32]Bennett, p. 14.
[33]Ibid., p. 137.
[34]Ibid., pp. 137–39.

by the following fall, and development of operational plans by the summer of 1989.[35] When asbestos-containing material was found, parents had to be notified.

Contrary to popular opinion, the EPA never issued a sweeping requirement that *all* asbestos be removed. Only if the ACM in schools were "significantly damaged" were they to be removed because frayed asbestos (the old spook, "friable asbestos"), it was believed, would release fibers into the air. Demolition or substantial remodeling would also trigger abatement. Otherwise, drastic measures were unnecessary.

Public perception, fed by the EPA's exaggerated claims of asbestos in schoolrooms, blurred such distinctions. Asbestos in schools was viewed in the same light as a visitation of the plague. Overreaction to the risk led to many cases of costly and dangerous removal, a reflex action still observed in many districts, to the detriment of staff and resources.

Public Dictates and Private Costs

The regulation also had a ripple effect. In the commercial sector, fearful that the EPA would eventually mandate removal of any and all asbestos, whatever its condition, many building owners decided to get rid of it, whatever the cost. The reluctance or refusal of banks to lend on asbestos-containing buildings, coupled with the concerns of current and prospective tenants, undoubtedly hastened many such decisions.

On the housing front, the specter of asbestos complicated the purchase of a home, increasing costs for both buyers and sellers. Real estate brokers and owners fearful of liability pressed for inspection requirements, and inspections became more frequent. In theory that benefited buyers by providing them with more information and enabling them to make a rational appraisal of the risk. In practice, however, thanks to entrenched fears, a finding of asbestos often produced panic and led to lengthy negotiations between the parties. In many cases a coat of paint on the asbestos-containing troweled ceiling would have effectively encapsulated the fibers, but the EPA had thoroughly convinced the public that "one fiber can kill." As a result, sellers often undertook expensive removal projects or tried

[35]Ibid., p. 226.

to split the costs of removal with buyers who, especially in the frantic real estate market of the 1980s, were often so desperate for housing that they were willing to share the expense in order to obtain the property. Sometimes the contract was simply rescinded, leaving the seller to search for other buyers and the buyers scrambling for another property, both expensive and time-consuming enterprises.

Whatever the outcome, the toll in dollars and distress was generally needless.[36] Asbestos remains in countless homes, in thousands of schools, and in more than 730,000 commercial buildings in the United States. Hence, the ongoing debate about management and removal.[37] The level of risk from those sources, however, is so small as to be insignificant.

Levels of Exposure

Despite frequent references to measured levels of asbestos fibers in the air, most people have little idea of the meaning of the term. Two convenient comparisons may provide some perspective. One comparison is with the concentration of fibers in outside air, which is as low as the concentrations can go. The other is with the permitted concentration in workplace air. Over the years OSHA has dropped the permissible levels of exposure to asbestos in the workplace from 5 to 0.1 fibers per milliliter of air (f/ml).

Essentially, all measurements of asbestos in indoor air have resulted in concentrations that are comparable to those in outside air.[38] Those measurements mean that asbestos in buildings poses about the same risk as asbestos in outside air. Concentrations in buildings are typically 1/200th to 1/500th less than the permitted occupational exposures.

The Discomfort of Uncertainty

What are the risks from the low concentrations of fibers inside buildings? The Health Effects Institute-Asbestos Research group

[36]A little-noted complication of removal remains the issue of ownership and liability. Once removed, ACM are tagged with the name of the person who orders and pays for the removal. Although the ACM may be buried fathoms deep in a landfill, that person and his estates remain liable for any ill effects they may create.

[37]Energy and Environmental Policy Center.

[38]Morton Corn, "Asbestos in Buildings: Some Lessons," *Health and Environmental Digest* 5, no. 3 (November 1991): 1–3; Michael Gough, "Asbestos in Buildings: The Emergence of Policy," *Health and Environmental Digest* 5, no. 9 (November 1991): 3–5.

extrapolated from information about past cancer rates resulting from high exposure levels to predict the risks from indoor exposure.[39] It concluded that the risk was on the order of one additional cancer per million exposed people. That estimate, however, is necessarily uncertain.

The HEI-AR estimate of the cancer risk is based on a linear, no-threshold model. Such models incorporate the idea that risk decreases with exposure but that risk does not reach zero until exposure reaches zero. Many scientists believe that there are exposure levels above zero that do not carry a risk; many more believe that risk increases very slowly at exposure levels near zero and more rapidly at higher levels. Models incorporating either of those ideas—that there is a threshold exposure below which there is no risk or that there is a "hockey-stick"-shaped dose-response curve such that risks increase very little at low doses—would produce risk estimates far below those of the HEI-AR. In other words, many scientists would argue that the estimates based on linear, no-threshold models that incorporate the "one-fiber-can-kill" idea are exaggerated.

Dose and Response

To avoid the charge of casually dismissing the "one-fiber-can-kill" hypothesis, it seems advisable to examine the debate. In 1976 Russell Peterson, chairman of the Council of Environmental Quality, told Congress, during hearings on the Toxic Substances Control Act, "No level of asbestos fibers in tissues is regarded as safe—a single fiber may initiate a response."[40] As one critic pointed out, however, asbestos is present in nature, a constituent of the air we breathe and the water we drink. That being so, ". . . *all* Americans have been inhaling, drinking, eating, and washing themselves with asbestos fibers all of their lives."[41]

---

[39]Health Effects Institute-Asbestos Research, "Asbestos in Public and Commercial Buildings," Cambridge, Mass., 1991, Executive Summary, pp. 1–4.

The HEI is an independent, nonprofit scientific group created by congressional mandate in 1988 and supported by the federal government, including the EPA and industry. It sought to determine airborne asbestos levels in buildings and to assess the comparative advantages of various management and abatement strategies. This document is cited hereafter as HEI-AR.

[40]Quoted in Efron, p. 407.

[41]Ibid., p. 407.

The "single-fiber" theory, however, remains the most important source of scientific disagreement about asbestos. According to that view, reducing the dose—that is, the number of fibers—to minuscule amounts reduces the *probability* of contracting cancer, but some risk remains at all nonzero exposures. In fact, the problem raised here is also that posed by such disparate environmental realities as radon and electromagnetic fields. The predicted harm is so low that it cannot be measured; therefore, it cannot be disproved. To prove a negative is impossible.

The EPA, all federal regulatory agencies, and HEI-AR assume that use of the linear, no-threshold model is appropriate. They give two reasons: the first is that it may be predictive; the second is that it is "prudent" because it almost certainly does not underestimate the risk. The linear, no-threshold model has one other advantage: it is simple.

For example, HEI-AR estimates that workers exposed to asbestos at 10 f/ml for 8 hours per day, 5 days per week, 50 weeks per year, for 20 years had an increase in cancer equivalent to 200,000 fatal cancers per million. (The increase brings their total fatal cancer risk to about 400,000 per million. Their "background risk," the same as all Americans', is about 200,000 per million, to which must be added the workers' risk from asbestos.) Risks for today's workers are based on the same length of exposure time, but the concentrations of asbestos are now set at no higher than 0.1 f/ml, 1/1,000th of the high exposures in the past. The new limit is associated with a risk of about 2,000 asbestos-related cancers per million workers.

Concentrations of asbestos in buildings are from 200 to 500 times lower than the occupational level, and the corresponding risks are calculated to be between four and six asbestos-related cancers per million people exposed. The estimated asbestos-related deaths are based entirely on extrapolation; no one can point to a person who died from lung cancer or mesothelioma and say that exposures to asbestos in buildings caused that person's death. Except in occupational situations, it is impossible to point to the source of the exposure.

Lowering the Scale

Research from other sources suggests that even the relatively low risk estimates of the HEI-AR study may be too high and that threshold levels may indeed exist. Geologist Malcolm Ross notes that

Canadian health studies "show that populations can safely breathe air and drink water that contains significant amounts of chrysotile fiber. These studies also show that there is a "threshold" value for chrysotile asbestos exposure below which no measurable health effects will occur."[42] Ross is careful to make distinctions: "The same fiber-dose response relationships observed for chrysotile asbestos do not hold for crocidolite asbestos. Health studies ... show it to be much more hazardous than chrysotile—with respect to mesothelioma, perhaps 100 to 200 times more hazardous." As for amosite, the hazards "are more difficult to assess."[43] Agreed, but rational distinctions have at least been made.

Another recognized authority in the field, Brooke T. Mossman, associate professor of pathology at the University of Vermont, asserts that "evidence that asbestos causes cancers in individuals at low levels of fibers found in indoor and outdoor air is lacking."[44] While recognizing the problems created by asbestos in the "unregulated workplace" of the past, she insists that "A compendium of information suggests that asbestos-related cancers are dosage dependent, thus invalidating the 'one-fiber-can-kill' hypothesis."[45] Mossman is also co-author of the previously discussed paper published in *Science*, which concludes, ". . . examination of combined data from published risk estimates shows that risks of asbestos-related total deaths ... due to exposure in schools are magnitudes lower than commonplace risks in modern-day society."[46]

The present-day risk of mesothelioma from asbestos in buildings, however, "is miniscule." There are about 1,500 cases of mesothelioma annually in the United States. Death rates from the disease have increased over the past 20 or 30 years in males over 65 years of age who have a history of past occupational exposure, whereas death rates for females have declined slightly or remained constant. The analysis concludes, "These results support the concept that asbestos in buildings is not an important risk factor, as one would

[42]Ross, p. 97.
[43]Ibid.
[44]Mossman, "Asbestos."
[45]Ibid.
[46]Mossman et al., p. 299.

expect increased mesotheliomas in both males and females in this case."[47]

That analysis and a variety of studies, referenced by Mossman and her associates, suggest strongly that panic is unjustified. In absolute terms the very low levels of asbestos generally present in indoor air pose an infinitesimal risk. The risk becomes even more manageable when compared with other dangers. The article in *Science* includes a table estimating the annual rate of deaths from asbestos exposure in schools, for students with an average lifetime expectancy of 75 years, at less than 1 per million (0.0005 to 0.093). Vaccination for whooping cough in the 1970s posed a much greater threat, the estimated deaths being 1 to 6 per million. High school football in the same decade carried an estimated mortality risk of 10 deaths per million. For children aged 1 to 14, the estimated risk from accidents in the home was 6-fold higher, or 60 deaths per million. As might be expected, long-term smoking carried an estimated risk several magnitudes higher: 1,200 deaths per million.[48]

Reason Asserts Itself

The slight risk of lung disease from low levels of asbestos and the much higher risks attendant on removing it have consolidated support for less drastic approaches. The EEPC study had sounded an early warning: "There is a reasonable possibility that removal of asbestos may actually increase exposure to building occupants . . . fiber concentrations can increase following abatement."[49] Finally, "Given revised estimates of public health risk . . . and the cost for removal, it is reasonable to reevaluate the federal policies and requirements related to asbestos in buildings."[50]

The HEI-AR report declares,

[47]Mossman et al., p. 299. The incidence of mesothelioma is, so far as is known, unaffected by smoking; "the disease is equally prevalent in smokers and nonsmokers alike." See Ross, "A Survey of Asbestos-Related Disease," p. 61.

[48]The table estimating risk from asbestos exposure in schools compared with other risks in the United States used data from six published risk estimates in which total deaths from lung cancer and mesotheliomas attributable to asbestos exposure over a lifetime were estimated per 1 million students exposed to 0.00024 fibers per cubic centimeter of air, the mean airborne concentration found in schools, for five school years, beginning at age 10. Mossman et al., p. 299.

[49]Energy and Environmental Policy Center, no page.

[50]Ibid.

There does not appear to be sufficient justification on grounds of risk to the health of general occupants [of buildings] for arbitrarily removing intact ACM from well-maintained buildings. The potential risk to custodial and maintenance workers "when ACM is disturbed is greater and, therefore, would appear to be the primary consideration in determining . . . remedial action."[51]

Mossman and her associates echo those misgivings: "As a result of public pressure, asbestos often is removed haphazardly from schools and other public buildings even though most damaged ACM is in boiler rooms and other areas which are inaccessible to students or residents." The consequences of such removal are frightening, for it "can lead to increases in airborne concentrations of fibers . . . sometimes for months afterwards." Even more alarming, "Asbestos abatement has led to the exposure of a large new cohort of relatively young asbestos removal workers."[52] In other words, abatement elevates health risks, leading to an *increased risk* of lung cancers and asbestosis.

The HEI-AR report presents another cogent argument for careful analysis rarely heard in media accounts: will the replacement materials be safer than those being removed? Ross had warned of specific dangers from replacements as early as 1984, noting that the replacement of chrysotile in drum brake linings might increase automobile accidents. The chance of such an increase "due to a possible inferior substitute must be weighed against the probability of anyone being harmed by the small amounts of chrysotile emitted by drum brakes."[53] According to Ross, "All the substitutes for asbestos are, in fact, carcinogenic. . . . Ceramic fibers, rock wool, fiberglass, all have been found carcinogenic in laboratory animals."[54]

Another problem, less often discussed, is still of concern. Will not the disposal of the removed asbestos "simply move the potential danger from one location to another?"[55] The presence of asbestos in a landfill, for example, may preclude construction near the site

[51]HEI-AR, pp. 1–12.
[52]Mossman et al., p. 299.
[53]Quoted in Bennett, pp. 76–77.
[54]Ibid., p. 85.
[55]HEI-AR, pp. 1–8.

because of fears that the asbestos will somehow escape and contaminate the atmosphere. Since naturally occurring asbestos "contaminates" the air we breathe and the water we drink, the anxiety seems misplaced.

The Leviathan's Response

The HEI-AR report and the papers by Mossman and others, incorporating careful and peer-reviewed research, have provided invaluable information. But what effects have they had?

Reevaluating and redirecting federal policies once they are in place is a Herculean task. The EPA has responded slowly, reluctantly, and with halfhearted reassurances. It relies on the presence of asbestos in schools and in more than 730,000 public and commercial buildings[56] to sustain anxiety. The Asbestos Hazard Emergency Replacement Act of 1986 is still the law of the land and will remain so until Congress acts.

In 1989 the EPA's Office of Toxic Substances called a public meeting in Washington, D.C., to discuss whether AHERA should be extended to buildings other than schools and it later hired the Conservation Foundation to hold additional meetings with representatives of the real estate and building industries. The Conservation Foundation report, issued in June 1990, reflected a division of opinion. The enormous costs involved may have had more to do with the reluctance of certain members to espouse extension of the act than did the minuscule threats to public health posed by asbestos in buildings.[57]

In 1990 the EPA departed from its course of pushing for removal as the only permanent solution. In its "Green Book" of that year, *Managing Asbestos in Place*, the EPA cautioned that remediation demands careful appraisal of the options to determine which will be most effective in reducing current or potential exposures for those

---

[56]"Asbestos Removal, Health Hazards, and the EPA." Council Report, *Journal of the American Medical Association* 266, no. 5 (August 7, 1991): 696, reprint. The number constitutes 20 percent of all government, residential, and private nonresidential buildings, a formidable bulk.

[57]Ibid.

in the buildings.[58] The agency was clearly backpedaling. Although it still insisted that "all fibers are of equal concern" and the Clean Air Act continues to require removal during renovation and demolition, in most other instances in-place management would suffice.[59] Finally, in its 1992 "Advisory to the Public on Asbestos in Buildings," the EPA made a startling admission. After years of insisting that "one fiber can kill," it asserted, "The present scientific evidence will not allow us to state unequivocally that there is a level of exposure below which there is a zero risk, but the risk at these low levels in fact could be negligible or even zero."[60] The wealth of data indicating that disease was a function of the degree of exposure was having an effect.

The 1990 Green Book sets forth guidelines for in-place management for building owners and workers confronted with fraying asbestos or the prospect of renovation: encapsulation (covering the ACM with a sealant), enclosure (surrounding the ACM with an airtight barrier), encasement (similar to encapsulation but using a hard-setting sealant). It also gives "helpful hints" on the hiring of asbestos consultants, recommending those who are registered and/or board certified and warning against possible conflicts of interest. The ethical standard of the building trades applies to asbestos abatement as well: in general, those who make the diagnosis should not do the work.

The final section leads the reader through the labyrinth of OSHA, AHERA, and the EPA National Emission Standards for Hazardous Air Pollutants. It highlights the OSHA eight-hour "time-weighted average limit (TWA)" of 0.2 fibers per cubic centimeter (f/cc) to which an employee may be exposed over a normal work shift. Promulgated in 1986, the TWA has now been reduced to 0.1 f/cc.[61]

---

[58]Environmental Protection Agency, Pesticides and Toxic Substances (TS-799), 20-T-003, *Managing Asbestos in Place, A Building Owner's Guide to Operations and Maintenance Programs for Asbestos-Containing Materials* (Washington: Government Printing Office, July 1990), p. 31.

[59]Environmental Protection Agency, Office of Pollution Prevention and Toxics, *A Guide to Performing Reinspections under the Asbestos Hazard Emergency Response Act (AHERA)*, EPA 700/B-92-001 (Washington: Government Printing Office, February 1992).

[60]The "Advisory," signed by William K. Reilly, then EPA administrator, introduces a five-point guide, summarizing the agency's position. Ibid., pp. H-2 to H-6.

[61]A cubic centimeter is about the size of a cube of sugar.

The Green Book aims to protect the custodial and maintenance workers whom Selikoff and others have predicted will be the "third wave" of workers suffering from diseases caused by exposure to asbestos. The goal is laudable, but the book falls short of meeting it.[62] Compiling an elaborate guidance manual without differentiating among the risks posed by the various types of asbestos does little to allay anxiety. The guide fails to emphasize the additional risk borne by smokers. As taxpayers, custodial and maintenance workers bear some of the costs of publication. The amount of benefit they are receiving for their money is open to question.

The publication of the 1990 Green Book, which affirms the federal government's slow acceptance of the evidence about the risks posed by asbestos, makes it interesting to review the comments of Marvin Schneiderman, an author of the draft-summary "Estimates Document." Belatedly, carefully, and conditionally, he acknowledged the error of that report. "We made the inappropriate estimate that short-term exposures were just as nasty . . . as long-term exposures." That, in itself, is an astounding statement. Although it may be unfair, one question comes irresistibly to mind: where else but in government would a group of scientists disregard such basic ideas as the relation of levels and duration of exposure to risk? Schneiderman also tried to pass the buck, adding "Selikoff had worked on this a great deal, and because we had no good estimates from the Bureau of Labor Statistics . . . , we did what scientists so often do, which was to use Selikoff's estimates without questioning them."[63] The admission is astounding; it is also mistaken. The mission of scientists is to ask questions: if the authors of the "Estimates Document" adopted estimates unquestioningly, they betrayed their calling.

The EPA Overreaches

While scientific information about the low risks to building occupants and outrage at the costs of abatement were driving the EPA to modify its asbestos-in-schools approach, the agency plunged

[62]Council Report, *Journal of the American Medical Association*, p. 697. Workers involved in the mining and milling of asbestos ore in the early 1930s and 1940s constitute the "first wave"; the "second wave" includes pipe fitters, shipyard and insulation workers, and users of asbestos-containing products during World War II and into the 1960s.

[63]Reynolds, p. 560.

ahead on another asbestos front. In 1989 it made use of Section 6 of the Toxic Substances Control Act to initiate a ban on the manufacturing, importation, and processing of almost all products containing asbestos. By 1997 the ban would have affected approximately 94 percent of U.S. production and importation of the mineral. Fortunately for the many industries dependent on asbestos for its resistance to heat and friction, the courts struck down the ban.

A manufacturer of friction products brought a case against the EPA in the Fifth Circuit Court (*Corrosion Proof Fittings v. The Environmental Protection Agency*) to protest the ban on the use of asbestos in friction products, such as brake drum and disk brakes, asbestos-cement pipe products, gaskets, roofing, shingles, and paper products.[64] In October 1991, the court rejected the proposed ban, asserting that " ... the costs of the asbestos ban were too high relative to the benefits."[65] In a broader context, the court's decision may have provided an opening wedge, encouraging studies of cost-effectiveness that are now beginning to command increasing attention and respect.

Costs: Anxiety Attacks

Whatever agencies do and courts decide, the word "asbestos" engenders fear, and the media can fuel the concern of an already fearful public. The depth and tenacity of that fear became clear in December 1993, when an asbestos spill on the San Francisco Bay Bridge connecting San Francisco to Oakland and the East Bay shut the span's eastbound traffic for eight hours, infuriating thousands of commuters. The asbestos program manager of San Francisco attempted to calm the disquiet by pointing out that exposure of short duration in the open air was unlikely to have long-lasting effects. A public health official also suggested that a commuter driving through the dust should simply keep the windows of the car shut and wash the vehicle later with soapy water. Despite such reassurances, the transportation authority closed the lower deck,

---

[64]*Corrosion Proof Fittings, et al., Petitioners, v. The Environmental Protection Agency and William K. Reilly, Administrator, Respondents*, No. 89-4596. U.S. Court of Appeals, Fifth Circuit, 947 Federal Reporter, 2d Series (October 18, 1991) at 1202–30.

[65]George L. Van Houtven and Maureen L. Cropper, "When Is a Life Too Costly to Save?" Resources for the Future, Discussion Paper CRM 93-02, Washington, July 1993, p. 7.

fearing a future public health threat.[66] In fact, drivers were unlikely to be harmed; the clear and present danger was to the workers cleaning up the spill, and even they were unlikely to be affected, given outdoor exposure and the winds sweeping the fibers off the bridge.

A San Francisco radio talk show host called Ross, one of the leading experts on asbestos, to ask what should be done. He replied: "Bring out the fire hoses and wash the mess into the bay. . . . This asbestos spill is about as dangerous as sunshine. It isn't going to hurt anyone."[67] No one ever heard that reassuring message because the radio station never broadcast it. A newspaper report of the incident speaks of a "technical glitch."[68] Ross himself believes that he was cut off on purpose. After all, "Once they [the radio people] have alarmed the populace they would not want to lose face and admit the whole thing was overblown."[69] They may have saved face but anxious commuters spent hours in the traffic jam created by the overblown report.

Costs: The Schools

Bad government policy, fueled by scientific extrapolations best described as "inconclusive" and lurid media accounts, have created an enormous actual and potential financial burden, especially for schools. Whatever the actual cost of removing asbestos-containing material, the estimates are astronomical to begin with and keep rising. In 1988 the EPA's price tag for about 107,000 primary and secondary schools was a minimum of $3.4 billion.[70] Adding public and commercial buildings pushed the figure to $53 billion. The eventual addition of another 733,000 sites forced the agency to estimate $100 billion to $150 billion for removal and renovation.[71]

---

[66]Barry Witt, "Bay Bridge Asbestos Spill Causes All-Day Traffic Jam," *San Jose Mercury News*, December 8, 1993, p. 3B.

[67]Reed Irvine and Joe Goulden, "Asbestos Panic Button," *Washington Times*, December 22, 1993.

[68]Ibid.

[69]Letter from Ross to the author, November 7, 1995.

[70]Council Report, *Journal of the American Medical Association*, p. 696. The Council Report cites the *Wall Street Journal*, September 8, 1988, p. B1.

[71]Ibid.

Financially, the schools have suffered severely. Over the past decade Houston has spent roughly $46 million to remove asbestos from 70 schools; another 170 remain. Oakland, Michigan, calculated its costs at $112 million. In 1989 Catholic schools in that state estimated that meeting federal standards would cost them $75 million,[72] a particularly burdensome requirement since Catholic schools receive no public money. The idea that buying textbooks might be a preferable alternative seems to have received little attention.

Asbestos removal not only is expensive but also carries risks for abatement workers, even when it is done correctly. Nevertheless, a removal industry has sprung into being. Spending for asbestos control in 1987 was $1.8 billion; two years later it had climbed to $4.2 billion. Reports of the exaggeration of the dangers have had an effect, however. By 1991 spending had dipped to $2.7 billion.[73] Whether the decline will continue in response to the revised EPA guidelines and ever-present budgetary constraints is the subject of debate. It may be that the firms that used to remove asbestos will simply turn their attention to lead.[74] Recent reports do indicate that lead abatement is increasing at a rapid rate.

It is hardly surprising that inspection of schools for asbestos and removal of asbestos could generate corruption. What else could be expected from a program based on fraudulent science and fueled by panic? New York City schools have been hard hit.

In August 1993, city officials announced that asbestos inspections carried out over the past decade were completely unreliable. It turned out that Robert Pardi, who headed the schools' Asbestos Task Force, had signed many inspection forms when no inspection had been carried out. (Even if the inspections had been carried out, they would have bordered on useless: they depended on visual inspection of asbestos-containing materials, a procedure never shown to be predictive of asbestos levels in the air.)[75]

Following the August 1993 announcement, Mayor David Dinkins ordered an emergency reinspection program for the schools. The

[72]Ibid.

[73]Jay Mathews, "To Yank or Not to Yank," *Newsweek*, April 13, 1992, p. 59.

[74]Jay Mathews, "The Heat Cools on Asbestos Removal," *Washington Post*, December 31, 1992, p. D10.

[75]Gough, pp. 81–85.

inspection delayed school opening, complicating the lives of parents as well as teachers, who faced making up the days later in the school year. It also had the unexpected consequence of increasing injuries to children. Schoolrooms and schools are relatively safe places. When the schools were closed, the children were in unsupervised places and incurred more injuries. A subsequent investigation revealed in the New York City schools asbestos program a wide range of sloppy practices that had hampered inspections and cost money.

The revelation that the inspection program was a joke resulted in a panic about risks to children in the schools. It was well known by 1990 that the levels of asbestos in schools, even those with damaged ACM, were very low and presented little or no risk. That information failed to reach the public, and people reacted with outrage that their children were being exposed.

The *New York Times,* in its issue of September 4, 1993, ran an article stating that there was ". . . virtually no risk . . . unless asbestos is removed improperly . . ." and that "virtually all the relevant scientific data have been ignored . . ." creating ". . .an unneeded epidemic of fear." Mossman and 16 colleagues submitted a letter to the *Times* substantiating the news report and presenting the rationale for management in place. It was never published.[76] Whether that single letter would have made a difference is doubtful. But had the press interviewed responsible scientists about the issue, it is possible that the public would have formed a more balanced approach to the "crisis."

As it was, parents turned angrily on the Board of Education, charging that the board had exposed their children to risk. The board and the schools responded with the hasty reinspection and some asbestos removal, which cost a school system plagued with leaking roofs, broken windows, nonfunctional bathrooms, and a "backlog of 44,000 repair orders" roughly $100 million.

In addition to the incompetence and credulity of the school administration, the episode revealed the lack of tolerance for risk on the part of the parents involved. Interviewed by John Stossel for ABC's *20/20,* one mother declared that no risk at all was acceptable. Asbestos had to be removed. Given the dearth of reliable information,

---

[76]Photocopy of the letter in the possession of the author.

especially about the dangers of removal, her reaction is understandable.[77]

Michigan vs. New York

Partially as a result of the press's failure to publicize the importance of risk appraisal, the costly, often unnecessary, and potentially risky abatement programs have taken on a life of their own. There are points of light, however. Propelled by John Schwarz, a state senator who is also a practicing physician, Michigan has moved to establish rational standards for dealing with the substance in the schools. After careful study Schwarz became convinced that properly managed asbestos-containing building materials presented a relatively low risk compared with the potential risks and high costs associated with removal. He also stated that Michigan's Asbestos Management Act mirrored the EPA policy clarification of 1990 in noting that asbestos removal was often not the best course of action and that stirring up the fibers could actually create a risk. Unfortunately, neither the EPA, nor Michigan, nor AHERA, the federal act requiring schools to manage asbestos, had established objective standards for maintenance versus removal.

The senator asked the Detroit public school district for information about its experience in asbestos management. An internal document sent to the senator's office from the office of the Detroit Public Schools showed a dramatic difference in cost for different modes of management. Maintaining intact asbestos in place would entail for the district a one-time cost of approximately $2 million, depending on the need to rewrap, encapsulate, or remove the material or simply leave well enough alone; removing asbestos completely would mean spending roughly $25 million.[78] Maintenance was clearly cost-effective, and a review of studies on schools indicated that risks to health from maintaining asbestos in place were so low as to be nonexistent.

The Michigan legislature, in tandem with Gov. John Engler, moved to establish standards that would obviate risky, expensive, and unnecessary asbestos removal. In May 1993, the legislature passed

[77]The program aired on April 22, 1994.

[78]Facsimile of the results of a study of Detroit Public Schools, dated January 29, 1992, which reviewed the analysis of asbestos received from the office of John Schwarz, Michigan State Center. In possession of the author.

189

the Michigan Asbestos Management Act, which controls the removal of asbestos from schools. Three months later the governor issued an executive directive outlining in-place asbestos policy for state buildings. Guidelines now specify that schools and state-owned or state-operated buildings may remove asbestos only under one or more of the following conditions:

- Removal is less costly than in-place management.
- Removal is incidental to normal maintenance or repair.
- The level of airborne asbestos fibers exceeds 0.01 f/cc (the occupational exposure limit).
- Renovation or demolition will break up asbestos, requiring removal.
- In-place asbestos has suffered significant damage.[79]

The guidelines aim to allay public anxiety while protecting health. In addition, the savings should allow the schools to spend money on books, computers, and staff, expenditures with potentially larger paybacks than abatement.

The Michigan statute has had a ripple effect in other states. Ohio, Hawaii, and Pennsylvania are considering legislation to mandate in-place management of intact asbestos. Louisiana seems close to introducing a bill. Such rational reappraisals are long overdue.

The Federal Government: Unheard Reassurance

Although the EPA failed to supply reasonable guidelines for schools, it provided them to building owners and employees in the 1990 Green Book, which stresses the protection of the health of custodial and maintenance workers who may be exposed to asbestos in the course of their daily routines.[80] As noted, the agency's emphasis was shifting from encouraging removal to providing ways of living with asbestos. Unless demolition or renovation requires removal, the guide recommends "a proactive, in-place management program."[81]

That publication outlines the provisions of the Asbestos Ban and Phasedown rule of July 1989 (which was, as noted, overturned by

[79]"Michigan Establishes Criteria for Asbestos Removals in Schools and State Buildings" (Washington: August 11, 1993). Photocopy in the possession of the author.

[80]*Managing Asbestos in Place.*

[81]Ibid., pp. vii, viii.

the courts) but emphasizes that it does not require the removal of asbestos-containing materials currently in buildings.[82] It reassures the reader once again that AHERA pertains only to schools. The iterations suggest an uneasy awareness that the EPA has been largely responsible for the widespread perception that removal constitutes the best, indeed the only, option.

Abatement and Maintenance: Dollars and Dust

As a rule of thumb, OSHA regulates types of occupational exposure that are associated with risks of greater than one additional cancer per thousand workers. The risk from asbestos at 0.2 f/cc over an eight-hour period, the standard established by OSHA in 1986, was greater than that, leading OSHA to lower the standard by half, to 0.1 f/cc in August 1994. Prompted perhaps by complaints from unions that the previous level failed to protect their members, particularly in the auto industry, the new regulations covered almost 4 million workers dealing with asbestos in construction and general industry. The estimated cost was $361 million annually for items such as worker training, improved ventilation, and the cleanup of sites from which asbestos has been removed.[83]

The new regulations impinge on building owners and contractors, affecting housing by increasing the costs of maintenance and construction. Two new housekeeping requirements mandate the method of caring for asbestos-containing flooring material, thermal system insulation, or deteriorated ACM. Sanding asphalt and vinyl flooring, for example, is prohibited, while the manner of disposing of dust and debris is carefully specified.

Record-keeping requirements have been revised. Construction contractors must keep employee training records for at least one year beyond the last date of employment, establish and maintain records of employee exposure measurements and medical surveillance monitoring for the duration of employment *plus 30 years* [emphasis added], and make the records available to the employee upon written request.[84]

[82]Ibid., p. 2.

[83]Asra Q. Nomani, "Clinton Plans Broader Rules for Asbestos," *Wall Street Journal,* August 8, 1994, p. 2B. The new standard was published in the *Federal Register* on August 10, 1994.

[84]David Wilson and Scott Nathan, "New Asbestos Standards," *The Law and the Land* 9, no. 2 (Fall 1995): 7.

The costs of compliance go a long way toward explaining the depreciation in the value of commercial buildings, estimated at $1 trillion.[85] And the convoluted regulations do not guarantee safety. Ripping out asbestos is still a dirty job, posing risks to workers from exposure to asbestos dust as well as from on-the-job accidents.

Costs: Commercial Buildings

To protect against any future liability, owners and managers may decide to discard management in place in favor of removal, however costly. One outline on abatement, entitled "Challenges Posed by Large-Scale Asbestos Abatement Projects in Occupied High-Rise Buildings," begins by noting that "the potential liability asbestos creates for commercial building owners is staggering"; later it says, "Its presence in commercial buildings is already having severe financial effects."[86] The appraisal of costs is sobering:

> Even though the relationship between disease and exposure to the low levels of asbestos found in office buildings is unclear, building owners are being faced with declines in rent and property values of as much as one-third or more in addition to ... legal liabilities. Obtaining financing ... is also becoming more difficult.... property managers are finding corporate tenants reluctant to lease space ... and are put at a disadvantage to newer buildings which do not contain asbestos.[87]

The writer acknowledges that options other than removal "deserve serious consideration" but never considers them. Given the economic factors outlined above and the liabilities involved, he concludes that "the only permanent solution, and the most cost-effective in the long run, is total removal."[88]

He then proceeds to detail "The Team Approach," which will include not only the owner and the contractors, who take major

[85]Malcolm Ross, "Failed Policy on Asbestos Abatement," *Washington Times,* October 8, 1993, p. B3.

[86]Nicolaus P. Neumann, "Challenges Posed by Large-Scale Asbestos Abatement Projects in Occupied High-Rise Buildings," pp. 160–167. In *Environmental Engineering,* ed. Joseph F. Malina Jr. (New York: American Society of Civil Engineers, 1989), p. 161.

[87]Ibid., p. 161.

[88]Ibid., p. 162.

roles, but bit players, such as the building's support and public relations staff, to say nothing of the certified industrial hygienist or the asbestos contract manager. The musical *A Chorus Line* may have had fewer characters.

Months of advance planning resemble preparations for D-Day. The complexity of the procedure, which proceeds floor by floor, soon emerges:

> After demolition, the heating-ventilation-air conditioning systems' (HVAC) supply and return ductwork is blanked, or locked airtight, within the work area. Returns for the floors above and below are sealed, creating positive pressure in those areas and isolation of the working area.[89]

When abatement is complete, the "trace fibers are affixed in place" and the "asbestos-contaminated wastes are double-bagged in 6-mil labeled polyethylene bags" for transportation to a licensed landfill. "Although asbestos is not classified by the Department of Transportation as a hazardous material, it must be transported in an enclosed vehicle or container."[90] All that remains for the asbestos abatement contractor, the owner, and the architect or the certified industrial hygienist is to follow up and write detailed reports.

The cost is astronomical, but the concluding paragraph of the chapter provides the rationale: "providing a safe indoor environment for building tenants and property *that is liability-free for the building owner and management firm*" (emphasis added). The fear of litigation drives the engine. The writer makes no mention of relative risk, assuming that any and all asbestos poses a threat. Indeed it may, but generally to the financial rather than the physical health of those involved with an asbestos-"contaminated" building.[91]

Costs: Public Buildings

A practical example of the way in which the fear of potential liability overpowers the data and the arguments produced by scientists comes from Stanford University. In the fall of 1993 the Hoover Institution, which is affiliated with Stanford, announced that it was

[89]Ibid., p. 163.
[90]Ibid., p. 166.
[91]Ibid., p. 167.

moving all personnel out of one of its three buildings because asbestos had been discovered in the air ducts. Only two offices had airborne fiber levels above OSHA's permissible limit, evidently as a result of the air that was blowing through the ducts, and the elevation even there was slight. Closing the affected offices and replacing the air ducts might have been a cost-effective solution, but the mere presence of ACM foreclosed a rational appraisal of alternatives. The decision to remove all ACM came almost immediately. The specter of liability loomed, and the cost of abatement evidently appeared trivial in comparison with the cost of a lawsuit. Moreover, the university could have lost its insurance coverage had it failed to take steps that could be defended as minimizing risk. So the building was closed for three-quarters of a year and costs ballooned.

In accordance with California's Connelly Bill (AB 3713) and its own "Asbestos Information and Management Program," Stanford now notifies its employees annually of buildings with ACM.[92] The announcement can clearly be justified as honoring the "right to know" of those working within the university's boundaries, but the actual notice provides too little information to quell and just enough to cause alarm. The 1994 notification states, "ACM's in buildings pose no risk to health unless asbestos fibers become airborne . . . and are inhaled. Asbestos does not pose a health hazard when it is in good condition and undisturbed." All well and good, but the outline itself does little to dispel the notion that one fiber can kill. Buried in a footnote is the notation that Stanford has established an "action control level of 0.1 fibers per cubic centimeter," in accordance with the recommendations of the Environmental Protection Agency and of the National Institute of Occupational Safety and Health.[93] Of what importance is the "action control level?" The casual reader is likely to conclude that asbestos, whatever the concentration, remains hazardous, despite the reassurance that "airborne asbestos fiber levels in buildings are generally comparable to such levels in outside ambient air. . . ." Building occupants are warned against attempting removal by themselves, but the notice never suggests that smoking dramatically increases the risks from exposure.

[92]Memorandum to Stanford Building Occupants, "Annual Asbestos Notification," July 1, 1994.

[93]Ibid., p. 4.

Finally, the "Asbestos Tables, 1994" provide a list of all buildings followed by symbols indicating the presence or absence of asbestos.[94] A "P" warns simply that ACM *may* be present. The tables include a notice that polarized light microscopy is being used to analyze all samples but fail to note the results. That may be irrelevant since that particular assay will never detect the low concentrations of fibers that may be present. More sensitive, more difficult, more expensive transmission electron microscopy is necessary for such work.

The expense of monitoring all buildings and of publishing the annual report must be considerable. Like many major universities Stanford in 1994 had been experiencing a "budget crunch" that led to cutbacks in staff. Yet it was allocating and continues to allocate scarce resources to an expensive and time-consuming monitoring protocol. A tally of costs and benefits might suggest, at the very least, greater emphasis on information and less on inspections.

Costs: The Automobile Industry

Despite the striking down of the ban on friction products containing asbestos by the courts in *Corrosion Proof Fittings,* fear of the material and of possible lawsuits led to the introduction of substitutes. That has been particularly notable in the case of brake linings. Although asbestos linings are still used to some degree by certain manufacturers, all will soon be asbestos free.

Is that an advantage? Do substitutes pose a danger? The heat resistance of asbestos constituted its major advantage, and industry representatives will admit off the record that asbestos was the best brake product ever, although "acceptable" substitutes are now in use. In that context "acceptable" means that the performance factor may be substantially the same but that the wear factor is 10 percent less. In other words, drivers will have to reline their brakes after 36,000 rather than 40,000 miles.

The reader may feel that the expense is justifiable, but the questions remain, Why was the substitution necessary? What are the benefits, if any?

[94]Ibid., pp. 1–6.

Liability and Litigation

The history of litigation on asbestos claims since the end of World War II more than justifies the fear of liability. As the incidence of asbestosis, mesothelioma, and lung cancer attributed to asbestos mounted, the victims took their grievances to the courts. Claims could not be filed against employers—workers' compensation laws prohibit such suits in return for fast action on medical claims and payments for disabilities—or against the government, even though it had mandated the use of asbestos in the shipyards. Claims against the companies that had manufactured the ACM were possible.[95] Companies that had manufactured asbestos, the most prominent among them being Johns-Manville, paid out millions in settlements; many, Johns-Manville being the foremost example, were driven into bankruptcy.

The companies involved sought indemnification from the U.S. government for damages and other legal expenses, claiming federal negligence in warning of the dangers of asbestos. The government retreated behind sovereign immunity and technical defenses and there ensued a virtual mudslinging match. A hearing held before the Subcommittee on Administrative Law and Governmental Relations of the House Committee on the Judiciary in August 1988 provides a fair sample of the charges and countercharges.[96] Former manufacturers of ACM were able to initiate the review as an attempt to reach a legislative solution to the problems of liability more equitable than that provided by the courts.

Rep. Austin Murphy of Pennsylvania noted that asbestos was used in 7,000 new and 67,000 reconditioned naval and commercial vessels during World War II. He added, "It is a matter of record . . . that the United States knew, during the 1940s, of excessive and unsafe exposure levels in the shipyards. . . . As early as 1941, a naval investigating officer reported, 'I am certain that we are not protecting

[95]Contractors who had operated the shipyards under contract with the government attempted the use of a "government contractor defense." They lost.

[96]U.S. Congress, House Subcommittee on Administrative Law and Governmental Relations of the Committee on the Judiciary, *Asbestos Claims/Claims Court Reference,* 100th Cong., 2d sess., August 10, 1988, serial no. 74.

the men as we should.'"[97] Although claims against the federal government amounted to $13.6 billion, "using defenses under the Federal Tort Claims Act, the United States has, to date, been able to shirk its responsibility owed to victims of asbestos diseases. Meanwhile, several major asbestos manufacturers have sought the protection of the bankruptcy code which has further delayed compensation to disease victims."[98] As of the date of the hearing, the government had settled directly with only one group of plaintiffs, a settlement then 10 years old.[99]

The attorney for the Department of Justice claimed that Johns-Manville had known of the dangers of asbestos "over a decade before the Government" and that the federal government was already paying heavily for the damage done "under FECA, Social Security disability insurance, Medicare/Medicaid, and other health and income maintenance programs."[100] That may well be true, but the printed testimony includes several references to cases in which the "discretionary function exception of the Federal Tort Claims Act" shielded the government from financial responsibility, as it was intended to do.[101]

Whatever the legal feinting, it seems clear that the negligence of the U.S. government contributed to the suffering and death of those

---

[97]Ibid., p. 19. An attorney representing former manufacturers of asbestos-containing materials asserted, "In the course of preparing our clients' claims . . . we have uncovered evidence showing: (1) that as early as 1932, U.S. Government health officials, including officials of the Public Health Service, participated in an epidemiological study that linked even low-dose asbestos exposure to the development of disease." The government failed to publish the results of its investigation, allowed unsafe levels of exposure to asbestos dust during World War II, and refused to declassify World War II shipyard surveys until the 1980s. As late as 1982, "rip-out" operations routinely exposed Navy personnel to high levels of asbestos dust (p. 68).

[98]Ibid., p. 19.

[99]Ibid., pp. 10, 19.

[100]Ibid., p. 2.

[101]Ibid., pp. 15–17. The First Circuit, for example, dismissed on discretionary function grounds *Shuman v. United States* 765 F.2d 283 (1st Cir. 1985), a direct suit against the United States brought by a private shipyard employee. The Fifth Circuit and the Northern District of California dismissed the claims of former merchant seamen on the same grounds: *Gordon v. Lykes* 835 F.2d 96 (1988) and *Smith v. United States*, No. C86-5626 (1987). At the time of the hearings several public shipyard cases were inactive, awaiting rulings by the appellate courts.

exposed to high levels of asbestos. Wartime pressures result in trade-offs, in this case, health versus the building of ships. Nevertheless, the federal authorities remain morally culpable. They knowingly withheld information that might have made it possible for workers to evaluate the risk, quit the job, demand higher wages as compensation for the danger, or insist on reforms in the workplace.[102] In fact, the fear of labor unrest, combined with pressure to launch as many ships as possible in as little time as possible, militated against disclosure. Precautionary measures that could have reduced risk were never taken. Ventilation was poor; respirators, even when available, were not mandatory. As a result, smoky, dusty working conditions aggravated the risk.

Even filing claims was difficult, at least originally. Lung diseases related to asbestos have a long latency period—10, 15, 20, or even 45 years—so the difficulty of diagnosing the condition and then ascertaining its cause exacerbated the problem. Once claims had been adduced and cases litigated, delays in awarding compensation, whether from government-mandated programs or from private companies, added to the burden of those with asbestos-related disease. In a final ironic twist, attorneys' fees and legal costs often gobbled up much of the payments.

Given the long latency period and the lure of contingent fees, however, claims are still being filed and pending cases clog the judicial system. In 1991, 2,000 new cases were being filed each month while 115,000 claims in asbestos cases were working their way through the courts.[103] Those numbers have risen. In 1995, 55,000 new personal injury claims were filed; more than 100,000 personal injury cases were pending.[104]

In 1993, 20 former asbestos manufacturers, calling themselves the Center for Claims Resolution, and lawyers claiming to represent

[102]For a fuller treatment of risk and information, see Kip Viscusi, *Risk by Choice* (Cambridge, Mass.: Harvard University Press, 1983). "Market Forces and Inadequate Risk Information" and "Controlling Risks through Individual Choice," chapters 4 and 9, are particularly relevant.

[103]Suzanne L. Oliver and Leslie Spencer, "Who Will the Monster Devour Next?" *Forbes*, February 18, 1991, pp. 76, 79.

[104]See, for example, Form 10-K, "Annual Report," filed by Owens Corning with the Securities and Exchange Commission for the fiscal year ended December 31, 1995. Note 21, "Contingent Liabilities/Asbestos Liabilities," details the numbers of claims.

future asbestos victims reached what appeared to be a creative solution to the litigation problem. The manufacturers and the attorneys agreed to a $1 billion settlement to settle up to 100,000 future claims over the next decade. An out-of-court system was to cap awards, setting out objective medical standards of qualification. According to the agreement, future claimants were entitled to remove themselves from the settlement and remained free to file suits in the future by filing an "opt-out" notice with the U.S. District Court in Philadelphia by January 24, 1994.[105]

In the course of events, the agreement came to nothing because the U.S. Court of Appeals for the Third Circuit threw it out. The decision turned on whether class-action settlements could be used to resolve future claims from people who did not yet know whether they were sick. The court held that the thousands of claims raised different legal and factual issues. In addition, it raised questions about the inability of future claimants to opt out of the agreement and about the conflicts between those who had become sick since 1993 and those who were still well.[106]

Although the companies involved represent no more than one-fifth of the asbestos industry, the case inspired close scrutiny for its possible effect on similar lawsuits nationwide. The U.S. Court of Appeals for the Fifth Circuit is now reviewing the class-action settlement involving claims that may arise in the future against the Fibreboard Corporation, which also made asbestos.[107] If the Fifth Circuit agrees with the Third, the floodgates will open and litigation will swamp the courts.

Despite charges that industry has simply been seeking to escape liability, it is clear that many of the claims were and continue to be questionable: various sources estimate the number of those actually ill at no more than 50 percent of those filing.[108] Attorneys have employed questionable tactics as well. In *Cimino, Raymark et al.*, litigated in Beaumont, Texas, in the early 1990s, attorneys for the

---

[105]"Deal Sets Terms for Future Asbestos Claims," *San Jose Mercury News*, December 11, 1993, p. 10D.

[106]Barry Meier, "Court Tosses Out an Asbestos Deal," *New York Times*, May 11, 1996, pp. 1, 19.

[107]Ibid., p. 19.

[108]C. Edley and P. Weiler, "Asbestos, A Multi-Billion Dollar Crisis," 30 *Harvard J. on Legis.* 384 (1993), at 393.

plaintiffs "created a class of 2,300 oil refinery workers and their families." Among the 2,300 plaintiffs, Gary Friedman of the Texas Lung Institute diagnosed more than 1,300 cases of cancer and 972 of pleural thickening. Yet doctors who reexamined some of the plaintiffs found that more than 50 percent of those reexamined "showed no sign of asbestos exposure."[109]

Who profited? Friedman, owner of the Texas Lung Institute, whose main business was screening workers referred by plaintiffs' attorneys and unions. Between 1984 and 1991, when *Forbes* published an article outlining the problem, the institute had earned "at least $4 million in revenues." By 1991 the firms of lawyers Walter Umphrey and Wayne Reaud had "collected over $57 million in contingency fees from pretrial settlements and would, on paper, be entitled to another $430 million" if the case were fully upheld on appeal. The 2,300 plaintiffs had "already collected an estimated $62,000 each from defending companies that have opted to settle out of the suit." Companies choosing to go to court found that jury awards started at $540,000, virtually guaranteeing an appeal.[110] The case exposes the weaknesses in the tort system's rules for assigning blame and assessing fair compensation, as well as the fear of punitive damages that motivates many companies to settle out of court.

Walter Umphrey, Wayne Reaud, and the Texas judicial system remain a center of controversy. The state is known for a handful of "plaintiff-friendly" jurisdictions, chief among them the city of Beaumont, "the Tort Capital of America." A backlog of 40,000 asbestos cases now clogs the state court. Tort reformers estimate that more than four-fifths of the plaintiffs are not even from Texas. As a result of a Texas Supreme Court decision in 1990, Texas judges could no longer dismiss out-of-state cases or foreign plaintiffs in personal injury cases. The Texas legislature did override the decision in 1993, but a loophole was engineered to benefit (it is claimed) members of the plaintiffs' bar who contributed to the campaign of former Democratic Governor Ann Richards. "The new law allows judges to dismiss out-of-state cases *except* those involving railroads, aircraft crashes and asbestos."[111]

[109]Oliver and Spencer, pp. 77–78.

[110]Ibid., p. 78.

[111]"Asbestos Audacity," in "Review and Outlook," *Wall Street Journal*, April 1, 1996, p. A14.

The decision was a boon for the plaintiffs' bar. Umphrey's firm, for example, won $26.5 million for 10 plaintiffs in 1994 from a Houston jury. In the meantime, as judges spend one month each year handling asbestos cases, the entire state subsidizes out-of-state lawsuits.[112]

It would be unfair to focus solely on Texas; the problem spans the nation, involving not only lawyers but also physicians and testing companies that have found the lure of profits to be made from asbestos suits irresistible. In 1990 a federal judge "excoriated two lawyers who set up a mobile van unit equipped with physicians and X-ray machines that traveled the country in pursuit of clients with asbestos-related disease."[113]

Owens Corning, which once made asbestos-based building insulation, has recently filed suit against three companies that test people for asbestos contamination, "alleging that the firms falsified thousands of test results that were later used in settlements of lawsuits." The company charges not only that those companies violated industry pulmonary testing standards in order to produce "false positives" but also that they "sold the results to plaintiffs' attorneys representing possible asbestos-contamination victims who then sued the company."[114] They also charged higher fees.

The suit has provoked the usual outcry from those who oppose attempts to stem the floodtide of litigation. Although he claimed to be unfamiliar with the suit, Baltimore lawyer Peter Angelos, whose firm has hundreds of asbestos-related suits pending against Owens Corning, declared, "To have these people casting aspersions at others is, to say the least, bizarre, ludicrous, and outrageous." That he and his firm stand to profit handsomely from those cases, he never mentioned. In the nonprofit arena, Brian Wolfman, representing Public Interest Litigation Group of Washington, D.C., said he "was concerned that Owens Corning was attempting to divert attention from its own alleged wrongdoing by filing the suit."[115] The strategy seems to be this: when in doubt about the soundness of your position,

---

[112]Ibid.

[113]Oscar Suris, Arnold Ceballos, and Richard B. Schmitt, "Owens Corning Sues over Tests for Asbestos," *Wall Street Journal*, June 21, 1996, p. A3.

[114]Ibid.

[115]Ibid., p. A6.

impugn the motives of your opponent, a surefire tactic for gaining the support of those easily swayed by emotional appeals.

In tandem with the suit against the testing companies, Owens Corning is pursuing a "global settlement" of thousands of other claims. Unfortunately, the attempt comes at an inauspicious time. As noted previously, in May 1996 the Third Circuit Court threw out a class-action settlement involving 20 producers. Although Owens Corning did not participate in the case, the legal precedent could place obstacles in the path of any massive agreement.[116] Nevertheless, a successful attack on allegedly fraudulent claims could signal a new era in asbestos-related litigation. Many companies might delay settling in favor of looking first at the circumstances underlying the claims.

Should those claims prove fraudulent, it might become possible to reduce the current buildup of asbestos-related litigation. In March 1996 Owens Corning alone had a backlog of 156,000 claims; the case in question involves an additional 25,000. The company has already established a reserve fund of $1.1 billion to meet claims from 1991 to 1999; additional reserves for claims after 1999 also total $1.1 billion. So great has been the strain on the company's finances that only in June 1996 did it approve its first dividend in years.[117]

Despite the charges of fraud and corruption, it should be kept in mind that certain of the claims put forward seem likely to have merit. At the same time, court dockets abound with claims that are virtually groundless. For example, one 75-year-old retired tire worker claimed that past asbestos exposure caused him shortness of breath. A lifetime smoker, he walked five miles per day. But in December 1990 a Los Angeles jury awarded him $155,000. Such frivolous suits go far beyond the claims filed against asbestos manu-facturers for asbestos-related disease. As the authors of the *Forbes* article noted, "Our populist-leaning courts are turning the asbestos issue into a giant lottery in which almost anyone can win and the consumers of America must ultimately pay."[118]

The burden is staggering. In 1991 it was estimated that "asbestos litigation ha[d] cost defendants and their insurers about $7 billion

---

[116]Ibid.

[117]Ibid., pp. A3, A6.

[118]Oliver and Spencer, p. 76.

... most of that going to lawyers and experts. Pending cases could cost another $20 billion, based on an average historical total cost of $170,000 per claim. But this total may be too low." The final tab could reach $50 billion or even $100 billion.[119] The ongoing payouts in Texas and the reserves of Owens Corning suggest that the authors of the 1991 analysis may have underestimated that total. Given the limited amount of damage now traceable to asbestos, it seems a high price to pay.

The avalanche of cases has benefited attorneys more than those filing claims. The costs of the plaintiffs have risen to astronomical ·heights while the expenses of litigation and settlement have burdened the insurance system. In 1981 one analysis supplied the following breakdown:

> For every $2.71 paid by defendants and insurers, defense litigation expenses are an estimated $1.00, plaintiff's litigation expenses are an estimated $0.71, and the plaintiff receives $1.00. The plaintiff receives an estimated 37 percent of the total expended.[120]

A 1993 statement lacks the same precision, but it underlines the costs of the system: "Adding the overhead costs of both the judicial and insurance systems, asbestos litigation consumes two dollars of society's resources in order to deliver a single dollar to people who were exposed."[121]

For those who have actually suffered from asbestos, it must seem a tragically paltry return. For the litigating attorneys, the fees are golden. For reformers, the long and tawdry tale underscores the necessity of tort reform.

The litigation will prove lengthy, costly, and of little avail to the defendants. Claims may clog the courts, but time is running out. Those who developed disease from exposure during and after World War II are dying, and the curtain is beginning to fall on the final act of asbestos as part of "the war effort." The government's willingness to jeopardize the lives of its own citizens has never been fully explored. Historical perspective, however, enables one to suggest

[119]Ibid., p. 79.
[120]Cross, pp. 95–96.
[121]Edley and Weiler, p. 393.

that the EPA overreaction to asbestos remaining in the man-made environment may have its roots in the prompting of a guilty federal conscience.

Costs: The Private Home

The same situation can be observed in the real estate community, where the response to suspicious substances has at least one certain result: it increases the cost of home ownership. The scenario develops as follows. To avert the charge of concealing a defect, contracts for the sale of homes routinely specify the presence or absence of asbestos; if the seller is uncertain or suspects that asbestos may be present, the buyers may call in a home inspector to examine the property. (To protect themselves, sellers sometimes have an inspection performed even before the home goes on the market.) If, however, the house is relatively old and fraying asbestos is seen or suspected, the buyer may well want a test for airborne fibers, thus driving up the costs. Because the buyer normally pays the inspector, a young couple with few resources confronted with a potential asbestos problem may well decide to look elsewhere. Older houses are generally cheaper, so the young couple may have to scale down their expectations and buy a smaller or less desirable house—if, in fact, they manage to stay in the housing market at all.

Should the buyers decide on a fiber count and it then proves to be high, the costs of removal or encapsulation are likely to become the subject of lengthy negotiations between buyer and seller. In an active market, the buyers will be at a disadvantage unless they can muster the funds necessary to cover the cost of the work. More affluent or less risk-averse buyers may have their offer accepted. In a sluggish market, the seller may well decide to underwrite the expense rather than lose a willing buyer and be left with a "contaminated" house. A common solution is an agreement to share the costs. The buyers get a house, although it has taken more of their resources than they had expected; the seller can take his diminished equity and move elsewhere, in all probability to a newer house, one without asbestos.

Whatever the result, it is unlikely that a clear understanding of the nature and risks of asbestos will have determined the outcome. The literature on asbestos is extensive, but few people have the time and the funds to do in-depth research. Even professionals in the field, worried about possible lawsuits, will err on the side of recommending removal. So the fear of illness or the fear of litigation will have motivated the decision. It is certain only that testing and possible abatement will be expensive and that a number of marginal buyers will find it impossible to compete for the property.

The specter of disease and liability fuels the process, which moves inexorably onward, raising anxiety and suspense in almost equal proportions. The seller orders an inspection; if he or she pays for it, the cost is added to the purchase price. Almost every party to the transaction—the inspector, the broker, the title company—now feels compelled to carry insurance against possible malpractice. If insurance is already carried, then the coverage may be increased. The premiums constitute a cost and the cost is passed on to the buyer, as an elevated price or in the form of a difficult and protracted negotiation. Commissions, it should be noted, are negotiable and may rise in compensation if the cost of transactions becomes much steeper. If the price goes high enough, of course, the purchaser will be unable to obtain a loan and will be driven out of the market or, possibly, to a smaller, less desirable property. Thus, the emphasis on eliminating risk is also eliminating homebuyers by placing one more rung on the financial ladder that they may not be able to tolerate.

Buyers and sellers are far from alone. Companies dealing with repair and improvement are scarcely immune to anxiety. In the Washington, D.C., suburbs, a homeowner whose basement had flooded had to call six companies before finding one willing to deal with the removal of damaged, asbestos-containing tile. There was no question of competitive bids. The owner, relieved to have discovered a solution, simply agreed to the estimate. Paying the bill entailed juggling tuition payments, but there seemed to be no alternative.

Asbestos in decorative ceilings poses less difficulty. A fresh coat of paint will encapsulate straying fibers. Tests have shown that even bouncing balls off such a ceiling has little effect. For buyers and sellers, however, the cost of the painting adds to the cost of the house: the seller, trying to recoup those costs, generally raises the sales price. There remains as well the possibility that an anxious buyer will insist on removal, thus increasing not only the costs but, more important, the risks of exposure by elevating the level of airborne fibers. For a home of moderate size, the cost of removal may easily run between \$6,000 and \$8,000. If neither the buyer nor the seller is willing and able to pick up the tab, the contract may collapse.

Estimates for the overall cost of removing asbestos from public, private, and commercial buildings now run between \$50 billion and \$100 billion.[122] Although the precise figure may be in dispute, it is obvious that the housing sector has contributed a significant share.

Costs: The Public Sector

Given the inability of most tenants in public housing to defend themselves against the bureaucracy, their problems with asbestos take on a poignant dimension. In January 1994 the U.S. Department of Housing and Urban Development evacuated 27 families from the Tyler House Apartments in Washington, D.C.—a project scheduled for renovation—after water pipes burst, sending water that contained asbestos down on some of the tenants. The sixth floor had already been evacuated at a moment's notice in August 1993 when asbestos was discovered during renovation.[123]

The 1994 evacuation was carried out in similar fashion. One resident reported that her daughter had called her at work saying that "someone" had knocked on the door and ordered the family to leave with no more than a change of clothes. The management firm responsible for the evacuation referred all questions to HUD, which initially refused to respond. Journalistic probing eventually unearthed a one-page report showing elevated fiber levels in one stairwell, but the HUD representative claimed he had no time to go through reports on general levels in the building or in recently tested apartments.

At no time did the agency or the management company attempt to explain the problem. As one resident noted, "I don't know that much about asbestos, but I want to know, and they are not telling us enough." Many tenants were too frightened to discuss the issue. Indeed, one resident had allegedly lost his job with the management company for circulating a memorandum critical of the contractor and urging residents to speak up about the asbestos. Meanwhile,

[122]Ross, "Failed Policy," p. B3.

[123]Cindy Loose, "27 Families Evacuated," *Washington Post*, January 1, 1994, pp. B1, B5. All quotes in the following paragraphs are from this article.

"the asbestos problem" has doubled the cost of renovation, from $8 million to $16 million, but there has been no official justification for the additional expense.

Unlike most reports on the schools in the *New York Times*, coverage of the evacuation in the *Washington Post* included interviews with several asbestos specialists, one of whom claimed that minute amounts of the material could cause serious problems. Others, however, "emphasized that the risk is very, very small." Despite the attempt to present a balanced view, the rhetoric of the article suggested that understanding of asbestos is still limited. The building was spoken of as "asbestos-*contaminated*," and the cold water pipes "sent a cascade of water through *contaminated* areas" (emphasis added). The government had provided $4,000 to each of the 19 families evacuated in August to replace some belongings left behind "because of possible contamination."

The real victims were those evacuated. As one specialist noted, "The stress of leaving all your possessions and not knowing what is going to happen . . . could be worse than the risk from asbestos."

Conclusion

The ill-advised policies of the EPA, reflected by HUD in its evacuation of the Tyler House Apartments, have inflicted astronomical costs on the general public. One study has calculated that the EPA has been willing "to impose costs on society approaching $49 million in some instances to avoid having exposure to asbestos trigger cancer in one person."[124] An even more startling figure emerged from a review of 41 studies on asbestos by Harvard's Center for Risk Analysis. Broadening the ban on uses of asbestos and lowering the already low permissible exposure levels would have a median cost per year per life saved of $1,865,000, an expenditure difficult to justify under any foreseeable circumstances.[125]

---

[124]John M. Berry, "What's a Life Worth to EPA Regulators? Try $49 Million," *Washington Post*, February 24, 1994, p. D1. The article refers to the Cropper and Van Houtven study cited earlier, highlighting the difference between the value set on a life by the EPA and the value set by individuals on their own lives in assessing the risk of death from occupational hazards. The EPA's valuation is about 10 times greater.

[125]Tammy O. Tengs et al., "Five-Hundred Life-Saving Interventions and Their Cost-Effectiveness," *Risk Analysis* 15 (1995): 369–90.

Despite the studies by qualified researchers, the specter of danger created by the draft-summary "Estimates Paper" of 1978 and the EPA's onslaught against asbestos in schools continues to haunt the homebuying public, raising costs long after the stated rationale for the original policies has all but collapsed. The reluctance, not to say refusal, of the EPA to modify its position significantly in accordance with research findings has undermined its credibility within the scientific community. At the same time, the government has shown no great desire to educate the public concerning that research and the greatly reduced risks from asbestos that have followed reductions in workplace exposure. As a result, many consumers remain aware only of the "scare stories" about asbestos, and assertions long out of date cast a long and costly shadow over the home-selling and homebuying public.

4. Electromagnetic Fields: New Hazard or Media Hype?

To the long and growing list of speculative risks faced by home-buyers, add high-voltage powerlines. The lines are undoubtedly ugly, but their aesthetics are a relatively minor concern. Far more important, especially for the homebuyer, is the fact that the lines generate electromagnetic fields that some claim may cause cancer, especially in children. The evidence of increased cancer is not only small and inconclusive but contradictory. Furthermore, with reference to residential exposure, studies that include actual measurements of magnetic fields do not confirm the cancer increases reported in studies that rely on surrogate measures. Still, the perception of risk has raised fears and lowered property values across the country. By just how much is a subject of dispute, since the evidence in terms of lowered asking prices and expired listings has often been anecdotal. At least one all-inclusive estimate of costs goes as high as $1 billion per year, which covers not only property values but research—both scientific and "pseudo-scientific"—litigation, and the expenditures required for "satisfying people's fears."[1] In any case, it is clear that the strategy of "prudent avoidance" adopted by many utilities and government at all levels has imposed signifi-cant costs on rate payers and, more generally, on all taxpayers.

A Technical Overview

The transmission of electrical power from the generator to the ultimate user of an electric blanket or toothbrush, a microwave oven, or a television set produces "electromagnetic fields"; so do the electric motors in household appliances. While "EMF" is used in the popular literature to refer to electromagnetic fields or "mag-netic and electrical fields," experts prefer the terms "power fre-quency fields" and "extremely low frequency" ("ELF") fields to

[1]Thomas G. Donlan, "Power-Line Fearmongering," Barron's, October 9, 1995, p. 38.

refer to the fields generated in the transmission and use of electrical energy. EMF is generally used in this chapter except in quoting or paraphrasing a technical source.

Because the electrical and magnetic fields associated with power-lines (see the Appendix) do not generate enough energy to break chemical bonds (as X-rays and ultraviolet light can do) or to cause electronic excitation or heating (as microwaves can do), it would seem reasonable to conclude that power frequency fields were unlikely to cause biological effects. In opposition to such theoretical arguments are epidemiologic studies that associate EMF with cancer, some of them proposing mechanisms through which EMF could have biological effects. Three mechanisms have been proposed: induction of electric currents by magnetic fields, direct effects on magnetic biological material, and effects on rates of certain chemical reactions. However, "when quantitatively analyzed all these mechanisms are found to require fields in tissue that far exceed the fields that are induced by typical environmental exposures."[2]

Electrical fields and magnetic fields, often treated as a single entity in the popular press, are separable and have distinct characteristics. Electrical fields associated with power frequency lines are measured in volts per meter (V/m). They exist whenever voltage is present and regardless of whether current is flowing but have very little ability to penetrate buildings or human skin. Magnetic fields are measured in terms of a unit of flux density called "Tesla" (T). In the United States, the unit generally used is the "Gauss" (G): 10,000 G = 1 T and 1 G = 100 mT. Magnetic fields exist only when current is flowing, but they are difficult to shield and penetrate buildings and people easily, a critical distinction in any discussion of biological effects. Moulder and Foster summarize the preponderance of knowledge when they say that any biological effect ". . . must be due to the magnetic component of the field, or to the electric fields and currents that these magnetic fields induce in the body."[3] Although power-frequency magnetic fields do induce electrical currents in the

---

[2] J. E. Moulder and K. R. Foster, "Biological Effects of Power-Frequency Fields as They Relate to Carcinogenesis," *Proceedings of the Society for Experimental Biology and Medicine* 209 (1995): 318. That paper is referred to in the text as PSEBM.

[3] Ibid., p. 310.

body, at power frequencies the currents induced are too small to produce notable effects.

In considering exposures, it is important to distinguish between distribution and transmission lines. Since the strength of an electric field is proportional to the voltage of the source and its distance from the observer, "the electric fields beneath high-voltage transmission lines far exceed those below the lower-voltage distribution lines." In contrast, the strength of a magnetic field is proportional to the current in the lines, so that a low-voltage distribution line with a high current load may produce a magnetic field that is as high as that produced by some high-voltage transmission lines.

> In fact, electric distribution systems account for a far higher proportion of the population's exposure to magnetic fields than the larger and more obvious high-voltage transmission lines.[4]

The "larger and more obvious" transmission lines, the ones on high metal towers, have created the most concern, even though their distance from people and the nature of the current they carry mean that they are not the major source of exposure to magnetic fields. Impossible to ignore, their presence has fueled the anxiety of owners and homebuyers; accumulating evidence suggests that they have depressed property values as well.

Less obvious and easier to overlook are the smaller wires emanating from the substations and the transformers (including, in many areas, telephone-pole-mounted transformers) of the electrical distribution system that carry current into the home. Those way stations step down the voltage but increase the current load and, thus, the magnetic fields, making them the major source of exposure.

The Origins of the Debate

The debate about the health effects of EMF has been raging for nearly 20 years, dispassionately in peer-reviewed journals, both here and abroad, more heatedly in the popular press. Its origins illustrate the shaky foundation of such controversies.

On the scientific front, two studies by Nancy Wertheimer and Edward Leeper can serve as a starting point. The first, a case-control

[4]Ibid.

study of childhood cancers, was based on the *"potential* [emphasis in original] current flow suggested by different wiring configurations (nearness and size of wires, closeness to origin of current, etc.)" of outdoor powerlines. Such "wirecodes" served as an index of exposure. Published in 1979, the study reported an above-average incidence of childhood cancers, especially leukemia and tumors of the nervous system.[5]

The second, a 1982 case-control study of adults living near distribution wires, reported an association between adult cancer and proximity to high current configurations (HCCs). Although the association was "highly significant," it was "considerably weaker" than the association with childhood cancer noted in the previous study. Moreover, the cancers of significance were those of the nervous system, uterus, and breast, and lymphomas, not leukemia.[6] In other words, both studies were "positive" in showing an association between EMF and cancer but congruent only for cancers of the nervous system and contradictory for total cancers and especially for leukemia.

Two years later, controversy over "Project ELF," the U.S. Navy communication system in northern Wisconsin, brought renewed attention to electromagnetic fields. The system, which operates in the extremely low frequency range, consists of several hundred miles of antenna used to contact submerged submarines. Michigan and Wisconsin opposed it for a variety of reasons, among them questions about how adequately the environmental impact statement had dealt with potential effects on health. John Moulder, who has documented much of the EMF debate, noted: "The 1984 trial was the first major airing of the 'powerline-cancer' issue."[7] Wisconsin obtained an injunction, but the circuit court overruled it "on a 'technicality' having nothing to do with the science or the Environmental Impact Statement." Wisconsin dropped the case. The project was built and

---

[5]N. Wertheimer and E. Leeper, "Electrical Wiring Configurations and Childhood Cancer," *American Journal of Epidemiology* 109 (1979): 273–83.

[6]N. Wertheimer and E. Leeper, "Adult Cancer Related to Electrical Wires near the Home," *International Journal of Epidemiology* 11 (1982): 345–55.

[7]John E. Moulder, electronic transmission, July 28, 1995. Moulder noted that land use issues and antinuclear war sentiments were also involved.

is still operational. Furthermore, the Navy strongly supports its continued operation.[8]

A third landmark was the New York State Powerlines Project, which ran from 1980 to 1987. The approval process for a proposed 765-kilovolt line brought an order from the New York Public Services Commission that the utilities spend $5 million on research. According to Moulder, "This was the first major influx of money into the field, and represented the first time that scientists who were not part of the 'EMF establishment' got involved in research in this area."[9]

The project funded, among others, an epidemiologic study conducted by David Savitz of the University of North Carolina and his colleagues that attempted to replicate the Wertheimer-Leeper research. The study was better designed and more extensive: investigators assigned wirecodes to houses blindly—that is, without knowing where children with cancer had lived.[10] In addition to assigning wirecodes, they measured indoor fields in most houses directly. Based on the wirecode estimates of exposure, Savitz's results confirmed those of Wertheimer and Leeper: there was a "possibly significant excess of leukemia" and an "excess incidence of brain cancer" for children with high-current-configuration wirecodes. Based on actual measurements of magnetic fields in the children's homes, however, there was no excess incidence of either cancer.[11] Because the first Wertheimer-Leeper study had not measured indoor magnetic fields at all, it provided no information about whether there was an unusual incidence of childhood cancers in association with measured exposures.

A later study, by S. J. London and her colleagues, published in 1991, highlighted the problems of measurement. A case-control

---

[8]Moulder has since confirmed the status of the project (personal communication with the author).

[9]J. E. Moulder, electronic transmission, July 31, 1995.

[10]The 1979 Wertheimer-Leeper study, short of funds, was not done blind, although a check on 70 case and 70 control addresses suggested a high degree of reliability. Wertheimer and Leeper, 1979, pp. 282–83.

[11]D. A. Savitz et al., "Case-Control Study of Childhood Cancer and Exposure to 60-Hz Magnetic Fields," *American Journal of Epidemiology* 128 (1988): 21–38, cited in Moulder, "Frequently Asked Questions (FAQs) on Power-Frequency Fields and Cancer," *Annotated Bibliography* (Milwaukee: Medical College of Wisconsin, 1995), p. C6. See also "Electromagnetic Fields," *Consumer Reports* 59 (May 1994): 355.

study of childhood leukemia in Los Angeles, it used measurements, wirecodes, and self-reported appliance use as indices of exposure. The results supported an association between childhood leukemia risk and wiring configuration, as had the first Wertheimer-Leeper study. At the same time, it reported no clear associations between leukemia risk and measured electric or magnetic fields.[12] The absence of a clear link between leukemia and magnetic field strength as determined by direct measurements of indoor fields thus cast doubt on the Wertheimer-Leeper results.

Measurement being the hallmark of science, the Savitz and London findings based on measurements of magnetic fields should be accorded more weight than the results based on wirecodes, which are only surrogate estimates of exposure. That has not happened. Instead, some proponents of the link between EMF and cancer have suggested that measurements of magnetic fields are not the proper measurement for exposure. Although they are uncertain of the proper measure, they are sure that it exists and that its measurement will confirm their beliefs. Neither the electrical nor the magnetic component of EMF, measured directly, is associated with increased cancer. The belief that there is "something else there" is more akin to magic than to science.

The New York powerline project also funded another study by Savitz and his colleagues on the possible link between magnetic field exposure from electric appliances and childhood cancer. Published in 1990, the study found that heated waterbeds and bedside electric clocks were unrelated to the incidence of childhood cancer. Prenatal electric blanket exposure carried with it a small increase in the incidence of childhood brain cancer but no significant increase in leukemia or overall cancer; no increased incidence of childhood cancer was found for postnatal use. By way of explanation, the study noted that electric blankets were a source of prolonged magnetic field exposure, "with levels up to 10 times background," and suggested that the blankets warranted "a more thorough evaluation."[13]

[12]S. J. London et al., "Exposure to Residential Electric and Magnetic Fields and Risk of Childhood Leukemia," *American Journal of Epidemiology* 134 (1991): 923–37.

[13]D. A. Savitz et al., "Magnetic Field Exposure from Electric Appliances and Childhood Cancer, *American Journal of Epidemiology* 131 (1990): 763, 771, cited in Moulder: "Frequently Asked Questions," p. C11.

Like others before and after him, physicist William R. Bennett Jr.[14] criticized both the Savitz and London studies for "inconsistencies between the high-current geometries (that in themselves are not adequately defined) and spot measurements of magnetic fields." In other words, the authors had given too much weight to wirecode information when they had more certain measurements. He also reported criticisms raised by others about the random-digit dialing used to select the comparison populations in both studies, a method that could have biased the reported results.[15]

The American Physical Society (APS), in its review of 16 papers that reported investigations of EMF and cancer rates, says that the 1979 study by Wertheimer and Leeper "triggered journalism that then created a large public response." It continues: "These results are greatly discredited by the totality of the 16 studies. The early results also were plagued by the fact that they reported an association with powerlines (wire codes) but they do not report an association with measured spot fields."[16]

The director of the compilation, Professor David Hafemeister, added a personal note: "The inconsistency in the results of these 16 studies is evidence of either a truly small or nonexistent risk, or else a measure of the confounders of different lifestyles, chemical exposures, etc."[17]

The technical comments in the APS paper on some of the individual studies that have played major roles in the EMF debate suggest that the analyses are often mutually contradictory. Others are internally inconsistent or methodologically flawed. Of the study of mortality among electrical workers conducted by Savitz and Loomis,

[14]Bennett is C. B. Sawyer Professor of Engineering and Applied Sciences and professor of physics at Yale University.

[15]William R. Bennett Jr., *Health and Low-Frequency Electromagnetic Fields* (New Haven, Conn.: Yale University Press, 1994), p. 7.

[16]American Physical Society, "Background Paper on Power Line Fields and Public Health," April 1995, IV, 1, p. 2. Electronic transmission: jmoulder@post.its.mcw.edu, May 16, 1995. Transmitted to the Panel on Public Affairs, American Physical Society, by David Hafemeister, Physics Department, California Polytechnic State University, San Luis Obispo, Calif. 93407. Text available from the American Physical Society: dhafemei@oboe.calpoly.edu or http://www.calpoly.edu~dhafemei.

[17]Ibid., IV.1, p. 2. Of the 16 studies referenced, 15 appeared in the December 1994 issue of *IEEE Spectrum;* the 16th is the Loomis study. As is the case there, Hafemeister places his own comments in brackets, preceded by his initials.

APS notes, "In contrast to other studies, these data do not support an association between occupational magnetic field exposure and leukemia but do suggest a link to brain cancer."[18] APS then compares these results to others in the literature: "Thus, Savitz's conclusion of no association with leukemia is in agreement with the California study but in disagreement with the Canadian-French and 1993 Swedish studies." On the other hand, for brain cancer, "Savitz quotes an RR [Relative Risk] of about 1.5–2.5 [meaning that the cancer risk was 1.5 to 2.5 times as high in the people living near the powerlines as in people living elsewhere] which is similar to the French-Canadian result of about 1.5, but in disagreement with the California and 1993 Swedish results of no association."[19]

Such contradictions, or at least inconsistencies, make it difficult to believe in a widespread menace. Indeed, the study goes on to cite an article in the *Washington Post* of January 12, 1995, which quotes Savitz himself as saying, "I don't want to downplay the adverse aspects of our findings, but one thing our study does is show once again there is not some public health disaster lurking out there."[20]

Confirmation of this view comes from yet another source. After a careful review of two recent Swedish studies, an Oak Ridge Associated Universities (ORAU) panel, which was itself in the process of publishing a report critical of a causal link between electric and magnetic fields and cancer, notes that "the findings of the two relevant studies [Feychting and Ahlbom, Tomenius] pointed in opposite directions." Following a detailed critique, the article concludes: "We have never stated that a causal association between EMF and cancer is impossible or inconceivable; we have indicated that the evidence for such an association is empirically weak and biologically implausible."[21] Once again, it is impossible to prove a negative.

---

[18]D. Savitz and D. Loomis, "University of North Carolina Study on Electrical Workers Mortality," *American Journal of Epidemiology* 141 (1995): 123–34. Cited in APS Background Paper, IV.3, pp. 3–5.

[19]APS Background Paper, IV.3, pp. 4–5.

[20]D. Savitz, January 12, 1995, *Washington Post*, quoted in APS Background Paper, IV.3, p. 5.

[21]Oak Ridge Associated Universities Panel on Health Effects of Low-Frequency Electric and Magnetic Fields, "EMF and Cancer," in "Letters," *Science* 260 (April 2, 1993): 13–14.

In their response to the Oak Ridge critique, Feychting and Ahlbom, authors of one of the Swedish studies, presented their own calculations showing 142 cases of all childhood cancers in children living within 300 meters of high-voltage powerlines, compared with an expected number of 138. They dismissed the Tomenius study, which contradicted their findings, as flawed in its measure of exposure and concluded that there were only six reliable studies, including one Danish report. Asserting that "the evidence on leukemia in children is actually fairly consistent," they added: "We agree with the ORAU panel that there is no known mechanism by which EMF might play a role in cancer development." Unlike the ORAU panel, which had suggested that "there are currently more serious health needs that should be given higher priority," Feychting and Ahlbom concluded by suggesting that further research might well be helpful in determining "an as yet unknown mechanism through which EMF interacts with human cells."[22] Given the impossibility of establishing the complete safety of an environmental agent, the lay reader and the researcher must both content themselves with a scenario suggesting the possibility, however remote, of a risk, however small.

As may be seen from this brief recital, inconsistency and contradiction characterize the studies of EMF and cancer. Such criticisms were generally ignored, however, as the controversy moved from academic journals and the discussions of public utilities commissions to the popular press.

Moving to the Popular Press

Paul Brodeur, writing for the *New Yorker*, played a major role in enlarging the debate. Beginning in 1990, he published a series of articles on the possible health effects of electromagnetic fields generated not only by powerlines but also by household appliances such as microwave ovens.

Two in-depth essays on cancer clusters proved particularly effective in sounding the alarm. The first, "Calamity on Meadow Street," dealt with cancers in three places: along Meadow Street in Guilford, Connecticut, where the houses faced a power substation; in Rowan County, North Carolina, in proximity to the Duke Power Company's

---

[22]Anders Ahlbom and Maria Feychting, untitled response in "Letters," *Science* 260 (April 2, 1993): 16.

Buck Steam Plant; and on Santa Rosa Lane in Montecito, California, near a substation at Montecito Union School.[23]

The second article, "The Cancer at Slater School," dealt with 14 cancers reported by teachers and aides at Louise N. Slater Elementary School in Fresno, California. Brodeur suggested proximity to the high-voltage powerlines on the south side of the school as the cause.[24]

Brodeur's interpretation of the Slater School situation was a major factor in the suit brought by 33 residents of Fresno against the Pacific Gas and Electric Company. Sixteen of the plaintiffs claimed that powerlines near the school had caused their cancers; 2 feared cancer; the remaining 15 alleged loss of "consortium" because of their spouses' cancers. The suit, *Hurd v. Pacific Gas and Electric*, aroused strong emotions among those who believed that the utilities were participating in a cover-up of real and deleterious effects on health.

The scientific evidence in *Hurd v. Pacific Gas and Electric* was questionable. Magnetic field readings taken in the school showed levels no higher than those in most homes; the state health department's study said that chance could account for the incidence of cancer among the school staff. The claims for health effects were dropped for nonscientific reasons when a California Court of Appeals ruled that an unrelated EMF suit should be handled by the California Public Utilities Commission, not the courts. The commission can modify powerlines for reasons of public safety but does not as a rule award money damages. The plaintiffs settled; the suit would not be refiled; and the company would pay its own legal expenses, an important provision since the plaintiffs might otherwise have been stuck with the bill, which was not inconsiderable.[25]

Jurisdiction became an issue in *Covalt v. San Diego Gas and Electric*, which was appealed from the Superior Court of Orange County to the California Supreme Court. Encouraged perhaps by cases in Florida, Kansas, and New York in which the courts have judged utilities responsible for loss of property values stemming from the fear of electromagnetic fields, the plaintiffs in *Covalt* have persevered,

[23]Paul Brodeur, "Annals of Radiation: Calamity on Meadow Street," *New Yorker* 66 (July 9, 1990): 38–72.

[24]Paul Brodeur, "Annals of Radiation: The Cancer at Slater School," *New Yorker* 68 (December 7, 1992): 86–119.

[25]"EMF Suit Runs Out of Power," in "Random Samples," *Science* 268 (May 12, 1995): 809; Donlan, p. 38.

the issue being the right to sue for compensation for reduced property values.[26] It's a subtle procedure. The plaintiffs call attention to
their health problems, publicizing the putative link between EMF
and health effects; when that fails they sue for reduced property
values. Probably nothing has contributed more to reduced property
values than these health claims.

The judicial process took time, but the plaintiffs were ultimately
unsuccessful. In August 1996, the California Supreme Court declared
that it had granted review to determine whether a previous case,
Waters v. Pacific Telephone Co., would bar "a superior court action
for property damage allegedly caused by the electric and magnetic
fields arising from powerlines owned and operated by a public
utility." The court affirmed the judgment of the court of appeals,
arguing that "such an action would impermissibly interfere with a
broad regulatory policy of the commission [the California Public
Utilities Commission] on this subject, and hence is barred."[27] The
decision sets a precedent and should make utilities breathe easier;
but in the court of public opinion, much of the damage to property
value has already been done.

The articles of Brodeur have been instrumental in spreading the
alarm. In his reporting Brodeur consistently highlighted the American and Scandinavian studies that had shown a positive association
between power-frequency lines and cancer. Inconsistencies and contradictions in the research reported simply disappeared. The electric
utility industry, which had funded and continues to fund research
in this area, was presented as unresponsive and faulted for failing
to educate the public on the dangers of power-frequency lines. The
EPA, by refusing to acknowledge the menace to public health, was
pictured as participating in a cover-up. In short, the federal government was "cautious at best, irresponsible at worst."[28]

The Debate Gathers Momentum

The tide of public anxiety began to mount. Public and private
utilities, in addition to several government agencies, were sponsoring multimillion dollar studies. In 1992 Congress mandated that

---

[26]Donlan, p. 38.

[27]In the Supreme Court of California: *San Diego Gas and Electric Company, Petitioner
v. The Superior Court of Orange County*, Respondent, *Martin Covalt et al.*, Real Parties
of Interest. Filed August 22, 1996, SO45854, Ct. App. 4/3 No. G016256.

[28]Brodeur, "Calamity on Meadow Street," p. 70.

the National Institute of Environmental Health Sciences (NIEHS) "commit millions of research dollars to lab studies on power-frequency fields." One commentator noted that the program "got a lot of attention from researchers not previously involved because it was a lot of money."[29] Whether those millions would produce results proportionate to the cost is an unanswered question.

Certainly it was a lot of money. The "Electric and Magnetic Fields Research and Public Information Dissemination Program" (EMFRAPID), sponsored as well by the Department of Energy, would cost $65 million over five fiscal years, 1993 through 1997. Half would come from the federal government, half from nonfederal sources. The program would have four components: health effects research, engineering, risk assessment research, and communication, including a clearinghouse for biomedical and engineering information.[30]

Since money did not really get to researchers until 1994, very little has yet been published. Communication efforts have been more visible: the program has, for example, distributed a public information booklet on electric and magnetic fields and electric power; a private organization, Information Ventures, evidently spurred by the program, has established a site on the Internet, "EMF-Link World Wide Web." A major purpose of EMFRAPID, however, was to determine which, if any, of the large number of reports in the field might be replicable; its greatest benefit may be to clarify which, if any, biological effects can be reproduced. From the scientific viewpoint, the program may be worthwhile. Should the taxpayers be supporting even half of the expenditures projected? It is certainly questionable.[31]

Whether it has been the infusion of money or increased interest in the field, the scientific community has intensified the hunt for possible effects. In May 1995, the APS noted that more than 1,000 papers had already been written on the ELF topic.[32]

---

[29]Moulder, electronic transmission, July 28, 1995, p. 2.

[30]The EMF Interagency Committee, "Progress Report on the Electric and Magnetic Fields Research and Public Information Dissemination Program," December 1995, pp. 1–4.

[31]Ibid. Moulder supplied an update on the status of the program, electronic transmission, July 10, 1996.

[32]APS Background Paper, I.i., p. 2.

Rational Reporting: The American Physical Society

The APS, on the well-founded belief that yet another study would be duplicative and expensive, decided to survey studies already completed and to draw its conclusions therefrom. Accordingly the POPA Study (Panel on Public Affairs: American Physical Society) examined the existing data, as well as the public response. The resulting "Background Paper on 'Power Line Fields and Public Health,'" scheduled to be updated periodically, reviews the analyses to date. If risk were a rational matter and if the public knew about the review, it might set the public mind at rest. But, given the high public anxiety surrounding the subject, perhaps the most that can be expected is a reduced level of concern.

Summary statements capture the thrust of the four technical sections of the APS report.

- Section III, "Reviews of the ELF Data," states: "None of the scientific panels that have carried out comprehensive reviews of the data has concluded that there is an established link between ELF and cancer."[33]
- Section IV, "Epidemiology," concludes: "The scientific panels that have reviewed the ELF epidemiology data have found them inconsistent and inconclusive."[34]
- Section V, "Biological and Biophysics Experiments," continues in the same vein: "The scientific review panels, the review articles, and the research papers that we have investigated do not claim a causal link between ELF and cancer. In addition, the review panels and review articles have pointed out that there is a large problem with replicating the experimental results."[35]
- Section VI, "Theoretical Mechanisms," is even more emphatic: "No plausible biophysical mechanism for the systematic initiation or promotion of cancer by these extremely weak ELF's has been identified." The critique then notes that the lack of epidemiologic and experimental evidence establishing a link between ELF and cancer "is consistent with the biophysical

[33]Ibid., II.2, p. 4.
[34]Ibid., II.3, p. 4.
[35]Ibid., p. 5.

calculations that rule out the carcinogenic effects because the thermal noise fields are larger than the fields from ELF."[36]

The concluding remarks of the section on "Theoretical Mechanisms," although technically dense, are worthy of emphasis:

> Since quantum mechanics, thermal noise fluctuations, and cancer promotion are all statistical effects, it is difficult to derive a proof that is a necessary and sufficient condition to preclude all cancer promotion.

In other words, it is impossible to prove a negative, a problem that plagues all analysis of risk. The paper goes on to conclude, however, that "these fundamental calculations are a significant guidepost to conclude that the ELF-cancer link, if any, should be extremely difficult to detect because of its small, if any, magnitude."[37] The reports of a menace to public health, it seems safe to say, have been greatly exaggerated.

The willingness of the APS to stake out a position in this troubled area is worthy of note. David Hafemeister, professor of physics at California Polytechnic State University and the coordinator of the APS paper, asserts that the views of physicists are relevant because they have "worked on many aspects of this multidisciplinary topic." Having asked ELF researchers their reaction to a statement putting forward "the simple concepts of (1) don't scare society with ELF, (2) don't spend billions to mitigate," he concludes: "It is my impression that the serious ELF professionals will welcome such an APS statement. And I think it is our professional obligation to speak up."[38]

Given the public hysteria on the subject, the reader can only agree.

The "Journalism" section of the APS report adds up the number of newspaper and magazine stories on ELF. They more than doubled from 1992 to 1993 (newspapers, from 233 to 548; magazines, from 101 to 216). Many of them were sensationalist or carried sensational headlines, such as "Warning: Electricity Can Be Hazardous to Your Health." The author of that section, presumably Professor Hafemeister, adds finally: "My conclusion is that the science and relative risk

[36]Ibid., II.5, p. 5.
[37]Ibid.
[38]Ibid., pp. 6–7.

methodology of ELF/EMF often undercut the quality of journalism in a free and fear-prone society."[39]

The magisterial statement issued by the APS Council to summarize its efforts merits lengthy quotation:

> The scientific literature and the reports of reviews by other panels show no consistent, significant link between cancer and power line fields. . . . No plausible biophysical mechanisms for the systematic initiation or promotion of cancer by these power line fields have been identified. Furthermore, the preponderance of the epidemiological and biophysical/biological research findings have failed to substantiate those studies which have reported specific adverse health effects from exposure to such fields. While it is impossible to prove that no deleterious health effects occur from exposure to any environmental factor, it is necessary to demonstrate a consistent, significant, and causal relationship before one can conclude that such effects do occur. From this standpoint, the conjectures relating cancer to power line fields have not been scientifically substantiated.[40]

The measured tone and careful wording of the statement command respect. If well publicized, it may prove effective in curbing, if not eliminating, the current climate of irrational fear. On the other hand, EMFs, like many other environmental factors, can be appealing to people searching for a cause for a terrible, inexplicable event, such as a childhood cancer, and that appeal can keep the putative link between EMF and cancer in the public eye. That is especially true when the putative link offers opportunities for lawsuits based on health effects or lost property values.

Frequently Asked Questions

A precursor of the APS paper and an ongoing source of reliable information in that area are the "Frequently Asked Questions (FAQs) on Power-Frequency Fields and Cancer" maintained by Professor John E. Moulder of the Medical College of Wisconsin and his colleagues on the Internet. Updated monthly, the questions are available to the growing number of people with access to the Internet. The

[39]Ibid., p. 7.

[40]Statement by the Council of the American Physical Society, April 22, 1995, pp. 1–2. Electronic transmission, May 16, 1995.

detailed answers and the carefully annotated bibliography provide a welcome resource for the anxious consumer.[41]

The questions add up to a cursory course in elementary physics. Such queries as "How do the power-frequency EM fields cause biological effects?" (#8) and "How are power-frequency magnetic fields measured?" (#30) receive a straightforward response. The writers neither intimidate nor patronize; they simply present the known universe.

In answer to the question "What is known about the relationship between powerline corridors and cancer rates?" they note that "Some studies have reported that children living near certain types of powerlines ... have higher than average rates of leukemia ..., brain cancers and overall cancer. ... The correlations are not strong, and the studies have generally not shown dose-response relationships. When power-frequency fields are actually measured, the correlation vanishes." The response is often keyed by letter and number to the annotated bibliography, giving those who wish to pursue the issue the means of doing so (#12).[42]

The difficulty of research in that area is also noted: "[A] simple overview of the epidemiology is impossible to achieve because the epidemiological techniques and methods of the exposure assessments in the various studies are so different" (#13). By avoiding the simplistic approach, the FAQs manage to suggest that hard and fast answers are difficult to find and a degree of skepticism may be advisable.

The FAQs note the role of false associations in epidemiologic studies, then stress a basic principle of statistics: association does not always mean causality, a point often lost in the accounts of possible relationships between power-frequency fields and cancer (#21B).

---

[41]Moulder, "Frequently Asked Questions (FAQs) on Power-Frequency Fields and Cancer." See ftp://rtfm.mit.edu/pub/usenet-by-group/news.answers/powerlines-cancer-FAQ or any other archive of USENET FAQ sheets. There are now two websites: Powerlines and Cancer FAQs: http://www.mcw.edu/gcrc/cop/powerlines-cancer-FAQ/toc.html and Static Electromagnetic Fields and Cancer FAQs: http://www.mcw.edu/gcrc/cop/static-fields-cancer-FAQ/toc.html.

[42]Ibid., FAQs, electronic transmission. Since the transmission used is unpaged, all references are to the numbered questions and are generally given in parentheses in the text.

The FAQs provide references both for "the strongest evidence for a connection between power-frequency fields and cancer" and "the strongest evidence against such a connection." They reference the relevant studies, leaving the reader with invaluable signposts. Indeed, the lengthy annotated bibliography may be the single greatest contribution of the FAQs to the debate. From "Recent Reviews of the Biological and Health Effects of Power-Frequency Fields" through "Regulations and Standards for Ionizing and Non-Ionizing EM Sources" (#A–#M),[43] the bibliography leads both the serious researcher and the nervous homebuyer through the forest of literature now surrounding the issue. It would be difficult to find a more dispassionate guide.

A particularly valuable aspect of the FAQs and of the paper authored by Moulder and Foster is the presentation of "Hill's criteria" used to assess epidemiological and laboratory studies of agents suspected of causing human disease. The criteria themselves— strength, consistency, dose-response relationships, laboratory evidence, plausible biological mechanisms—are discussed at length in the paper and the FAQs. Both the FAQs and Moulder and Foster emphasize that those criteria must be applied with caution: first, the entire published literature must be examined; second, the source documents must be reviewed directly; third, the criteria must be viewed as a whole, for no single criterion can be used to conclude that there is a causal relationship between exposure and disease; finally, support for individual criteria can be strong, moderate, weak, or nonexistent. Moulder has pointed out that satisfying each criterion is not a matter of "yes or no" but one of degree. The exact words used to describe degrees of support are a matter of personal preference.[44]

In their work, Moulder and Foster present a table (Table IV) that evaluates how well the epidemiologic and laboratory studies of power-frequency fields satisfy the Hill criteria. They interpret the support for a cancer connection as ranging from "weak-possible" (strength and consistency of association) to "weak" (specificity of

---

[43]Ibid., FAQs. The annotated bibliography is referenced by means of letters, A through M, rather than numbers.

[44]See FAQs, question 20. See also questions 20A, 20B, 20C, 20D, 20E, and Moulder and Foster, p. 314. Moulder clarified the use of the Hill criteria in a note to the author.

association) to "none-weak" (dose-response and laboratory evidence) to "none" (plausibility). Their overall analysis reinforces the conclusions of the APS study.

> Overall, application of the Hill criteria shows that the current evidence for a connection between power-frequency fields and cancer is weak, because of the weakness and inconsistencies in the epidemiological studies, combined with the lack of a dose-response relationship in the human studies, and the large unsupportive laboratory studies.[45]

Such careful evaluation finds no echo in popular discussions of EMF.

Another Rational Perspective

The Institute of Electrical and Electronics Engineers (IEEE) has published a recent and welcome contribution to the field, "Questioning the Biological Effects of EMF." In a field sorely lacking balanced perspectives, IEEE provides a rational view of the biology of electromagnetic fields, a complex subject that involves not only biophysics, medicine, and engineering but public health, risk assessment, tort law, and public policy as well.[46]

The collected articles begin with an historical introduction to the health effects of EMFs, and additional articles by, among others, John E. Moulder, who maintains the Frequently Asked Questions Internet site, and Kenneth R. Foster, the coauthor of the PSEBM article cited previously, highlight particular areas of concern, such as the studies of power-frequency fields and carcinogenesis and the much-debated question of biological mechanisms. Those concerned with public policy will find "The Role of Science in EMF Litigation," by Mark A. Warnquist and his associates, troubling. The outline of cases traces the expansion of scientific debate into tort law, suggesting that public utilities and the plaintiffs' bar are likely to pay increasing attention to "prudent avoidance," "notwithstanding the uncertainties in the science."[47] Anxiety and costs can only rise.

[45]Moulder and Foster, p. 314.

[46]"Questioning the Biological Effects of EMF," *IEEE Engineering in Medicine and Biology* 15 (July/August 1996): 23–103.

[47] Ibid.

If the compendium can clarify the controversy and lead to a more reasoned assessment of risk, it will have provided a public service. It is, in any case, an essential reference.

Reporting and Publication Bias in the Professional Literature

Stated crudely, bad news sells better than good. The corollary in the professional literature is that "positive studies," those that show associations between risks and health effects, ". . . are more likely to be published than negative studies. This can severely bias meta-analysis studies such as those discussed. . . . Such publication bias will increase apparent risks" (FAQ: #21D). The bias is so pronounced that it causes authors to be reluctant to submit negative studies.

One published Canadian study, for instance, showed an elevated risk of leukemia in electrical workers. The follow-up study, which showed a deficiency of leukemia, was never published, but there is no evidence that the authors ever submitted it for publication. The maintainer of the FAQs goes on to observe: "This is an anecdotal report, but *publication bias, by its very nature, is usually anecdotal*" (FAQ: #21D). [Emphasis added.] The comment should put even the casual reader on guard. Given the opportunities for partiality underlying publication, the papers that finally appear in the pages of professional journals may be telling only part of the story.

Publication bias is not restricted to epidemiologic studies but applies to laboratory studies as well since "it is much easier to publish studies that report effects than studies that report no effects." The maintainer notes two cases in which "reports of failure to replicate [were] not published, so only the positive report is currently in the peer-reviewed literature" (FAQ: #21D).

The related issue of "'reporting bias'" covers "both situations where multiple studies are done but only some are reported, and . . . situations where abstracts and / or press reports emphasize unrepresentative subsets of the actual study." For example, the FAQs cite three "Swedish" studies, two published and one unpublished:

> The original unpublished report used a number of different definitions of "exposure," and studied both children and adults. Of all the comparisons, the most significant correlations were found for childhood leukemia and calculated

fields. The first published version[48] omitted details of some of the exposure definitions that showed no relationships, and omitted the adult studies.

The abstract of the English-language version emphasized the groups, exposure definitions and cancer types for which there were significant relationships, and the press reports were based largely on that abstract. The recent publication of the adult portion of the study,[49] which shows no statistically significant relationships between exposure and cancer incidence, has received virtually no press coverage.

The result is that a handful of significantly positive associations have been emphasized from a much larger group of overwhelmingly non-significant associations" (#21D).

Given the technicality of often conflicting reports in the scientific community, a clear need exists for careful journalistic coverage. But such care is a rarity.

Recent Press Coverage

Charles C. Mann presents a meticulous analysis of the problems with press coverage in a 1995 issue of *Science*: "The media tend to report each new study in isolation, as a new breakthrough. Such reporting, some scientists say, is encouraged by press releases put out by journals and researchers' institutions." Whoever is to blame, one epidemiologist noted that the result is "'just too many false alarms. When we do have a serious message, I fear it won't be heeded. . . .'"[50]

Coverage of two large studies on occupational exposure to electromagnetic fields provides examples of such false alarms. Both studies appeared in the *American Journal of Epidemiology*; both were covered by the *Wall Street Journal*. The first study, of French and Canadian electric utility workers, "found no link between EMF and 25 of the

[48]M. Feychting and A. Ahlbom, "Magnetic Fields and Cancer in Children Residing near Swedish High-Voltage Power Lines," *American Journal of Epidemiology* 7 (1993): 467–81.

[49]M. Feychting and A. Ahlbom, "Magnetic Fields, Leukemia, and Central Nervous System Tumors in Swedish Adults Residing near High-Voltage Power Lines," *Epidemiology* 5 (1994): 501–9.

[50]Charles C. Mann, "Press Coverage: Leaving Out the Big Picture," *Science* 269 (July 14, 1995): 166.

27 varieties of cancer in the study; the exceptions, two rare types of leukemia, had a weak and inconsistent positive association with EMF." The headline in the *Wall Street Journal* read, "Magnetic Fields Linked to Leukemia."[51]

The second study, covering American workers at five U.S. utilities, "found no association between exposure to EMF and 17 of 18 types of cancer, including the leukemias linked to EMF by the first study. The sole exceptions were eye and brain cancers—conditions that had shown no link to EMF in the first study." The headline in the *Wall Street Journal*? "Link between EMF, Brain Cancer Is Suggested by Study at 5 Utilities."[52]

A comment by the writer of one of the articles affords some insight into the problem: "'People are not interested in what diseases [a risk factor] doesn't cause, but what it might cause. . . . We've had this argument with scientists many times. . . .'"[53] Viewed in that light, reporting becomes a matter of catering to the public taste. The reader may be entitled to demand a warning label: "Read with caution. The views expressed are not necessarily those of the researchers or the scientific community."

Two Views from the *Wall Street Journal*

The *Wall Street Journal*, one of the country's leading national newspapers, has published not only articles but also op-ed pieces about EMF. The next two sections describe the different messages conveyed.

EMF Causes Cancer (Maybe) and Depresses Home Values

A 1993 article in the *Wall Street Journal* on the effect of powerlines on home sales suggests the way in which this "handful of significantly positive associations" receives emphasis. The effects of this emphasis may be far-reaching on the real estate market. Articles about home values have a ready audience. The millions of homebuyers are exquisitely sensitive to negative influences on their property values. For almost all, a house represents their most significant investment, the repository of their life savings as well as of their hopes for security in retirement.

[51]Ibid.
[52]Ibid.
[53]Ibid.

In outlining a legal battle between homeowners and the San Diego Gas & Electric Company, Alix Freedman, writing in the *Wall Street Journal*,[54] touches on the drop in property values due to "a *perceived* health risk" [emphasis in original]. Such a perception is almost impossible to erase, for it rests essentially on neighborhood rumor and popular reports and easily becomes grounds for lawsuits. Freedman also sketches the scientific debate, which has continued for 20 years, and notes, "Although risks are believed to be low, some scientists have found an association between childhood cancer and power lines and similar risks among occupationally exposed workers."[55]

Freedman then cites "researchers from Sweden's prestigious Karolinska Institute [which] reported finding up to a fourfold higher leukemia rate among Swedish children living near power lines."[56] It is reasonable to infer that the researchers referred to are Feychting and Ahlbom. A preliminary report (in Swedish) of their work had been followed by a more extensive analysis published in English by the *American Journal of Epidemiology*.[57] Freedman evidently relied on the abstract of that journal article, since he focuses on childhood leukemia, fails to note that the Swedish researchers in the full-length paper in English reported no overall increase in cancer for any measure of exposure, and omits their careful qualifications of exposure by distance. The summation, "No increase in cancer was found for measured fields," given in the FAQs simply falls through the cracks.[58] To buttress the case, Freedman goes on to cite another Swedish study, this time by the National Institute of Occupational Health, showing that "male workers exposed to approximately the same levels of EMF had three times the rate of a certain kind of leukemia."[59]

---

[54]Alix M. Freedman, "Power Lines Short-Circuit Sales, Homeowners Claim," *Wall Street Journal*, December 8, 1993, p. 1B.

[55]Ibid.

[56]Ibid.

[57]M. Feychting and A. Ahlbom, "Magnetic fields and cancer in children residing near Swedish high-voltage power lines," *American Journal of Epidemiology* 7: 467–481, 1993.

[58]Moulder, "Frequently Asked Questions (FAQs) on Power-Frequency Fields and Cancer," v3.1.1, June 19, 1995, *Annotated Bibliography*, p. C19. See also p. C21.

[59]Freedman, p. 1B.

As partial balance, Freedman states that other studies have found no unusual incidence of cancer or other health problems among exposed workers and adds that "no one has figured out how EMFs may cause cancer and how much exposure might be perilous."[60] That reassurance is likely to fall on deaf ears. It can also be interpreted as a "cover-up" by the scientists who failed to "find something" or by the government agency or company that funded the studies and bought off the scientists. By highlighting without qualification one finding that could be a cause for alarm in research emanating from a highly regarded institution, the article has managed to deepen the concern of the average reader and the uncertainty of the homebuyer.

The controversy within the scientific community has significant repercussions for the general public. It would require substantial grounding in physics and biophysics to translate the debate into nontechnical terms. Without such a technical background, the journalists have some excuse for sounding the alarm. Even moderate appraisals, unfortunately, tend to frighten a public already fearful of unseen threats from the environment.

A Moderate View

The *Wall Street Journal* also published an op-ed piece by William R. Bennett Jr., which cast grave doubt on the EMF-cancer connection.[61] Bennett underscores two basic problems with the epidemiologic studies: marginal statistical accuracy—that is, samples too small to produce meaningful results—and susceptibility to systematic error. A disease like childhood leukemia, he notes, is extremely rare. Since there are only a few cases per 100,000 people annually, "it is hard to obtain large enough samples to permit meaningful analysis." A difference of one or two cases between the exposed and the control groups can result in a percentage of incidence of disease high enough to appear significant. "But as the size of the sample groups has increased in these studies, the percentage 'effect' has declined."[62]

Numerous sources of systematic error complicate the matter. Bennett summarizes the major difficulties:

[60]Ibid.

[61]William R. Bennett Jr., "Power Lines Are Homely, Not Hazardous," *Wall Street Journal*, August 10, 1993, p. A10.

[62]Ibid.

The population groups are often of different ages, socioeconomic classes and races. Leukemia primarily attacks older
people and white male children under the age of five. Without sorting the people in the exposed and control groups
according to such categories, the epidemiological data are
not meaningful.

He also underlines two other sources of systematic error, economic
factors and different work environments. Poorer people are often
forced to live next to eyesores such as transformer substations and
transmission lines. In general, they are also more subject to disease.
Studies tend to ignore the "natural tendency" for disease to be
correlated with such locations. (It should be noted, however, that
neither childhood leukemia nor brain cancer is higher in lower socioeconomic groups.)[63] At the same time, "the populations sampled
usually have different work environments and spend unequal
amounts of time in the 'exposed' area." Other risk factors are sometimes ignored. For instance, "If someone spends his working hours
exposed to carcinogenic solvents, it is irrelevant that he lives near
a power line."[64]

Finally, Bennett notes that all studies to date have been retrospective, rather than prospective. A retrospective study is "subject to
the vagaries of individual memory, inaccuracy . . . and personal
prejudice." Most important for an accurate appraisal of any possible
threat, there has been no day-to-day monitoring of "actual individual
exposures to electromagnetic fields." [65]

Bennett reports that the absence of any connections between measured magnetic fields and cancers, as well as the absence of any
theory based on known physical and biological properties to explain
any risk, have led some proponents of such risks to propose a "biological resonance process that magnifies people's sensitivity to magnetic fields . . . triggered by the frequency of power lines." Bennett
dismisses this as a "far-fetched hypothesis" put forward by "alarm-
ists." There exists "No plausible physical explanation for such an

[63]Moulder, electronic transmission, November 26, 1995.
[64]Bennett, "Power Lines Are Homely, Not Hazardous," p. A10.
[65]Ibid.

effect." Moreover, "the resonance explanation could not work simultaneously in the U.S. and Europe, where the power line frequencies are different."[66]

Another Moderate Voice

Moderate voices have been raised elsewhere in the popular press. An issue of *Consumer Reports* devoted to domestic risks carried an extensive report on electromagnetic fields. Although the writer began with a discussion of the Wertheimer-Leeper study, he went on to note: "Neither the original study by Wertheimer and Leeper nor the epidemiological studies that followed have added up to scientific certainty." Laboratory studies had not been very helpful and, in addition, "few of the studies have passed the most basic test of scientific validity, being replicated in somebody else's laboratory."[67]

There was also a reasonable sketch of costs and benefits. The writer suggested that a *"possible* health hazard" justified taking simple steps inside the home to reduce exposure [emphasis in the original]. He noted, however, "The larger dilemma is whether the risks justify making major changes in our huge, complex electric-power system," changes that would be very costly. While citing M. Granger Morgan and the doctrine of "prudent avoidance," the writer did highlight the enormous costs that the precept would impose.[68]

The moderate tone and general balance of the article contrasted with the polemics of Brodeur, who advocates preventive measures, such as burying or rerouting powerlines without consideration of costs.[69]

Costs

There is great uncertainty about the risks—if any—from EMF, but there can be no doubt about the costs, including the money needed for more research and the costs imposed by "prudent avoidance." "Prudence" can cause utility companies to bury power transmission lines and rate payers to pay for them as well as for electrical

---

[66]Ibid.

[67]"Electromagnetic Fields," *Consumer Reports*, p. 354.

[68]Ibid., pp. 354–5.

[69]P. Brodeur, "Department of Amplification: Annals of Radiation," *New Yorker* 66 (November 8, 1990): 134–50.

appliances that have been reengineered (and cost more) to reduce magnetic fields. Beyond "prudence," legal suits seeking recovery for alleged health effects and for far more certain reductions in real estate values, if successful, will increase utility costs and rates even more. Finally, many homeowners will see their principal asset decrease in value.

The Call of the Grant

Wherever there is technical uncertainty, there is a call for yet more research. A workshop sponsored by the Electric Power Research Institute (EPRI), a research group funded primarily by the electrical utilities industry, highlights that approach. The "Introduction" to the published proceedings states:

> In the case of EMF [that is, the implications of EMF for human health], both the epidemiologic evidence and the picture of human exposure are incomplete, the toxicologic studies have been mostly negative, the evidence for cellular damage is weak, and the proposed mechanisms are speculative.[70]

The layman might reasonably conclude that there was little to be gained by pursuing the matter. Wrong! The workshop published nine "Directions for New Research"—research without certain outcomes but certain to require substantial funding.[71]

EPRI has already spent $75 million on research and has plans to spend $50 million more over the next five years. Meanwhile, as already noted, the U.S. Department of Energy has authorized $65 million for the five-year research and public information EMF*RAPID* program to be administered by the National Institute of Environmental Health Sciences.[72]

Expenditures like that are exactly what the APS study did not suggest in its review of existing research. Study after study has failed

[70]Electric Power Research Institute (EPRI), Proceedings: Health Implications of EMF Neural Effects Workshop, May 17–21, 1992, Asilomar Conference Center, Asilomar, Calif.; August 1994: TR-104327; Research Project 2965–99; 2964–06, pp. 1–2.

[71]Ibid., p. iv.

[72]Tekla S. Perry, "Today's View of Magnetic Fields," *IEEE Spectrum* (December 1994): 19. Considering the quality of "public information" thus far provided by sources accessible to the lay reader, there is little hope that the EMF*RAPID* study will settle the issue or allay anxiety.

to resolve the debate; it is unlikely that another thousand or so will do more than spend dollars that might well be put to use elsewhere to greater effect.

Whatever its cost, "research" has an undeniable appeal. Few organizations or people affiliated with them like making decisions, and even fewer like making them when the information is uncertain. Research holds out the promise that issues will be clarified and that any required decisions will be universally justifiable. Even if the research fails to pan out, decisionmakers can put off making definite pronouncements while they wait for more information. In the meantime, delay absolves them of blame. They can never be called to account—they are simply awaiting the next study.

The Costs of "Prudent Avoidance"

"Prudence" has taken on a new coloration in the debate on powerlines. Granger Morgan, head of the department of engineering and public policy at Carnegie Mellon University, first articulated "prudent avoidance" for EMF. It is an apparently commonsense approach that says: We are not too sure of the risk, if there is one, but we should take steps to avoid that risk, however small, if avoidance does not cost too much. Commonsensical or not, it provides little direction for behavior. A person who can force another person to pay for the avoidance is unlikely to show much prudence. One commentary on the issue straddled the policy fence adroitly:

> The fact that evidence exists suggesting enough of a potential problem to warrant further research means doing nothing may not be the best policy. Still there are enough unknowns . . . that spending millions to move power lines may not seem wise, either.[73]

The article then goes on to suggest several instances of actual or potential redesign for items such as electric blankets and video display terminals. The APS summary is far more pointed:

> "Prudent avoidance" would make sense if the ELF risk was documented and some measure of cost-effectiveness could be determined. This is not the case for the alleged adverse effects from ELF/EMF. Since prudent avoidance does not

[73]Ibid.

place a limit on mitigation costs, it allows fear to propel society's institutions to spend more than $1 billion per year ($23 billion in total by 1993). Prudent avoidance runs counter to the prioritization of spending on a cost-effectiveness basis.... [It] essentially states to the public that there is a likely possibility of danger to them and that we should begin to spend money to mitigate the risk, if any.[74]

"Prudent avoidance" thus becomes a convenient cover for vast expenditures. According to the APS, "The vague concept of 'Prudent Avoidance' has been used by at least eleven utility commissions to promulgate regulations on ELF because the science connection between EMF and cancer has not [been] demonstrated."[75] Hafemeister adds:

Thus, prudent avoidance opens the political path for the utilities and other bodies to spend money without a scientific basis for concern.... In our free society, this open-ended, unbounded approach to risk mitigation allows a fearful public to use the threat of litigation to remove the "phantom effect." As long as the rate payers and others will cover the costs, the utilities and others have little incentive to take on litigation in this area.[76]

A later note is even more emphatic:

I agree with the critics of "prudent avoidance" who have call[ed] it "the abandonment of science," "the triumph of fear of the unknown over reason," and "being so vague as to be useless." This makes for regulation by fear and without substance. Prudent avoidance is a delight for plaintiff lawyers since it is essentially a conclusion that the danger is probable.[77]

State utility commissions have responded. They are now pressuring utility companies to reduce exposures. In 1993, for example, the California Public Utilities Commission required utilities "'to reduce the existence of [electromagnetic fields] through the implementation

---

[74]APS Background Paper, II.6, p. 5–6.
[75]APS Background Paper, VII.1, p. 8.
[76]Ibid., pp. 8–9.
[77]Ibid., p. 10.

236

of no-cost or low-cost steps,'" defined as 4 percent of the total cost of a budgeted project.[78] It is difficult to translate 4 percent into "no-cost" or even "low-cost" measures, but the commission may have access to other definitions. An article in an engineering society journal claims that design changes can be implemented "at little cost in new construction" but provides no figures.[79]

Regulation at the state level is now firmly in place and federal regulation may not be far behind. Counties in eight states—Montana, Maine, New Jersey, New York, North Dakota, Oregon, Illinois, and Florida—have imposed limits on the electrical fields associated with transmission line rights-of-way. Florida and New York have also adopted magnetic field strength limits, and such limits are pending in New Jersey.[80]

The response to EMF stands as a paradigm of the public response to risk. Insistence on the impossible—that is, the absence of risk—leads to tolerance for the irrational and to policies that have little in common except fear and escalating budgets.

Should the country be spending large sums of public money on a vague menace? Resources are finite; research on power-frequency fields bids fair to be an insatiable drain on public and private funds.

It is instructive to examine the position of the National Electricity Safety Board of Stockholm, Sweden, enunciated in 1994.

> Our current knowledge about how magnetic fields affect humans is not sufficient. We therefore do not have sufficient grounds to determine limit values. But the suspicions of a connection between magnetic fields and cancer are such that we recommend a certain caution. Therefore . . . *if such can be done within reasonable costs* [emphasis added], strive to design and/or place new power lines and electrical facilities so that magnetic fields are limited. . . .
>
> In our society we must constantly evaluate how much money we shall invest in health and the environment. . . . As far as we know today, magnetic fields from power lines could cause

[78]Perry, p. 22.

[79]Ibid.

[80]William R. Hendee and John C. Boteler, "The Question of Health Effects from Exposure to Electromagnetic Fields," *Health Physics* 66 (February 1994): 132.

> two cases of childhood leukemia per year [in Sweden]. The
> costs to eliminate those eventual cases are very large.[81]

Here is prudent avoidance again; but it is somewhat balanced by recognition that the risk will affect very few people or, perhaps, no one. However tragic those few cases, funds are limited. Acting prudently means considering the greater good for the greater number of people.

It is worth noting that Florida's magnetic field limits, established in 1989, were "based on what existing technology can meet, not on health data," according to an official of the state's Department of Environmental Regulation. In other words, the fear of liability, fueled by public anxiety, drives the standards, rather than an objectively evaluated menace to public health. That fear is also driving up costs in states that have imposed limits.[82] In addition, such "technology-based" standards, not uncommon in environmental health regulations, leave unaddressed the issue of whether those technology-based limits are protecting the public from any harm at all.

Professor Hafemeister has little patience with such an expedient. Taking issue with Morgan and "prudent avoidance," he notes that Morgan "seems to have placed great reliance on well-known discredited work . . . has failed to examine the risk factors by type of cancer, an approach which shows glaring inconsistencies. Lastly, his writings should be updated to take into account the new work of Savitz and others." Morgan is held responsible for increasing public fears: "Morgan's [sic] is concerned that public perceptions may drive regulations rather than scientific fact, but yet I conclude that it is his own papers which have pushed the ELF-risk process away from science and towards irrationality."[83]

What *Does* It Cost?

Projected costs would alarm even the casual reader. Without considering attempts to reduce the ELF[84] fields from appliances within

---

[81]Moulder, electronic transmission, July 20, 1995, pp. 3–4. Moulder was kind enough to supply a translation of the statement by the Swedish government.

[82]Karen Fitzgerald, "Part 2: Societal Reverberations" in "Electromagnetic Fields: The Jury's Still Out," *IEEE Spectrum* (August 1990): 28.

[83]APS, Background Paper, VII.1, pp. 9–10.

[84]Bennett, *Health and Low-Frequency Electromagnetic Fields*, pp. 165–6. ELF, or extremely low frequency, fields are defined by international convention as within the band from 30 to 300 Hertz (Hz). A Hertz is itself a unit of frequency: 1 Hz = 1 cycle per second.

the home, which are considered in the next section, one study calculates the following mitigation costs:

- $90,000/mile for delta design above-ground transmission lines to reduce magnetic fields by 45 percent
- $2 million/mile to bury transmission lines in fluid-filled steel pipe to reduce magnetic fields by 99 percent
- $1 billion to limit magnetic fields to 10 mG (milliGauss) at edges of rights-of-way for planned new transmission lines
- $3 billion to $9 billion to reduce magnetic fields at homes where grounding systems are the dominant source
- $200 billion to bury transmission lines nationwide near homes with fields greater than 1 mG
- $250 billion to reduce average exposure to less than 2 mG from all transmission and distribution lines[85]

The Missouri Public Service Company has made its own estimates. Reconfiguring a 345-kV line would cost about $200,000 per kilometer for the simplest above-ground method and $1.5 million per kilometer for the most effective option, underground pipes.[86] Even in a world long accustomed to billion dollar budgets and trillion dollar debts, expenditures of such magnitude raise questions.

Domestic Exposure

Scientific debate aside, "prudent avoidance" has an ironic ring because it is literally impossible to avoid exposure. To begin with, the only effect magnetic fields are known to cause in the human body is the generation of electrical currents. Electrical currents, however, occur naturally in the body, and Bennett states that "In some cells of the body, these fields can be millions of times greater than those resulting from power lines."[87] Moreover, "the Earth's magnetic field is hundreds of times larger than any power distribution line field at ground level. Riding a bicycle or driving an open car through the

---

[85]APS Background Paper, VII.5, "GAO ELF Mitigation Costs," pp. 12–13. The paper is citing a publication of the General Accounting Office, "Electromagnetic Fields," GAO/RCED-94-115.

[86]Perry, p. 22.

[87]Bennett, "Power Lines Are Homely, Not Hazardous," p. A10.

Earth's magnetic field creates at least as much electric field inside the body as do power lines."[88]

A power-frequency magnetic field in excess of 5 G is necessary to induce electrical currents of a magnitude similar to those that occur naturally in the body. The fields within the right-of-way of a high-voltage transmission line can approach 100 mG (0.1 G), 50 times below the level needed to induce similar currents in the body, and the fields fall off sharply with distance. Even 10 meters from a distribution line, fields will be 2 to 10 mG, far below the 5 G needed to induce currents equivalent to those that occur naturally in the human body; at the edge of a high-voltage transmission right-of-way, the fields will be between 1 and 10 mG.[89]

Since it is so generally ignored, it is worth re-emphasizing the point made at the beginning of this chapter concerning relative exposures from transmission and distribution lines. Given the characteristics of electric and magnetic fields, "electric distribution systems [the lines running into houses, which are generally low-voltage but carry a high current load] account for a far higher proportion of the population's exposure to magnetic fields than the larger and more obvious high-voltage transmission lines" [which hang from high metal towers].[90] Bennett was right: the giant lines are "homely, not hazardous."

Moreover, everyday activities, such as riding a commuter train, can produce high levels of exposure. Bennett reports the Amtrak Metroliner from Washington to New York generated "peak fields of up to 646 mG [approximately one-eighth of the 5 G necessary to induce electrical currents equivalent to those occurring naturally in the body] ... inside the train at sporadic intervals of one or two minutes duration, with an average value over a four-and-half-hour trip of 126 mG." A different wiring arrangement on the New York-New Haven run reduced peak fields "to only about 300 mG, with an average value over the whole two-hour trip of about 35 mG."[91] Elsewhere, the fields were lower: "Apart from electrified railroads,

[88]Ibid.

[89]Moulder and Foster, "Biological Effects of Power-Frequency Fields," pp. 310–11; Moulder, FAQs, 3.1.1, question 10.

[90]Ibid., p. 310. See also Bennett, "Power Lines Are Homely, Not Hazardous," p. A10.

[91]Bennett, *Health and Low-Frequency Electromagnetic Fields*, p. 45.

magnetic fields of larger than 10 mG were seldom encountered in normal travel except under high-voltage transmission lines."[92] For those still nervous about EMF, flying would seem to be the safest mode of travel. Commuters, of course, have little choice. In fact, it may be a Hobson's choice in any case, since flying would increase exposure to ionizing radiation.

Fields within homes vary from more than 1 G a few inches from certain appliances to less than 0.2 mG well away from those appliances. Activists who claim that a level above 2 to 3 mG is dangerous generally ignore the magnetic fields created by such household appliances as toasters or vacuum cleaners, which produce some of the highest levels of exposure. The fields from appliances fall off very rapidly with distance, so a few centimeters means a substantial drop. A coffeemaker generates a magnetic field of 230 mG at a distance of 2 centimeters (cm), 90 mG at 4 cm, and 26 mG at 10 cm. At the same distances, an electric can opener generates a field of 12,400 mG, 10,400 mG, and 2,080 mG, respectively.[93] Thus, homes miles away from high-voltage transmission lines exhibit power-frequency fields by virtue of the electricity residents use—yet residents seem reluctant to ascribe ill effects to their blenders.

Compare these everyday exposures of hundreds and thousands of mG with fields approaching 100 mG within the right-of-way of a high-voltage transmission line. Brewing coffee takes only a few minutes but produces about the same level of exposure; opening a can with an electric can opener produces far higher exposures during the time of operation; other appliances in the home generate magnetic fields of varying strengths and duration. However, the comparison to 100 mG within the right-of-way is not the reasonable one; the reasonable comparison is with the much weaker fields farther from the right-of-way of a transmission line. The typical exposures at the edges of rights-of-way are 1 to 10 mG. By that analysis, exposures from transmission lines have little effect on total exposures.

[92]Ibid., p. 56.

[93]Alix M. Freedman, "The Gaussmeter: A Hot New Gadget," *Wall Street Journal*, December 8, 1993, p. E1. See also Moulder, FAQs, 3.1.1, question 10; Bennett, *Health and Low-Frequency Electromagnetic Fields*, pp. 61, 62, 64–65. Bennett's Table 2.8, listing domestic magnetic fields, is particularly helpful.

Even occupational exposures, such as those sustained by arc welders and electrical cable splicers, are relatively low. Although occupational exposures in excess of 1 G (1,000 mG) have been reported, typical mean exposures range from 5 to 40 mG, again far below the level needed to induce electrical currents of a magnitude similar to those found naturally in the body and little different from those of other individuals.[94]

The Effect on Property Values: Risk Perception and the Homebuyer

Nowhere has the effect of the EMF controversy been shown so clearly as in the pricing of homes. Clarifications and reassurances have failed to dissipate the fog of fear surrounding the powerlines. As one commentator noted:

> After years of agitation, it no longer matters if you and all the Ph.Ds in the nation believe that there's no danger to the occupants of your house from the electromagnetic fields of a nearby power transmission line. You will find it hard, perhaps even impossible, to sell it. And you may find it hard to dismiss the temptation to sue somebody to make good your loss.[95]

That analysis has the sad ring of truth.

An expert can dismiss the alarm surrounding power-frequency lines as an "electromagnetic hoax," but the popular impression of risk continues.[96] Why should that be so? There may be a general mistrust of large companies, such as the electric utilities, and of government agencies. Fear of involuntarily imposed risk undoubtedly adds to the concern. The reports and studies circulated in the scientific community are poorly disseminated among the general public and, even more important, poorly understood. That is particularly unfortunate since they are generally reassuring. The result, however, is ongoing tension between fear of exposure to an

---

[94]Moulder and Foster, pp. 310, 311; Moulder, FAQs 3.1.1, questions 8, 10.
[95]Donlan, p. 38.
[96]Bennett, "Power Lines Are Homely, Not Hazardous," p. A10.

unknown peril and "society's need to have reliable electric power and electric products at an affordable price."[97]

One sign of widespread anxiety is the popularity of the Gaussmeter, a hand-held measuring device that provides a digital readout of the strength of magnetic fields. The Gaussmeter has become a popular item in the consumer market, despite its price ($200 to $600) and the difficulty of interpreting the readings. When even experts have problems, homebuyers are likely to find themselves at sea.

Costs have been mounting. One real estate analyst estimated recently that "electrophobia" was costing the country some $1 billion annually in reduced property values, higher electricity rates, and litigation expenses.[98] Florig makes clear that losses in property values, delays in constructing needed transmission and distribution lines, shielding of workers, and reconfigurations of household appliances may push that figure much higher in the future. He finds such ad hoc responses costly and suggests that additional research to settle the issue might be economically justified.[99]

Just how difficult the uncertainty can make the search for a home is seen better through anecdote than statistics. The account of the search conducted by one homebuying couple illustrates the problem.[100]

Although Palo Alto, California, is considered expensive, even for the Bay Area, the couple in question thought the city particularly desirable because of its schools and were willing to stretch their finances to purchase a home. After several disappointments, they found an affordable property. There was one catch: looming over its 8-foot-high side fence was a 20-foot-high power substation. The house itself was larger and more attractive than anything else in their price range. A comparison with a house down the street, well away from the substation, suggested the reason. The proximity of the substation, they estimated, meant an asking price $40,000 to $50,000 lower than that of the roughly comparable property.

---

[97]H. Keith Florig, "Containing the Costs of the EMF Problem," *Science* 257 (July 24, 1992): 468. Florig takes care to define the sociopolitical and ethical concerns underlying the debate.

[98]"Electromagnetic Fields," *Consumer Reports*, p. 354.

[99]Florig, p. 488.

[100]The couple, friends of the author, requested anonymity.

This couple was unusual. Both had graduated from a technical university and were willing to explore. They read articles, but none of the research dealt with magnetic-field levels below 1 mG. They consulted friends, even checked out a Gaussmeter from the city. The readings were low. The substation, being new, had been built to minimize magnetic fields. Fields in most of the yard measured between 1 mG and 2 mG—in most of the house, 0.5 or 0.6 mG. Measurements in other houses on the market were around 0.2 or 0.3 mG, not a great difference.

In the foregoing case, knowledge was of little help. The couple's conclusion records their puzzlement:

> So after two weeks of fairly thorough investigation, we had no idea how bad it was to live next to that power substation. We did not know how risky it would be for children. We did not know whether or not electromagnetic fields were ever a health threat. We didn't even know if we should buy any house without borrowing a gauss meter to check it out first.

The couple found a reasonably priced house in a slightly less convenient area of the city. At the time of this writing, the listing on the house located next to the power substation had expired. Roughly comparable homes in the neighborhood have sold for more than its asking price.

The Effect on Property Values: Risk and the Courts

Florig estimates a $1 billion loss for properties near enough to transmission lines to have EMF levels that exceed typical household background values.[101] That is an easy-to-remember number in thinking about the possible costs of the EMF scare, but it is only an estimate. The effect on property values of the uncertainty surrounding power-frequency fields has yet to be fully determined. There is "anecdotal evidence and on-going litigation" but "very little hard data." In other words—and greatly complicating cost estimates—for some time to come, the perception of risk is likely to prove of greater importance than any number of studies, whether or not they support the perception. As Moulder notes, "If buyers start requesting

[101]Florig, p. 469.

magnetic field measurements, no telling what will happen, particularly since measurements are difficult to do and even more difficult to interpret."[102]

In the courts, that perception of risk has often proved persuasive, bolstering the claim for damages as compensation for lost property value. In a landmark California case, *San Diego Gas & Electric Company v. Daley*, the U.S. Court of Appeals, Fourth District, affirmed the decision of the lower court, concluding:

> The trial court here was correct . . . that the truth or lack of truth in whether electromagnetic projections caused a health hazard to humans or animals was immaterial. Rather the question was whether the fear of the danger existed and would affect market value.
>
> . . . . In the final analysis, we are concerned only with market value. Although these studies [referred to in the trial] may show objectively the complete safety of these structures, we are not convinced that certain segments of the buying public may not remain apprehensive of these high voltage lines, and therefore might be unwilling to pay as much for the property as they otherwise would.[103]

In other words, public fear, even if unreasonable, can lead to a loss in property value and that loss is entitled to compensation. The court awarded Daley damages and litigation expenses.

A dozen states and the 6th U.S. Circuit have adopted the majority view espoused in that case, creating shock waves in the utility industry. New cases alleging EMF liability are being filed at the rate of about one per month, signaling not only the aversion to risk of many consumers but the eagerness of attorneys in a litigious society to file claims. There are thousands of circuit miles of high-voltage transmission lines in the United States and an additional 12,600 miles are scheduled for construction before the year 2000 to service new generating plants and the growth in demand.[104] As a result, the

---

[102]Moulder, FAQs 2.5, part 4, question 28, May 12, 1994, pp. 3–4.

[103]*San Diego Gas & Electric v. Daley*, 253 Cal. Reporter. Reptr. 144 (Cal. App. 4 Dist. 1988), pp. 152–3. The case was argued and won on the grounds of eminent domain, since the utility had in fact condemned part of Daley's property. It was not, therefore, a victory for the "takings" clause of the Fifth Amendment.

[104]Florig, p. 469.

number of workers and the numbers of children and adults in residences who are exposed to moderately increased EMF levels will inevitably rise and with those numbers, quite probably, the incidence of litigation.

Later Developments

Recent decisions may be moderating the rush to adopt the policy enunciated in *Daley*. In one case, a California Superior Court judge ruled that electromagnetic fields from high-voltage electric lines near three San Clemente homes had not affected property values. Evidently relying on previous case law, the homeowners had argued that "mere perception" of a possible health hazard had lowered the values of their homes. The judge disagreed, ruling that the lines did not represent a "condemnation" or "taking" of the properties for which the utility would be required to pay condemnation.[105] Although the case is being appealed, San Diego Gas & Electric, the defendant, as well as the utilities industry as a whole, see the decision as a possible new trend in EMF litigation.

On the occupational front, a recent case, *Pilisuk v. Seattle City Light*, merits attention as "the first 'EMF' worker's compensation case to be fully litigated against an electric utility." Moreover, the issue of causation was "directly addressed in a situation where there was unquestioned occupational exposure."[106]

Robert Pilisuk, an apprentice and electrician-constructor with Seattle City Light, died of leukemia in 1989. His widow sued for a pension on behalf of herself and the claimant's beneficiaries on the grounds that his occupational exposure to "electromagnetic radiation" had led to his cancer. The Department of Labor and Industries denied her suit. The appeal resulted in lengthy testimony to determine whether Pilisuk's employment had been the proximate cause of his cancer.

Witnesses testified that the associations in epidemiologic studies between electrical occupations and leukemia were weak and that laboratory studies did not support such a link. The witnesses stated

[105]Walt Albro, "EMFs Don't Affect Property Values, Court Rules," *Realtor News*, June 6, 1994, p. 4.

[106]John E. Moulder, summary of *Pilisuk v. Seattle City Light*, electronic transmission available from ftp.//ftp.mcw.edu/pub/emf-and-cancer. All quotations refer to this electronic transmission.

that laboratory studies show EMF causes some biological effects in cells, but there is no necessary connection between those effects and leukemia. Moulder gave several examples of substances that cause biological effects in cells but are not health hazards. Finally, several witnesses asserted that "EMF is not involved in the initiation of leukemia." Nor is it a promoter. The court affirmed the original decision.

Although those decisions may be sending a hopeful signal to the utilities, they are weak reeds, too fragile to support major policy decisions. Faced with the possibility of escalating litigation, ballooning insurance costs, and additional costly regulation, many utilities are opting for "prudent avoidance." They are reconnecting phases on certain transmission lines so that magnetic fields partially cancel each other out and reconfiguring others. They are also carefully weighing alternative possibilities in siting new lines or cranking up the current on already existing circuits. These efforts are ongoing, although studies in which measurements of magnetic fields were made show no associations even close to significant between the fields and cancer rates. For new transmission and distribution lines, they have become more willing to consider burying the cables, although the cost is astronomical, 2 to 10 times that of overhead lines.[107]

That figure may be too low, according to specialists in the field. But such an expenditure may be good public relations. Buried wires are closer together, so burying does reduce fields because it causes phase cancellation.[108] Given the never-ending controversy, the utilities may be willing to shoulder the cost and, in due course, pass the cost onto the rate payer. A competitive market has so far kept them from doing so, but there are no guarantees for the future.

Practical Consequences

What does the uncertainty mean to the homeowner? If the amount of land deemed suitable for development shrinks, the price of homes will rise—a straightforward function of supply and demand. By the same token, as the demand for electricity rises but anxiety impedes the construction of new high-voltage transmission lines, limiting

[107]Fitzgerald, p. 31.
[108]Moulder, electronic transmission, November 26, 1995.

power delivery, supply will be constricted, costs will rise, and outages will become more common. It may take several years for rates to rise enough to become apparent to consumers, who generally think of electricity as a low-cost utility. Nevertheless, those higher rates will surely materialize unless the problems created by perceived risk are resolved.[109]

Without a clear-sighted appraisal of risk, resolution is likely to be difficult. While public awareness of the possible hazards posed by high-voltage lines has been increasing, the demand for electricity has been increasing as well. Despite the potential risk, consumers seem happy with their air conditioners, their microwaves and power mowers, and even, to some extent, with homes built almost in the shadow of powerlines. Although the unaesthetic appearance of the lines and the noise attendant on transmission make such properties less attractive, they are also lower in price than comparable homes situated elsewhere. Those willing to accept the drawbacks may feel that they have found a bargain. Knowing, however, that such a house may be difficult to resell, they may hesitate, as did the couple in Palo Alto.

Gas and electric bills, however, are unlikely to remain constant. Increased costs for utilities aiming at "prudent avoidance" will certainly push rates—and with them utility bills—higher for everybody, renters as well as homeowners. The expense of litigation, the payment of damages, and increased costs for insurance,[110] coupled with the cost of more expensive technologies, such as burying powerlines or reconfiguring the flows of current, will inevitably squeeze homeowners, unless they are willing to forgo modern appliances, return to candles, and adopt an "early-to-bed, early-to-rise" pattern of living.

The only recourse would seem to be an informed skepticism regarding the potential risks of exposure, coupled with a knowledgeable appraisal of the forces at work in the market. Unless a report

---

[109]The situation is particularly true if the increased cost affects secondary products that are power intensive, such as aluminum.

[110]Most utilities are self-insured for the first several million dollars of liability, above which they obtain excess liability coverage. The insurance structure may change in the future. In any case, the prospect of paying huge sums in damage claims will induce a prudent utility to increase its reserve fund—and its rates. See Roy W. Krieger, "On the Line," *ABA Journal* (January 1994): 45.

appears in a peer-reviewed scientific journal, the consumer should view it with reservations. Even articles in peer-reviewed journals may be flawed. Another decade or two of research may clarify the picture, but the homebuyer and the homeowner must make their decisions now.

If the perception of risk is likely to make selling a home difficult, then buying elsewhere, even at an increase in cost, may be prudent. Buyers who can ignore the aesthetic drawbacks and the noise of powerlines and substations may find that they can afford a slightly larger house with more amenities than they could otherwise. Transmission lines are highly visible so there is little risk of concealment. Much easier to conceal are other sources of high electromagnetic fields, such as distribution lines, ground currents, and old wiring. Those are typically products of high population density. In urban areas the buyer may wish to consult the local utility company before making a decision: most utility companies will be able to sketch the configuration of powerlines and estimate exposures. They will also loan Gaussmeters or make the measurements themselves. The final choice, however, as always, must be the consumer's.

The EMF/ELF debate highlights a philosophical issue central to controversies over real and putative hazards. How safe is "safe?" An unrealistic insistence on absolute safety, coupled with reliance on science to provide certainty, fuels all such debates. Moulder and Foster have looked into the future, and they are not sanguine about an early end to scare, uncertainty, and effects on housing:

> Public concern about electricity and cancer will continue either until future research shows that the fields are hazardous (an outcome we personally consider unlikely), or until the public learns that science cannot provide absolute guarantees that anything is absolutely safe (an outcome, unfortunately, that we consider equally unlikely).[111]

An understanding of the limits of science, the omnipresence of risk, and a willingness to accept the tradeoffs between hazard and safety imposed by everyday life may have positive effects on our psychological health and our budgets. The current, vague climate of anxiety is detrimental to both.

[111]Moulder and Foster, p. 321.

Appendix

The study of electric and magnetic fields is a well-established but highly technical academic discipline. A brief outline of the field may serve as a helpful postscript to the analysis. The electromagnetic (EM) energy associated with powerlines is part of the EM spectrum, all parts of which are characterized by their frequency or wavelength. The two are related: as the frequency rises, the wavelength shortens. Powerlines operate at low frequencies, so their wavelengths are thousands of miles long. Frequency is the rate at which the EM field changes direction and is usually given in Hertz (Hz), one Hz being one cycle per second. Since power-frequency fields in the United States vary 60 times per second, they are 60-Hz fields and have a wavelength of 3,000 miles; powerlines in most of the rest of the world operate at frequencies of 50 cycles per second or 50 Hz. Those extremely low frequency (ELF) fields are the type generated by most powerlines.[112]

The interaction of biological material with an EM source depends on the frequency of the source, so the EM spectrum falls into four divisions in terms of potential biological effects. The first or ionizing portion covers the very high frequencies typified by ultraviolet light and X-rays, which can cause direct damage because the EM particles or photons have enough energy to break chemical bonds. Such ionizing radiation is capable of breaking bonds in the DNA, the genetic material of the cell, killing cells or causing mutations or cancers. Ultraviolet light can also cause direct damage to tissues, as commonly demonstrated by sunburned children. Frequencies below those of X-rays and ultraviolet light—that is, the nonionizing portion of the EM spectrum—do not damage DNA because the photons lack the energy needed to break chemical bonds. Those are the frequencies generated by powerlines.[113] Given the widespread perception of risk, the point is worth emphasis.

The nonionizing portion of the EM spectrum itself falls into three categories. In the first, that of visible and infrared light, photon energy creates electronic excitation rather than ionization; in the second portion—that of microwaves, for example—the wavelength is smaller than that of the body but can induce weak electrical currents and cause heating. Power frequencies occupy the last category of the nonionizing spectrum. Their wavelength is much larger than that of the body, and heating via induced currents seldom occurs.[114]

A further distinction is made between radiation and fields, both of which can be produced by sources of EM energy. Radiation travels away from its source and continues to exist even if the source is turned off. In contrast,

[112]Ibid., p. 310.

[113]Ibid., p. 311.

[114]Ibid., p. 310. See also, Moulder, FAQs 3.1.1, question 3, June 19, 1995.

some electric and magnetic fields near an EM source are not projected into space and cease to exist when the energy source is turned off. The fact that exposure to powerlines occurs at distances that are much shorter than the wavelength of 50- or 60-Hz radiation has important implications, because under such conditions (called "near-field"), the electric and magnetic fields can be considered to be independent entities. That is in contrast to EM radiation, in which the electric and magnetic fields are inextricably linked. To be an effective source of EM radiation, an antenna must have a length comparable to its wavelength, and powerlines are clearly too short to be effective radiation sources. For all practical purposes, therefore, radiation from powerlines can be ignored; if there are biological effects, they are due to the magnetic fields, not to the nonionizing radiation.

If the electric and magnetic fields associated with power-frequency lines cannot break bonds because the energy per photon is too low and because these fields cannot cause electronic excitation or heating, it would seem reasonable to conclude that power-frequency fields were unlikely to cause biological effects. Could strong ELF magnetic fields set in motion more subtle biophysical mechanisms? Three such mechanisms have been proposed: induced electric currents, direct effects on magnetic biological material, and effects on rates of certain chemical reactions. The objection to induced currents noted previously—that they would be too small to cause notable biological effects—applies to the other two as well. In other words, "when quantitatively analyzed all these mechanisms are found to require fields in tissue that far exceed the fields that are induced by typical environmental exposures."[115] Reasoned analysis, however, seems to have little to do with the emotional controversy over the putative health effects of EMFs.

[115]Ibid., p. 318.

5. Haunted Housing: An Epidemic of Anxiety

The homebuyer's lot is not a happy one. Preoccupied with down payments, bridge loans, mortgage rates, termite inspections, and closing costs, the last thing homebuyers need is reports of cancer risk associated with radon, asbestos, and power fields (electromagnetic fields, EMFs) and the much publicized neurological risks from lead. But buyers do hear or read those reports, which too often create a climate of fear and recrimination.

Mortgage companies and brokerage firms may stress a home as essential to happiness and family life—"a man's home is his castle" goes the saying—but confronted with lengthy disclosure forms about risk after risk, homebuyers may feel as though they are embarking on a trip through a minefield when they inspect a house before purchase. Each new report of risk in housing adds to an "epidemic of anxiety"[1] that can be no less frightening than an actual plague.

This chapter revisits and underlines some of the uncertainty that underlies the science used to justify the campaigns against radon, asbestos, power-frequency fields, and lead. The term "uncertainty" is used so often that it has lost most of whatever effect it might once have had, but it is appropriate here. Time after time and for threat after threat, the evidence for toxic effects is based on extrapolation from measured effects—diseases and deaths—in highly exposed populations.

Efforts to demonstrate those effects in people exposed to the far lower levels that characterize housing fail to show increases in disease or death. In fact, the studies that are done and that could

---

[1]Gary Taubes, "Epidemiology Faces Its Limits," *Science* 269 (July 14, 1995): pp. 164–69. Taubes cites Lewis Thomas as the originator of the phrase "epidemic of anxiety."

possibly be done about residential exposure cannot detect the predicted tiny effects, if they occurred, or disprove them. The studies lack power because they are not nearly large enough. It would require studies of a magnitude far beyond what can be funded and managed to verify the estimated risks if those risks are to be translated into human harm. For instance, a study of tens of thousands of people with lung cancer would be necessary to verify the estimated lung cancer risk from indoor radon (see chapter 1). Such large studies are too expensive to contemplate and, even if funded, they would present major management problems.

Despite agreement that the results of studies of residential risks will be inconclusive, such studies go on all the time, usually supported by government funds. What happens to the results of such studies depends on what results are obtained. *By chance,* even if there is no connection between residential exposure and disease, the results of some studies will suggest a linkage. When that happens, the newspapers and television pour out stories of cancer risks from asbestos, EMF, or radon or stories about damaged IQ from lead. Other studies that find no indication of a linkage receive less attention. The homebuyer without the benefit of specialized knowledge can be left adrift between the publicized studies that "found an association" and those that did not.

In practice, the positive studies—those that suggest exposure to a risk has increased disease or death rates—are accompanied by such nostrums as "better safe than sorry" or "you can't prove it's not a risk" to justify taking action to reduce exposures. Lost in that common equation is the very real possibility that the risk does not translate into actual harm.

The homebuyer's lot is further complicated because a number of biases contribute to the number of positive studies and the publicity that they receive. Most scientists are reluctant to undertake studies that they know in advance are too small or otherwise compromised so that they will provide no clear answer. As a result, it is likely that scientists who undertake such studies believe or hope that the risk is actually higher than predicted and that the study will detect it. Professor John Graham, director of the Harvard Center for Risk Analysis, made that point when he said, "A lot of us scientists have motivations, as we build our careers, to exaggerate a particular possible cause of cancer that we're advancing as our own scientific hypothesis."[2] Scientists have many reasons to try to tease something dramatic from their data. For one thing, a study that "finds something" is far easier to publish than one that does not. For another, funding, especially from government agencies, is far more likely to flow to an investigator whose study "found something."[3] After all, doesn't that study need to be followed up with one that is bigger or more elaborate? Still another reason is the professional recognition that comes from publication and funding.

The source of funding can play a major role in the media's treatment of a study, which, in turn, largely determines whether the public will hear about it. In general, funding sources can be divided among government, industry, and environmental organizations. The media usually treat federally funded studies and federal-agency-endorsed studies respectfully. In addition, those studies can be promoted by the agencies, increasing the chances that the public will learn of them.

In contrast, industry-supported scientists are often viewed as hired hands at the beck and call of their paymasters. Inspection of the literature shows that to be untrue. Many of the epidemiologic studies that identified human risks in high-exposure occupational situations were industry sponsored, and the pages of occupational medicine journals are full of reports of studies conducted by "company docs." Industry has also sponsored some of the most important laboratory studies about risk. For instance, industry scientists conducted the single animal experiment that is the basis of almost every estimate of human cancer risk from dioxin. Nevertheless, industry-sponsored science is sometimes viewed with suspicion, and it is still tarred by some companies' compliance in covering up the consequences of workplace exposure to high levels of asbestos.

Other scientists receive funding from environmental organizations such as the Environmental Defense Fund or the Natural Resources Defense Council to conduct original research, to write reviews of the scientific literature, or to prepare position papers for the public or government agencies. The motives of scientists who receive support from environmental organizations are far less often called into question than are those of scientists who receive industry support. But

[2]John Graham, comments on NBC-TV, "Dateline," August 20, 1996.
[3]Steven Milloy, *Science without Sense* (Washington: Cato Institute, 1995), pp. 3–4.

both groups, being human, are subject to the pressures and tantaliz-ing inducements that Dr. Graham sees as sometimes affecting all scientists who investigate human risks.

Because motives are beyond the boundaries of this book, let us simply call this a draw. The more important point is that studies should neither be accepted nor rejected because of who funded them. Better to remain agnostic about an unexamined study than to toss it aside because of its source of funding.

The Role of Epidemiology

The source for all the information about the threats considered in this book is epidemiology. Epidemiology is the study of the distribu-tion of human diseases and their precursors. Epidemiologists played a major role in determining the causes of infectious diseases, and, in recent years, many have investigated possible connections between disease and chemicals and energy sources in the general environ-ment and in the workplace.

Studies of "environmental" exposure, such as occurs in the home, are investigations of rare events. As already mentioned, many of those risks are so small that no study can be devised to detect them. And no matter how carefully structured, some studies "will inevitably generate false positive and false negative results."[4] Media put out by journals and research institutions tend to publicize the positive findings, and the popular press reports them uncritically. Thus a study reporting a link between EMF and cancer reaches a wide audience. The results of the next study may point in the oppo-site direction, but the public is less likely to hear of it; even if it does, many people will only remember the first and scary outcome. In any case, journalists are rarely savvy enough or have enough time or space to suggest caution in interpreting the two studies.

Public Relations: The Media

The media uncritically repeat such administrative pronounce-ments as EPA's assertion that radon causes up to 30,000 deaths per year and thus stoke the flames of congressional outrage and public fear. Reporters generally lack scientific expertise; they are under pressure to make their news timely, and they find it easier to echo

[4]Taubes, p. 164.

the declarations of government agencies than to check other sources. Thus only one writer bothered to dig out the facts during the panic over asbestos in the New York City school system and found, of course, that the alarm was unwarranted. His report went all but unnoticed while the paper supposedly synonymous with journalistic integrity, the *New York Times*, chose not to publish a letter from some preeminent scientists that would have lessened the alarm. After all, bad news sells better than good.

Not to be outdone, the agencies, particularly the EPA, have learned how to manipulate the media. Thus we had alarmist ads showing a skeletal child in its mother's lap as a warning against the alleged dangers of radon and large posters in Washington, D.C., Metro stations giving an 800 number to call for information on RADON. As far as the public is concerned, rational risk analysis is all but nonexistent. As a result, the citizen is left little choice between alarm and apathy.

Perhaps because some members of the media have had time to reflect and to learn more about environmental scares, some of which affect housing, a skeptical eye is being brought to bear on reporting. In 1994, John Stossel of ABC News produced a special[5] that featured clips of a newsman reporting on environmental scares in the 1970s and 1980s. Stossel was that newsman, and his pointing to himself as an uncritical reporter in the past made his 1994 exposure of overblown fears that much more dramatic. Two years later, NBC's "Dateline"[6] broadcast a segment about environmental causes of cancer, and it too featured clips of old news shows that had uncritically reported various environmental scares.

Such revelations by major networks indicate that some news people are willing to treat "environmental news" with the same skepticism that is supposed to greet all news. Will that happen? Increased skepticism would benefit homebuyers as they confront the well-publicized risks that complicate obtaining a house. But it may be that revelations of past credulity will be but a tiny bump in the well-paved road of uncritical reporting.

[5]"Are We Scaring Ourselves to Death?" produced by John Stossel, ABC News, April 22, 1994.

[6]NBC-TV, "Dateline," August 20, 1996.

What to Believe?

According to epidemiologists interviewed for an article in *Science* magazine, convincing studies have to show "a very strong association between disease and risk factor and a highly plausible biological mechanism." A number of epidemiologists, some of whom had published erroneous results in the past, "say it is so easy to be fooled that it is almost impossible to believe less-than-stunning results."[7]

There are two general methods of investigating the strength of an association, both of which figure prominently in the *Science* article. The first is "statistical significance," which refers to statistical analyses designed to estimate the possibility that the connection between exposure and effect could have occurred by chance. The epidemiologists interviewed for the article worried that the tests could be deceiving because it is literally impossible to be aware of and to guard against all the factors in a study that could contribute to a false-positive finding. Simply stated, they were not certain that the criteria for statistical significance are sufficiently rigorous. Against that background, the EPA decision to eliminate statistical significance as a criterion in its evaluation of epidemiologic studies[8] about environmental causes of cancer[9] appears to be a further attempt to allow the agency to pick and choose results that it likes.

The second method for judging the strength of an association in an epidemiologic study is to examine the magnitude of the relative risk that exists between the exposure and the effect. Many of the scientists interviewed for the *Science* article insisted that effects observed in exposed populations need to be three or four times higher than those observed in unexposed populations (that is, the relative risks must be 3 or 4 or more) to be convincing. Few of the studies that the EPA relies on to point to risks from radon, asbestos, EMF, or lead achieve that criterion. Application of that criterion would reveal EPA estimates of the risks from residential exposure to be a house of cards.

Sometimes several different studies of a possible exposure-effects relationship detect small relative risks or produce some results that

[7]Taubes, p. 168.

[8]Milloy, "The EPA's Houdini Act," *Wall Street Journal*, August 8, 1996, p. A-10.

[9]Steven Milloy and Michael Gough, "The Environmental Cancer Epidemic That Never Was," *Regulation*, No. 2 (1996): 18–21.

indicate a connection and some that do not. "Meta-analysis" is a technique that combines the results from available studies, and it is often suggested as a method for obtaining the maximum information from epidemiology. It raises its own set of interpretive problems. When Gary Taubes, the reporter who wrote the *Science* article, asked epidemiologists "to identify weak associations that are now considered convincing because they show up repeatedly,"[10] some epidemiologists accepted the repeatedly reported weak associations as convincing and some did not.

Given those areas of dispute, the lay reader is well advised to read critically and skeptically the many popular accounts of the latest scientific findings. There should at least be a very strong association and a highly plausible biological mechanism. Applying the first criterion, if it includes requiring a relative risk of 3 or 4, would eliminate any connection between the risks discussed in this book and human health. Some scientists, however, object to the use of a relative risk as high as 3 or 4 as a criterion.[11]

Laying aside the criterion that relative risks should be 3 or 4 or more and applying the general criteria of strong association and plausible mechanism to the four risks discussed in this book separates them into two groups. EMF is in a category by itself. There is no strong association between exposure to EMF and disease even in workplaces where exposure is far greater than in homes. Moreover, as discussed in chapter 4, there is no plausible biological mechanism that can explain how EMF could cause cancer.

Asbestos and radon have certainly caused cancer in occupational groups, and decades ago lead caused terrible neurological diseases in highly exposed workers in highly polluted workplaces. The effects from those high exposures can be considered settled, but questions remain about whether the mechanisms that cause disease at high levels of exposure operate to cause disease at the far lower levels encountered in housing. Studies that have examined the effects of asbestos in buildings and of indoor radon on health provide no convincing or consistent evidence of harm, but they are not powerful enough to rule out the possibility that some small risk is present.

[10]Taubes, p. 168.
[11]Ibid.

The most important studies warning of risks from low-level lead exposure have focused on reduced IQ scores. A handful of studies, essentially those carried out by Dr. Herbert Needleman, have produced evidence of an effect on IQ at relatively low lead levels, but Needleman's studies have been attacked because of problems in methodology and reporting. Most telling, however, is the failure of Needleman's latest paper to find the effect anticipated (see chapter 2). That failure casts renewed doubt on the link between low-level lead exposure and decreased IQ.

The science is of fundamental importance, but it has limits. It cannot tell us definitely that no risks exist. It is impossible to prove a negative, and that is what would be required to be definite. Of equal importance is the fact that it is possible to go through information that is available about every imaginable connection between exposure and health effect and construct a case for its existence. The EPA often prepares a risk assessment and puts it out for public and scientific review. Members of the public, including scientists, may object to the assessment and its conclusions, but there is no formal method by which to force the agency to reconsider its risk estimates.

De Tocqueville in the 20th Century

Does EPA do a good job? Does it consider the science evenhandedly? A research report published by the Alexis de Tocqueville Institution in the summer of 1994 answers a resounding "No" to those questions. The report

> documents the misuse of science by the EPA, often aided and abetted by the environmental movement, to justify its decisions on four of the most current—and controversial—environmental questions: ... In all four cases, this report found that the EPA routinely ignores the economic costs of its policies and programs. Moreover, the report uncovers a common 'modus operandi' employed by the EPA by selectively using data, and misusing statistical analyses in order to exaggerate health and ecological risks.[12]

The authors scorn environmental policy decisions "based . . . on distorted information, laden with emotion."[13] Their analysis of risk,

[12]Gary Anderson et al., *Science, Economics, and Environmental Policy* (Arlington, VA: Alexis de Tocqueville Institution, 1994), p. 12.

[13]Ibid., p. 1.

sorely lacking in most government pronouncements, bears quoting at length:

> Before the government takes action to ban or restrict an activity or substance on the basis of its purported danger to our public health or ecosystems, it is extremely important that we know the degree of danger or risk based on generally accepted scientific principles. If science is debased in an effort to "do good," society ultimately may be left worse off. . . . First, if we debase the scientific method in pursuit of a political agenda, we are opening a Pandora's Box of misguided and costly regulations.
>
> Second, the number of dangers everyone encounters in everyday life are so numerous that if we do not carefully delineate the government's role in regulating such dangers there is essentially no limit to how much government can ultimately control our lives. Further, we must know the precise costs and benefits of every proposed environmental regulation in order to better target economic resources to reducing the most serious and probable risks and limit unnecessary economic hardships on consumers, businesses, and state and local governments.[14]

The issues raised are basic to the policy debate, although policymakers often seem unaware of them. As a result, the Pandora's Box has long been open and we have thousands of "misguided and costly regulations." Those regulations intrude daily on the lives of citizens, raising their costs and lowering their standards of living for little, if any, gain. Targeting of resources at the most serious concerns has been all but nonexistent. Instead we have a babble of conflicting voices, over which one hears the stentorian voice of the EPA announcing that doom is at hand.

The de Tocqueville report underscores the issues raised about radon in this book. It highlights the EPA's "Exaggerated Death Toll," based on studies of smoking miners, and notes the EPA's persistent refusal to underline the synergistic relationship between radon and lung cancer. It is "unsettling" to discover that "the EPA uses the separate estimates of risk for smokers, former smokers, and nonsmokers *averaged together* [emphasis in original] in order to generate

[14]Ibid.

a single 'average' risk for the total population. . . ."[15] The procedure masks the differences among the various groups. A nonsmoker or a former smoker, for example, would gain no precise estimate of his risk by referring to the "average" risk for everyone. Being misled in that way would indeed be "unsettling." At the same time, the "misleading picture" presented by the EPA "hid[es] the fact that smoking is the major component of these risk estimates."[16]

The agency clings to the linear, no-threshold theory for estimating risks. It ignores the Health Physics Society's conclusion that there is no justification for making quantitative estimates of risks from exposure to concentrations of less than 30 pCi/l of radon in air and that the risk is likely to be zero for lower exposures (see chapter 1). The EPA certainly ignores studies suggesting that there may be an inverse relationship between low levels of radiation and health. It refuses even to discuss the theory of hormesis and, in so doing, may actively harm the society it is supposedly protecting. As the de Tocqueville authors note, "If hormesis occurs with radon, at some point, efforts to reduce radon exposure will have a negative impact. . . . EPA's policy will be killing more people than it saves."[17]

The de Tocqueville study reviews the EPA's all too effective efforts to frighten families, noting, for instance, the agency's survey of radon in schools. The survey appears to have been intended to drive school boards into action just as the now discredited EPA survey of asbestos in schools drove many school boards to ill-advised "rip-it-out" campaigns. If families are frightened enough to insist on radon testing in all American primary and secondary schools, the bill will come to $138 million,[18] and far larger amounts would be needed for remediation. Those funds would be better spent on equipment and programs to improve teaching. In any case, without any further testing, simple analysis shows that in-school exposure to radon is a small to tiny part of total exposure,[19] and EPA claims that children were

[15]Ibid., p. 5.

[16]Ibid.

[17]Ibid., p. 7.

[18]Ibid., pp. 9–10.

[19]Office of Technology Assessment, *Risks to Students in Schools* (Washington: Government Printing Office, 1995), pp. 147–55.

more vulnerable to radon have fallen by the wayside because of lack of any support.

The report also outlines the EPA "Radon Partners" program in which the agency gives money to nongovernment groups that are "able to say things that the EPA knows are unsupported or even untrue."[20] The agency sends millions of dollars to such supposedly prestigious organizations as the American Lung Association, the National Safety Council, and the National Education Association. Not content with scaring parents, the agency evidently wants to frighten their offspring as well: it has financed hundreds of radon coloring books for distribution in the elementary grades. As the report points out, such behavior by private industry would be considered a conflict of interest,[21] but the EPA blithely ignores such minor ethical details.

Although the report focuses mainly on the development of policy rather than on the costs that flow from policy, it does include data on the expenditures mandated by current, muddled regulations:

> We are now spending close to $150 billion a year—$1500 per household—to comply with environmental regulations which, in turn, reduces the standard-of-living and economic growth. Therefore, a *responsible* [emphasis in original] environmental policy should avoid unnecessary burdens on the economy. It is clear that wasting economic resources has a negative impact on the health and welfare of American citizens.[22]

Regulatory costs are not the only ones imposed by EPA policies. As spelled out here, fear of radon, asbestos, EMF, and lead in housing generates many costs that are not lumped under "regulatory costs." If they could be totaled, they could be added to the $150 billion—$1,500 per household—that the regulations cost.

Can the Science Be Improved?

The difficulties that arise when science cannot answer the questions that are asked of it have been recognized for years, and there

---

[20]Anderson et al., p. 10.
[21]Ibid.
[22]Ibid., p. 1.

has been no shortage of suggestions for methods to "improve the science." So far, none of the suggestions has proved sufficient.

Congress writes the laws, appropriates funds for regulatory agencies, and oversees the policies and programs of those agencies. Given the widespread questioning of EPA activities, why can't Congress take the lead and judge the validity of the agency's risk assessments? Everyone knows the answer. Congressional committees and sub-committees are composed of lawyers, not scientists. As a result, most members of Congress have little or no idea of the science involved in disputed areas and are all too willing to rely on the accounts furnished by agency administrators. Worse still, many place great store by the testimony of the witnesses put forward by the agencies themselves. Congress simply lacks the technical expertise either to voice doubts or to search out countervailing views, and it fears appearing insensitive on issues that supposedly affect public health. Too often its legislative mandates undercut those in the agencies who might favor a more moderate approach.

Almost 20 years ago, the "science court" was advanced as a method for bringing better science to bear. The "court" had a variety of forms; basically, it was to be a group of qualified scientists who would sit as judge or as judge and jury, hear scientific evidence, and decide whether the data were convincing. Usually the idea of a court included provisions for attorneys and cross-examination.

There is little enthusiasm for the court idea now, one reason for its demise being the realization that many of the tricky "scientific" questions or uncertainties are not scientific. Instead, they are "trans-scientific," meaning that they are asked in scientific terms but impossible to answer with current scientific knowledge. For example, "Does indoor radon cause cancer?" is a scientific question. When, however, analysis of the studies that can be used to investigate the question reveals that the studies are not sufficiently powerful to answer the question, it becomes trans-scientific. That does not mean that a trans-scientific issue will always remain trans-scientific; new techniques or new insights may make it possible to address the issue scientifically. Here and now, however, many questions are trans-scientific and likely to remain so for some time. With that realization, the science court, which would consider only the science that could be brought to bear on an issue, lost much of its appeal.

Short of a science court that would make scientific decisions, there are many suggestions for and a few examples of committees of scientists who advise the government. As the controversies described in this book illustrate, none of the existing committees has distinguished itself as a source of reliable advice. Cynical Washington observers view many of the advisory panels as covers for congressional or regulatory indecision. While the committees deliberate, investigate, review, and write, the politicians and regulators can delay decisionmaking, claiming that they are awaiting more information.

Congress established the Scientific Advisory Board (SAB) of the Environmental Protection Agency to provide scientific oversight to the agency. The SAB argued against the EPA's proposed regulation of radon in water, and its deliberations may have influenced the decision of Congress to place a moratorium on that regulation in the early 1990s (see chapter 1). It is difficult to determine which carried more weight with Congress—the SAB's judgment or the cries of protest from the water utilities, which would have been forced to foot the bill. Certain it is that the SAB did take a stand on the issue and that Congress did place a moratorium on the regulation.

Nevertheless, there is little reason to expect great things of the SAB. The mechanisms by which its members are appointed are a general mystery. The chairman and committee chairmen are clearly political appointees, serving at the pleasure of the president and the administration, a procedure that underlines the political implications of the work of the board. Moreover, all the staff support comes from the EPA. No matter how independent some of the staff may be from the EPA's drive to regulate, the overwhelming dependence on EPA experts, reports, and staff support must inevitably bias the SAB.

There are alternatives to placing an advisory body in the agency it is to advise. For example, Congress established a committee in the Department of Health and Human Services to review and advise on the study by the U.S. Air Force of the health of Air Force personnel who sprayed Agent Orange. That might be a useful model, but it is extremely clumsy to consider setting up a new advisory body for every issue. Even if it were attempted, it can be expected that the number of critical, qualified scientists who would be willing to serve on such boards would be far fewer than the number of seats to be filled.

The best known source of scientific advice for the government has been around for well over a century. In 1863, during the Civil

War, Congress chartered the National Academy of Sciences as an adviser to the federal government. The academy selects its own members, and membership is a mark of scientific achievement. Like many scientists, academy members are not eager to participate in activities that take them away from their laboratories, field sites, clinics, and offices, and very few academy members serve on the "academy panels" that investigate the issues on which the government seeks advice. Those issues are generally identified by Congress, and Congress appropriates a sum of money to an executive branch agency that then contracts with the academy for a study. For example, in the 1996 Amendments to the Safe Drinking Water Act, Congress directed the EPA to contract with the academy for a study of the possible health effects of radon in water. Most of the academy's financial support comes from those contracts.

When requests for studies, with their accompanying hefty sums of money, arrive at the academy, the National Research Council, the Institute of Medicine, or the National Academy of Engineering, the operating arms of the academy, organize "academy studies" and set up "academy committees" that have few academy members. Whatever conclusion a committee may reach about the merits of an issue, it can be counted on to recommend more research. That is far from unexpected. More research might provide more information. If the information is incontrovertible, the decision to be made will be apparent to everyone and noncontroversial. What more can anyone in public life desire? Another good reason lies behind calls for more research: most of the committee members will benefit from the flow of more dollars into the research effort.

In addition to calls for more research, most academy reports contain "on the one hand, on the other hand" conclusions. Unsatisfying as such conclusions can be, they are expected. After all, if the answer were clear-cut, Congress would not have requested the study.

Justice Stephen Breyer has suggested another process for improving the government's technical decisionmaking: an interdisciplinary professional group within the executive branch that would review administrative rulemaking, including the scientific issues involved. Insulated from politics by the Civil Service, the members would be able to offer their expertise in their own fields to those seeking to reduce the role of bureaucrats.[23] Unless closely supervised, however,

[23]Stephen Breyer, "Solutions," in *Breaking the Vicious Circle* (Cambridge, Mass.: Harvard University Press, 1993), pp. 61–64.

civil servants will still look after their own interests. Moreover, the creation of a super-regulatory regulatory commission would simply establish another layer of bureaucracy atop the many layers already existing. "Philosopher kings" of that type have had poor track records, and Justice Breyer did not point to them in U.S. history. It is still possible that the idea will be fleshed out, but currently it appears to have died aborning.

The Office of Managment and Budget, which is located in the Executive Office of the President, has some parallels to Justice Breyer's suggestion, but it is now seldom mentioned as a brake on regulatory drive, probably because of politics. During the "Reagan years," the OMB was criticized because it was trying to block the programs initiated by the Democratic Congress. During the "Clinton years," the executive branch has been in the different position of trying to maintain and expand programs in the face of congressional opposition.

It is reasonably easy to propose constituting a new group of scientists to try to moderate the drive of Congress and the regulatory agencies to legislate regulatory solutions to every identifiable environmental concern. In practice, it would be exceedingly difficult. Who would fund such a group? Even if the executive branch or the Congress were of such a mind, funding by the federal government would increase the chances that one or another executive branch agency would capture the group.

Ideally, voluntary contributions from citizens, including scientists, would provide funding. There is no shortage of private-sector groups working to make regulations more rational, so such funding could in all probability be organized. But the idea will make sense only after thought is given to how the group would work. Such a group has a chance of success only if pledges of cooperation are secured from scientists with prestige sufficient to guarantee that they will be heard. The location of the group also raises problems. All universities are dependent on the federal government for part of their funding, so a group set up within a university department could be subject to political pressures. A free-standing organization is another possibility, but it might be subject to attacks because of its sources of funding (whatever they might be). The possibility of such attacks reinforces the idea that such an organization will succeed only if its scientific advisers or staff have excellent credentials and demonstrated integrity.

The science that underlies the furor over residential risks is uncertain and mechanisms to improve the science are far from clear, but there are few doubts about the costs imposed by government risk assessments and regulations. The costs are real, regardless of the reality or unreality of the risks that are used to justify the expenditures.

Cost

Scientists at the Harvard Center for Risk Analysis collated the costs of 500 "life-saving interventions" and published the results in 1995.[24] One of their analyses compared the median "cost per life-year saved" for interventions in medicine, injury reduction, and toxin control. The median cost per life-year saved ranged from a low of $19,000 for medicine, through $48,000 for injury reduction, to a high of $2,782,000 for toxin control.[25] The comparison of estimated costs at various regulatory agencies reveals that the Federal Aviation Administration saves one life-year for every $23,000, whereas the EPA requires the expenditure of $7,269,000, about 300 times as much, for the same (EPA-estimated) benefit.

Indeed, when one judges by the costs of programs, the EPA leads the pack of regulatory agencies. The number of dollars spent to reduce the EPA-identified risks is a great deal more certain than the risks themselves. If the number of cases of lung cancer that would be eliminated by controlling radon, for instance, is a great exaggeration, as seems likely, the unit costs are higher than estimated. As the preceding chapters of this book demonstrate, scientific considerations apart, the regulations promulgated by the EPA constitute an enormous drain on the economy.[26]

The costs per life-year for radon control underline the willingness of the EPA to expend vast amounts for questionable gain. Remediating radon in homes with levels of the gas greater than or equal

[24]Tammy O. Tengs et al., "Five-Hundred Life-Saving Interventions and Their Cost-Effectiveness," *Risk Analysis*, no. 15 (1995): pp. 369–90.

[25]As a "definitional goal" of the study, costs were to be expressed in 1993 dollars using the general consumer price index.

[26]On a cautionary note, Tengs et al. explain that the interventions described include those that are fully implemented, those that are only partially implemented, and those that are not implemented at all. Thus their conclusions pertain to cost-effectiveness of life-saving opportunities, not necessarily actual expenditures.

to 21.6 pCi/l, a very high level by most standards, would cost approximately $6,000 per life-year. Remediating radon only in homes with levels greater than or equal to 8.1 pCi/l, a level twice as high as EPA's "action level" but one tolerated without great alarm in Canada or Finland, could cost nearly six times as much per life-year, or roughly $35,000.

To remediate homes with radon levels greater than or equal to 4 pCi/l, the "action level" long proposed by the EPA, would boost the cost per estimated life-year saved to more than $140,000. The agency has long insisted that such a level poses a public health threat requiring remediation. Given the tendentious nature of its arguments and the soaring cost, it is permissible to question the wisdom of spending scarce dollars to counteract a threat about which there is, at the level of concern stipulated by the EPA, grave doubt.

The figure for the costs of radon reduction, reported in chapter 1, is easier to remember. It would cost $1 trillion, about half the current federal deficit, to reduce indoor radon concentrations to those found outdoors, the goal Congress set for the EPA.

In considering those estimates, it is worth recalling that the Health Physics Society cautions against making any quantitative risk estimate for exposures of less than 30 pCi/l and that the risks from lower exposures are as likely to be zero as anything else.[27] If the society is correct, every penny spent to reduce residential radon exposure is wasted.

The Center for Risk Analysis study does not detail costs for other interventions described in this book, but the cost of removing lead paint from public housing ranges from a few hundred to several thousand dollars per unit (chapter 2), and electric utilities are spending or contemplating spending billions of dollars to bury power lines (chapter 4). The dollars are real—the reasons for spending them uncertain.

Relative Risk and the Absolute

A critic is certain to declare, however, that no price can be set on a human life. There is an ethical reluctance to believe that dollars

[27]Health Physics Society, *Radiation Risk in Perspective*, a 1996 position statement available from the Health Physics Society, 1313 Dolley Madison Blvd., Suite 402, McLean, Va. 22101. The position statement refers to radiation exposure of less than 5 rem per year as too low to be the basis for quantitative risk estimates; living in a house at 30 pCi/l of radon in air results in an exposure of about 5 rem per year.

and cents can be used as a measure of risk and protection from risk. The reluctance is surely understandable; in fact, the author shares it. But it is also essential to note that individuals evaluate risks and make tradeoffs on the most mundane levels every day. It is statistically safer to take a plane to visit friends and family than to drive a car, but some trips are too short for a plane or the cost of the plane ticket may seem prohibitively high, leading to a decision to use the car, despite the risk involved. In the events of daily life, there is often enough information available to make reasoned choices. Even more often, personal habits dictate choices; tradeoffs are not considered.

When the government refuses to acknowledge such tradeoffs, it leads to the imposition of vast costs that will make all of the individuals in a society worse off than they would be otherwise. Resources are finite. The unwise allocation of funds to protect against exaggerated risks or, in the case of lead, to make war against an enemy that has already decamped exacts a heavy price. W. Kip Viscusi, an analyst known for his work on risk, presents a compelling outline of the problem:

> Proposals to rationalize the regulatory process . . . may well be attacked as irresponsible and immoral since, in effect, lives will be traded off explicitly for dollars. But tradeoffs of this type are made implicitly by individuals and by all government policies that could have produced additional health benefits if more resources had been expended.[28]

Characterizing the current approach as "absolutist," Viscusi concludes that the justification for the approach

> rests on the illusion that society should not and, at present, does not trade off dollars for lives. The fundamental question that we must address is whether we should continue to sacrifice additional lives in an effort to preserve this popular mythology.[29]

The present course has nonmonetary costs as well. People hearing the drumbeat of "risk, risk, risk" must decide what action to take:

[28]W. Kip Viscusi, *Risk by Choice* (Cambridge, Mass.: Harvard University Press, 1983), p. 167.

[29]Ibid., p. 168.

270

whether to do nothing and feel guilty or to spend money and wonder if anything of value has been purchased. The government offers no dissenting voice from the prophets of doom, and citizens have to seek out such information on their own. Ironically, and by design, government programs that are supposed to inform are campaigns to instill fear. Fear, whatever its source, is a burden.

The Homebuyer's Dilemma

Epidemiology and the risk assessments based on it are all-important for the threats addressed in this book. The checks and balances that normally apply to regulations—that give regulated parties opportunities to object and to go to court to petition for redress—do not apply to risk assessments. Neither indoor radon nor residential asbestos nor EMF is regulated, so "getting the science (or, more correctly, the risk assessment) right" or, at least, "better," is the only check and balance on EPA efforts directed at those risks.

Once the government identified, publicized, and exaggerated risks, sellers and brokers, worried about possible liability, and buyers, worried about their health and regulations that might be forthcoming, acted to defend themselves. The lengthy disclosures now routinely included in sales contracts, the increased emphasis on inspections, and the establishment of escrow accounts for possible remediation represent protection from liability. Granted, inspections for asbestos and radon are aided and abetted by EPA programs that certify people to do the work, but the government does not require them. (In fact, the speed with which the real estate industry has adopted disclosure statements casts doubt on any need for a federal requirement.)

All of the regulatory reforms, had they been enacted, would have had no effect on the problems buyers and sellers of homes confront because of radon and asbestos. Fear takes the place of regulation—fear of being sued, fear of compromising one's health or the health of one's children. The resultant costs of inspections and remediation have become part of the sales contract and are visible to everyone connected with them.

EMF costs do not appear on a contract, but EMF can decrease the value of a home. Most often the culprit is power transmission lines or power distribution lines. The seller, unable to force the utility company to bury them, pays for the assumed risk in a reduced price

271

when he tries to sell his house. The reduction does nothing to help the home owner, nor does it protect the utility company from liability. There are more direct costs as well. Practicing "prudent avoidance," the utility can bury the lines, site new lines elsewhere, rethink plans for expansion, and pass the costs on to rate payers—and utilities are doing so. As a result, costs are likely to rise for everyone.

Lead paint is different; it is regulated. Its sale to the construction industry and thus to consumers was legally banned nearly 20 years ago; statutes, rules, and regulations prohibiting its use and governing its removal in federally constructed or assisted housing date back to the early 1970s. In 1996, regulations reached the private homeowner. As of September 6, 1996, an owner of four or more housing units, any of which was built before 1978, when lead paint was banned, must tell a prospective buyer about any lead hazard in the building, give the buyer a pamphlet about the hazards of lead paint, and allow him or her 10 days to have the house inspected for "unacceptable levels of lead" before becoming obligated under the sales contract. That rule might appear to spare anyone who owns less than a small apartment building. Not at all. The *Washington Post* has pointed out that an individual who owns his own house, a weekend house at the beach or mountains, and two rental units is subject to the law.[30] In any case, after December 6, 1996, every owner, including the private homeowner, must comply with the notification rules. The penalty for noncompliance is $10,000 and possibly imprisonment.

The regulation of lead in public housing requires all taxpayers to pay for the "get-the-lead-out" programs. Given $1,000 to spend on bettering the chances of a poor child for a successful life, some people at least would prefer to spend those dollars on improving the local school and on making sure the child goes to that school. The lead in bullets, it has been pointed out, is a greater threat to many children than the lead on the walls, but the Department of Housing and Urban Development (HUD), directed by Congress, goes after the lead paint and lead dust. It removes lead or, more accurately, as reported in chapter 2, it makes efforts to remove lead, efforts that have met with indifferent success when measured by reduced lead levels in the housing or in the children. Success in

[30]Kenneth R. Harney, "Deadlines Nearing for New Rules on Lead-Based Paint," *Washington Post*, August 23, 1996, pp. E-1, E-12.

terms of higher IQ or in terms of school performance, the hoped-for improvement, even if realized, would be so small that evidence of it would escape detection.

Given the wide-ranging and expensive effects of EPA risk assessments, the regulatory process with its hearings, balancing of views and opinions, and opportunities for legal interventions seems almost attractive. But there is no way of knowing what would have happened if radon, asbestos, and EMF had gone through the regulatory process. Open argument and discussion might have produced more rational and less expensive policies, as it has done (so far) with EPA's attempted regulation of radon in water (see chapter 1), but that is not the only possible outcome. A $10,000 fine and imprisonment seem rather severe penalties for not telling someone of the hypothetical risk from lead paint.

Another example related to housing underlines the fact that the regulatory process does not guarantee the correct conclusions and illuminates the arbitrary nature of government analysis and cost-benefit calculations. To protect buyers of mobile homes from confronting a market in which some mobile homes are built to withstand gale- and hurricane-force winds and some are not, HUD instituted its "Wind Rule," which requires mobile homes built for sale in certain coastal areas of the Gulf and Atlantic Coasts, Hawaii, and parts of Alaska to be manufactured to meet government specifications. The developers of the rule ignored convincing evidence that the highly competitive mobile-home market is supplied by many different manufacturers and that retailers, mobile-home operators, and other mobile-home owners are well aware of the structural quality of the various models. Ignoring that information, the rule writers said that the government had to intervene to protect bu rs because the buyers lacked sufficient information—a "market ure," beloved by regulators. The consequence of the rule is to c up the prices of mobile homes, especially those at the low end of the price range, and to deny the possibility of homeownership to people who currently purchase those models.[31]

If the fears engendered by EPA's risk assessments are justified—and that seems very unlikely—lives are at stake. If they are not—

---

[31]L. D'Alessi, "Error and Bias in Benefit-Cost Analysis: HUD's Case for the Wind Rule," *Cato Journal* (forthcoming).

and that is very likely—housing costs are being driven up needlessly. The EPA apparently thinks that the scientific niceties—considering studies and analyses that provide no support for its position, acknowledging uncertainties, weighing the benefits of spending money differently—are inconvenient. It prefers to operate in a vacuum characterized by good intentions and claims that it is protecting the public. The intentions and the promotional hype, however, seem to have done little so far except to frighten homebuyers and sellers with stories based on questionable hypotheses and to drive up costs. As repeated time and again in this book, any improvement in health will be so small as to escape detection. There may well be none at all.

Absolute safety and a risk-free society are not of this world. Yet the EPA, often encouraged by Congress, continues to act as though all hazards can be eliminated. Far from being a reasonable goal, that is an exercise in futility. Everyone who owns a home or who wants to be a homeowner—all citizens, in fact—has reason to object to the EPA's pursuit of the impossible. If Congress hears the objections and acts, there is hope that the agency will back off from its risk assessments and there will be resulting reductions in fears of liability and regulation. The alternative is to watch the costs of haunted housing soar.

Index

About the Author

Cassandra Chrones Moore, an adjunct scholar with the Competitive Enterprise Institute and the Cato Institute, writes frequently on regulation of housing, trucking, trusts, and pensions. After earning her bachelor's and master's degrees from Harvard University and her doctorate from the University of Michigan, she spent several years learning the practical side of real estate, first as an agent and broker, then as a director with the National Association of Realtors. She later served as the first executive director of the Interagency Council on the Homeless. As a result of her experiences in real estate and in government, she began a series of policy studies that led eventually to *Haunted Housing*.

Cato Institute

Founded in 1977, the Cato Institute is a public policy research foundation dedicated to broadening the parameters of policy debate to allow consideration of more options that are consistent with the traditional American principles of limited government, individual liberty, and peace. To that end, the Institute strives to achieve greater involvement of the intelligent, concerned lay public in questions of policy and the proper role of government.

The Institute is named for *Cato's Letters*, libertarian pamphlets that were widely read in the American Colonies in the early 18th century and played a major role in laying the philosophical foundation for the American Revolution.

Despite the achievement of the nation's Founders, today virtually no aspect of life is free from government encroachment. A pervasive intolerance for individual rights is shown by government's arbitrary intrusions into private economic transactions and its disregard for civil liberties.

To counter that trend, the Cato Institute undertakes an extensive publications program that addresses the complete spectrum of policy issues. Books, monographs, and shorter studies are commissioned to examine the federal budget, Social Security, regulation, military spending, international trade, and myriad other issues. Major policy conferences are held throughout the year, from which papers are published thrice yearly in the *Cato Journal*. The Institute also publishes the quarterly magazine *Regulation*.

In order to maintain its independence, the Cato Institute accepts no government funding. Contributions are received from foundations, corporations, and individuals, and other revenue is generated from the sale of publications. The Institute is a nonprofit, tax-exempt, educational foundation under Section 501(c)3 of the Internal Revenue Code.

CATO INSTITUTE
1000 Massachusetts Ave., N.W.
Washington, D.C. 20001